FEMINISM
AND
SCIENCE
FICTION

FEMINISM AND SCIENCE FICTION

Sarah Lefanu

INDIANA UNIVERSITY PRESS
Bloomington and Indianapolis

The publisher gratefully acknowledges permission to quote from the following works: *Trillion Year Spree* by Brian Aldiss, by permission of Victor Gollancz Ltd; *Heroes and Villains* by Angela Carter, copyright c 1969 by Angela Carter; *Thinking about Women* by Mary Ellman, by permission of Harcourt Brace Jovanovich, Inc.; *Contemporary Writers* and *The Captain's Death Bed and Other Essays* by Virginia Woolf, by permission of the estate of the author and The Hogarth Press, and of Harcourt Brace Jovanovich, Inc.; *The Ruins of Isis* by Marion Zimmer Bradley, published with permission of the Donning Company/Publishers.

© 1988 by Sarah Lefanu. First published in the United States by Indiana University Press, 1989.

Manufactured in the United States of America

Library of Congress Cataloging-in-Publication Data

Lefanu, Sarah.
   Feminism and science fiction.
   Bibliography: p.
   1. Science fiction--Women authors--History and
criticism. 2. Fiction--20th century--History and criticism.
3. Science fiction, American--History and criticism.
4. Science fiction, English--History and criticism.
5. Feminism in literature. 6. Feminism and literature.
I. Title.
PN3433.6.L4 1989   809.3'876   88-8555
ISBN 0-253-33287-7
ISBN 0-253-23100-0 (pbk.)

1 2 3 4 5 93 92 91 90 89

For Michèle
and
Chris, Alexander and Beatrice

Acknowledgments

I am grateful to Philip Mercer of the City Lit for encouraging my class on feminism and science fiction, and to my students for their insights and enthusiasm, especially Susan Beetlestone and Peter Warburton for his excellent bibliography, to Joyce Day of the Science Fiction Foundation Library at the North East London Polytechnic, and to Ros de Lanerolle and my colleagues at The Women's Press for their support and encouragement.

I should like to thank John Clute, Gill Durber, Juliet Girling, Joanna Russ, Daphne Tagg and Lisa Tuttle for their invaluable help with the manuscript. And to thank for their help in various ways, from the loan of books to extra child-care, Sabina Bowler-Reed, Giles and Patrick Collins, Colin Greenland, Dick Jude, Hannah Kanter, Roz Kaveney and Brian Stableford.

In particular I should like to thank Christopher Collins and Michèle Roberts, without whom I could not have written this book.

Contents

What women do is survive. We live by ones and twos in the chinks of your world-machine.

'*The Women Men Don't See*'
James Tiptree Jr

Introduction

In 1982 I started giving a series of classes on the subject of feminism and science fiction at the City Lit Centre for Adult Studies in London. I had been interested in the subject for some time, but as I read more, thought more and learned more from my small but enthusiastic group of students, I began to think about writing a book. I would never have begun it but for my friend Michèle Roberts, herself a novelist and poet, who insisted that I take time off from my part-time work at The Women's Press and generously funded a full week of childcare. I would not have had the courage to allow myself such a luxury, a whole childfree week to get on paper a hesitant, tentative plan. That original plan has long since changed, but my commitment to the project is a direct reflection of the commitment that Michèle offered to me. Throughout the writing of this book she has been a constant source of encouragement and support: I have felt stimulated by her questions, perceptions and criticisms and have relied on her at moments of crisis, both material – when my typewriter broke down she unhesitatingly lent me her own – and mental.

I gave my last class at the City Lit at the end of 1985. My second child was due early in the New Year, and I moved to Bristol with my family a month later. I don't know whether the classes could have continued: the Conservative government was getting into its stride with savage cuts in adult education and the marvellous variety of courses on offer at the City Lit was under threat. Meanwhile, however, The Women's Press science fiction list had been launched, in spring 1985. My involvement with that has given me enormous pleasure. Many of the books discussed on the following pages are now on that list.

This is a book about feminism and science fiction and the conjuncture of the two. I want to explore the question of whether science fiction, despite its preponderantly male bias, offers a freedom to women writers, in terms of style as well as content, that is not available in mainstream fiction. Further, does it offer a means of fusing political concerns with the playful creativity of the imagination?

Science fiction is popularly conceived as male territory, boys' own adventure stories with little to interest a female readership. This is true of the heyday of magazine science fiction, the 1930s and 1940s, but even then there were women writers, like C.L. Moore and Leigh Brackett, who may have assumed a male voice and non gender specific names to avoid prejudice on the part of editors and readers alike, but who were none the less there. Pamela Sargent gives a detailed history of these hidden women in the introduction to her first anthology of science fiction stories by women, *Women of Wonder*. There have always been women readers of science fiction, as Susan Wood pointed out in her article 'Women and Science Fiction'. It would be simplistic to assume that a lack of female characters in the science fiction of the time automatically excluded a female readership (just as the obverse, that female characters guarantee women's interest, is patently untrue): why and how we read books is a more complicated business.

And yet early twentieth- and mid-twentieth-century science fiction does lack women-identified women as writers and readers: women's participation necessitated becoming one of the boys, joining in on their terms, becoming a Female Man (this protective disguise is one of the subjects of Joanna Russ's classic *The Female Man*). However, it is a great mistake to trace the beginnings of science fiction only back as far as the magazine fiction of the 1920s. In *Trillion Year Spree* Brian Aldiss and David Wingrove, who define science fiction as 'the search for a definition of mankind and his status in the universe which will stand in our advanced but confused state of knowledge (science), and is characteristically cast in the Gothic or post-Gothic mode',[1] place the beginnings of science fiction one hundred years earlier, with Mary Shelley and *Frankenstein, or the Modern Prometheus* (1818)(previous non-realistic writings such as the flights to the moon described by Lucian of Samosata,

c. AD 150, or Bishop Francis Godwin in 1638, being ur-science ✓ fiction, fantastical rather than science fictional).

Contemporary science fiction does have roots in the nineteenth-century Gothic mode – though as I will argue it has roots elsewhere too – and contemporary feminist science fiction draws on what Ellen Moers has described as the female Gothic, as exemplified in the works of Ann Radcliffe. A parallel strand, that of contemporary feminist utopian writing, also has roots in the nineteenth century. Charlotte Perkins Gilman's *Herland* is a particular example of the uses to which the utopian form can be put as a critique of existing conditions and a vision of something different: a dual purpose that creates its own vital tensions and which resurfaces in the work of writers such as Marge Piercy, Sally Miller Gearhart and Joanna Russ. Interestingly, in the work of Charlotte Perkins Gilman we see the conjuncture of two important strands of nineteenth-century female thought: the socialist-inspired, pragmatic aspects of utopian writing, with their emphasis on social structure, and the more painful interiorisation of female experience, as exemplified in her story *The Yellow Wallpaper*. Both elements, the optimistic and the pessimistic, are offset by an implied or stated critique of a dominant male social and political system. And both, as we will see, appear in the work of women writing science fiction today.

But feminist science fiction does not follow simply and directly from the literary forms explored by nineteenth-century women writers. It is informed by the feminist, socialist and radical politics that developed during the 1960s and 1970s. Previous to the intervention by feminist writers in the late sixties and early seventies science fiction reflected, in its content at least, what could be called masculine concerns, based around the central theme of space exploration and the development of technology: masculine concerns because access to these areas was effectively denied to women in the real world, and science fiction, like all writing, is written from within a particular ideology. A truism perhaps, but worth emphasising in this instance because of the form's reputation for, and indeed its aspirations towards, being 'out of this world'.

For all its speculation on the consequences of scientific development, science fiction has been notably silent on the concomitant subject of social development, particularly as regards the personal and political relationships between women

4

and men. Joanna Russ has defined this as a failure of imagination, remarking on the extraordinary prevalence of what she calls 'intergalactic suburbia' in worlds and times light years from our own. Kingsley Amis, perhaps surprisingly, pointed out as early as 1960 that there was a strange lack of experimentation around sex; that while all else may vary, male/female relationships stay the same. His explanation is straightforward and honest: 'Though it may go against the grain to admit it, science fiction writers are evidently satisfied with the sexual status quo'.[2] Even in the 1960s, with the growth of left libertarianism and the move away from the exploration of outer space to that of 'inner space', as exemplified in the work associated with the magazine *New Worlds*, and the accompanying interest in 'personal relationships', sexual roles were not in themselves challenged.

What, then, *does* challenge the sexual status quo? I believe it has been challenged profoundly by the growth of feminism over the last twenty years. The feminist intervention in science fiction has not been an easy one: writers have had to struggle not only against the weight of the male bias of the form but also against the weight of a cultural and political male hegemony that underpins the form itself. However, women writers have been able to draw on the possibilities opened up by an important strand within science fiction that is in opposition to the dominant ideology, that, rather than celebrating imperialistic and militaristic glory, is subversive, satirical, iconoclastic. To quote Amis again, 'science fiction's most important use . . . is a means of dramatising social enquiry, as providing a fictional mode in which cultural tendencies can be isolated and judged.'[3]

One of the major theoretical projects of the second wave of feminism is the investigation of gender and sexuality as social constructs, thus posing a challenge to notions of a natural law regulating feminine behaviour and an innate femaleness that describes and circumscribes 'woman'. Feminism has drawn on a variety of theories and practices in this endeavour, from an emphasis on consciousness-raising as a means of transposing the experience of oppression from an individual to a wider, social level, to a development of psychoanalytic theory that explores the creation of the gendered subject within language and culture. Questions of class and race have pushed feminism further from the experience of individual oppression into a

wider political arena. The stock conventions of science fiction –
time travel, alternate worlds, entropy, relativism, the search for
a unified field theory – can be used metaphorically and
metonymically as powerful ways of exploring the construction of
'woman'. Feminist SF, then, is part of science fiction while
struggling against it.

In the following pages I shall describe the fruits of this
marriage between feminist politics and science fiction. The
freedom that SF offers from the constraints of realism has an
obvious appeal and has been exploited by mainstream writers
such as Margaret Atwood and Marge Piercy. Its glorious
eclecticism, with its mingling of the rational discourse of science
with the pre-rational language of the unconscious – for SF
borrows from horror, mythology and fairy tale – offers a means
of exploring the myriad ways in which we are constructed as
women.

Further, science fiction offers women new ways of writing.
Despite the growing popularity of the trilogy – an unnerving
prospect for the writer as she starts out – there is still a
privileged place for the short story within the body of SF. What
is perhaps most remarkable is the fluidity of form that SF allows:
the set length of the novel does not dominate. Writers can let
themselves experiment, writing and rewriting in short story,
novella or novel form. More than in any other form of fiction
there is an easy flow between writers and readers. Professional
writers often start out as fans, writing in fanzines or producing
their own. One does not have to be a professional in order to be
read. Ideas, themes and characters are borrowed, elaborated,
reworked by different people in different forms. One example
of this is the elaboration of the Kirk/Spock relationship in *Star
Trek* produced and written in a series of fanzines entirely by
women. Another is Suzette Haden Elgin's Ozark Centre for
Language Studies, where, amongst other things, she is developing the study of Láadan, the women's language of her novels
Native Tongue and *The Judas Rose*. Writers, C.J. Cherryh being
one example, may invent a universe and then invite other
writers to share it. There are many collaborations in SF, such as
in the rather unappealingly named Sime/Gen novels of Jac-
queline 'Lichtenberg and Jean Lorrah, and between Cynthia
Felice and Connie Willis. And the numerous SF conventions
bring together writers, fans and artists from all over the world.

All this leads to a breakdown of the conventional hierarchies between writers and readers, and challenges the conventional authority of the single author. Such an anti-authoritarian style has, potentially, a particular interest for women, for whom writing requires not just self-confidence, but the confidence necessary to break through what can be seen as a male-dominated world of ordered discourse, into a male-dominated world of professionalism.

'They wrote it, but they were a fad.' There is a trend current in science fiction to dismiss the writing of the 1970s and with it the extraordinary and exciting contribution made by women as writers, readers and fans. It is described in disturbing detail in an Open Letter to Joanna Russ by Jeanne Gomoll in the feminist magazine *Aurora*. Jeanne Gomoll sees her own experiences of fandom in the 1970s being written out of history by similar mechanisms to those described by Joanna Russ in her critical book *How To Suppress Women's Writing*. Russ has charted the myriad ways in which this is done ('She wrote it, but she had help', 'She wrote it, but she was an anomaly', and many others), and Jeanne Gomoll suggests that this tendency is now at work on feminist science fiction. She interprets the now-fashionable generalised attacks on the 1970s for being a 'me-decade' as being a disguise for more specific attacks on the gains made by the women's movement (and in Britain at least a similar accusation of selfishness and individualism run wild is used to attack the anti-authoritarian ethos of the 1960s, and to justify a return to so-called 'family values' and all that that implies about 'women's role').

In fact, huge numbers of us rejected the traditional role of anonymous, self-sacrificing helpmate that has so long trapped women in unhappy marriages and unrewarding jobs. We began caring for ourselves more than we cared for others. But the ironic judgment of the men who found *themselves* cared for less well than their fathers had been is that women who are not self*less* must be self*ish*. The phrase 'the me-decade' then, with its pejorative tone, rejects all of the positive, vitalising effects brought about by the healthier, stronger, more capable women flourishing among us. For that reason alone, it is an inappropriate label.[4]

The work of women writers, Jeanne Gomoll goes on, can be dismissed thus: 'They wrote it, but they were just part of the me-decade.' Pejorative labelling such as Gomoll describes suggests that neither the incursion of women writers into the field, nor their recognition therein, is significant. Yet it must be significant that while between 1953 (the year of its inception) and 1967 there were no women winners of the Hugo Award, between 1968 and 1984 there were eleven. Similarly, women's past activities as fans are being denied or ignored. 1974 saw the first 'women and science fiction' panel at a convention, one that was fought for by Susan Wood in the teeth of vociferous opposition from other members of the convention committee. Susan Wood died tragically young, but the conjuncture of women and science fiction went from strength to strength in the next years, with 'women and SF' panels at most conventions, women-only rooms, and a general flowering of writing, debate and discussion. But now, at 'fandom of the 70s' panels, says Jeanne Gomoll, 'I sit in the audience . . . and don't hear *anything* of the politics, the changes, the roles that women played in that decade (except sometimes a little chortling aside about how it is easier now to get a date with a female fan).'[5]

This, then, is one of the aims of this book: to chart that extraordinary relationship between feminism and science fiction that flowered in the 1970s and that continues to the present day. I would like to give the lie to a version of events that belittles the achievements of women *and our politics* in the 1970s, that seeks to dismiss them as faddish and passé. I hope to show that science fiction is one of those areas – and there are of course others – where the idea of feminism as a thing of the past can be resisted with spirit, as can the insidious notion of 'post-feminism'.

I shall look at English-language science fiction by both British and American writers. For although the political experiences of women in the two countries differ enormously in many respects, the particular circumstances of reading and marketing within science fiction override any clear distinction. The feminist texts, too, of the 1970s sped back and forth across the Atlantic.

I also believe that the anti-feminism of the present day is a powerful force in both Britain and America. The Thatcher–Reagan alliance seems to encourage imitative moves between the two countries. The growth of the New Right in Britain (who like to see themselves as having intellectual respectability) is not unrelated, I believe, to the growing power of the 'moral majority' in the USA, although I suspect they might not like the connection. Both promulgate an ethos of authoritarianism under the guise of 'responsibility'. Both governments seem determined to crush movements of organised labour, to attack civil rights and, in Britain at least, to undermine a socialised system of health care and education. Women are not the only victims of right-wing governments, but they are amongst the first. This, then, is common ground, and is likely to be reflected in contemporary science fiction.

I feel, therefore, that there is no justification for trying to delineate a British from an American feminist science fiction. The reader will see that the majority of work that I draw on is by American writers: there were, and are, more of them. There are probably a variety of reasons for this. An important one must be the greater market for all SF in the USA. Until recently, British publishers have not been encouraging towards women writers of science fiction. An indication of this can be seen in the publishing history of work by two long-standing British writers, Tanith Lee and Josephine Saxton, who for many years were published only in the USA and in translation.

The book is divided into two parts: an overview, in which I will mention a variety of work by women and look in detail at some of it, and four chapters on the work of individual writers: James Tiptree Jr (the pen-name for Alice Sheldon); Ursula K. Le Guin; Suzy McKee Charnas; and Joanna Russ.

In the first section of the book, the overview, I shall start by looking at the representation of women, or the lack of it, in science fiction, and ask whether this can, or should, reflect the experiences of women in the 'mundane' (to use a science fictional term) world. I will then raise some questions about the function of narrative, drawing on Rosemary Jackson's analysis of the 'fantastic' to explore the subversive potentialities of science fiction. I will describe some of the ways in which science fiction narratives allow the inscription of woman as subject, first by borrowing from Ellen Moers the concept of 'travelling heroinism', then moving on to look at different writers' use of the amazon-figure and the contradictions thrown up by role reversal as a literary strategy.

From narrative as analysis I will move to narrative as the telling of dreams: the traditional 'what if . . .?' of science fiction transformed into 'if only . . .'; then from dream to nightmare, from utopias to dystopias. I will return to woman as subject of her story, looking at the constitution of self and other and the expression of desire; this will lead to a description of the practitioners of what might be called 'women's science fiction' and I will contrast their aims and aspirations with those of the practitioners of 'feminist science fiction'.

What I hope to show overall is that the plasticity of science fiction and its openness to other literary genres allow an apparent contradiction, but one that is potentially of enormous importance to contemporary women writers: it makes possible, and encourages (despite its colonisation by male writers), the inscription of women as subjects free from the constraints of mundane fiction; and it also offers the possibility of interrogating that very inscription, questioning the basis of gendered subjectivity. I shall back up these ambitious claims for the potential of the genre by detailed reference to the writing of the many talented women who recognise and exploit its possibilities.

My overall desire is to communicate and pass on to others my own enthusiasm for these writers. My selection is personal: I have chosen to write about writers that I care about, and I have devoted the most space to those that I care about most passionately. This is not a definitive guide, and far from being a definitive interpretation. But the gaps will be filled, I hope, and alternative readings offered, by other enthusiasts.

PART ONE

1
Representation and the Natural Woman

In an essay first published in 1971 and reprinted in 1974 in the science fiction magazine *Vertex*, where it was greeted with a certain amount of male hysteria, Joanna Russ wrote: 'One would think science fiction the perfect literary mode in which to explore (and explode) our assumptions about "innate" values and "natural" social arrangements, in short our ideas about Human Nature, Which Never Changes. Some of this has been done. But speculation about the innate personality differences between men and women, about family structure, about sex, in short about gender roles, does not exist at all.'[1]

Joanna Russ decided, after some hesitation, to entitle her essay 'The Image of Women in Science Fiction' rather than 'Women in Science Fiction' because 'if I had chosen the latter, there would have been very little to say. There are plenty of images of women in science fiction. There are hardly any women.'[2] Do the arguments that Russ puts forward still hold true, or has science fiction changed to such an extent that they are no longer relevant? I hope to show in this book that science fiction *has* changed; that it has in fact been changed by writers like Joanna Russ herself, in her critical work and in her fiction, and by the work of other women writing in the 1970s and 1980s, who have recognised the enormous potential that science fiction offers for the speculation about gender roles that Joanna Russ couldn't find. I hope to show, too, how these ideas have come, in different ways and degrees, from the women's liberation movement, and how science fiction has indeed proved to be 'the perfect literary mode' for their expression in fiction.

A feminist critique of science fiction would not be possible without the pioneering work of Joanna Russ and her fellow American Susan Wood. Their interests are wide ranging and sophisticated; both of them are as concerned with the formal possibilities of science fiction as with its sociological subtexts. I think it is worth looking in some detail at the essay by Joanna Russ mentioned above as it offers such a clear and interesting analysis of the state of SF at the end of the 1960s and looks forward to the changes that were to come.

What does Joanna Russ mean when she says that there are no women in science fiction, only images of women? Are not all forms of representation, linguistic or otherwise, images, and in a relation not altogether straightforward to the 'real'? Is the 'real' what we are looking for in science fiction? Russ's answer, perhaps surprisingly, is yes; what is the point of any amount of speculation and extrapolation if it all takes place around the black hole of women's absence? The images of women reflect women only as seen by men. There are no women in science fiction, Russ is saying, that a woman can read about and say, 'Yes, that's me' or 'Yes, that could be me'. In the 1960s, Russ admits, more writers were concerned to show a two-sexed world, but the implications of what a genuinely sexually egalitarian society might be like were not faced. 'What is most striking about these stories', she says, 'is what they leave out: the characters' personal and erotic relations are not described; child-rearing arrangements (to my knowledge) are never described; and the women who appear in these stories are either young and childless or middle-aged, with their children safely grown up.'[3]

Russ's demand for the 'real' is then not so surprising: she is asking for a realistic premise to underpin science fictional speculation. In other words, how can gender roles, or the representation of gender roles, be challenged if recognisable female characters are simply not present?

In her essay Russ divides the work of women writers into four rough categories: ladies' magazine fiction ('in which the sweet gentle intuitive little heroine solves an interstellar crisis by mending her slip or doing something equally domestic after her big heroic husband has failed');[4] galactic suburbia, which, she maintains, is the most common form for women writers, and is often entirely female-free (if not, female characters tend to be wives and mothers, the backbone of the nuclear family); space opera (Leigh Brackett is given as an example here); avant-garde fiction. Even amongst the more adventurous women writers, amongst those who do create lively and active female characters, it becomes obvious that 'the conventional idea that women are second-class people is a hard idea to shake'.[5] It is worth noting here Russ's recognition of the power of a male value system. The development of any tradition of women's literature, in science fiction or any other field, takes place in relation to that value system. It cannot simply be ignored. The women writers that Russ refers to may show active and lively female characters, but these are still male identified. As with the male writers, very few attempts are made to show family, erotic or personal life.

Since the publication of Russ's essay the lack of speculation 'about family, about sex, in short about gender roles' has been rectified by writers like Suzy McKee Charnas, Sally Miller Gearhart, Marge Piercy and of course Joanna Russ herself. It is almost exclusively women writers who have taken up Russ's challenge, although there are notable exceptions amongst male writers, such as Samuel Delany. (There are also plenty of male writers who appreciate the current market value of appearing pro-feminist.)

Yet there were some women writers exploring those very areas before the 1970s. 1974 saw the publication of the first of Pamela Sargent's anthologies of science fiction stories by women, *Women of Wonder: SF Stories by Women about Women*. The cover illustration of the UK edition emphasises the womanish aspect: a bizarre be-spacesuited semi-prosthetic woman and baby, looking as if they come from the pages of a nineteenth-century manual on how to feed your baby in public without baring your breasts. The collection opens with Judith Merril's powerful 1948 story, 'That Only a Mother', which examines the human and psychological consequences of nuclear radiation and describes a woman's stubborn refusal to see her baby daughter's gross deformities. This story is not only unusual for its time, both in its sensitivity to the political issues and the significance it gives to a woman's experience, but also remarkable in science fictional terms for its insistence on the reality of emotional life. The setting may be Russ's 'intergalactic suburbia', with hubby away and wife at home bringing up baby, but the affect comes from the gut. This is a story in which that rarest of beings in the world of science fiction, a mother, is central and powerful.

From the 1950s Sargent includes Katherine MacLean's 'Contagion', which deals with the relationships between the women and men of a scientific expedition on another planet and what happens when their physical appearance changes so that they all look alike. It explores the question of how much we are what we look like. Again, the premise of the relationships is all-American healthily heterosexual, but the story's concern is with an inwardness lacking in much SF of the time. Marion Zimmer Bradley's 'The Wind People' concerns a mother and child: a careful and serious story about sexual needs and taboo. The stories from the 1960s in this anthology include Anne McCaffrey's 'The Ship Who Sang' (later developed into a series of linked stories, published as *The Ship Who Sang*), about Helva, a woman's mind in the body of a spaceship, and her love for her scout Jennan, who is killed on one of their missions. Writers of the 1970s are represented by Ursula Le Guin, Chelsea Quinn Yarbro, Joanna Russ and Vonda McIntyre, the last with the story 'Of Mist, and Grass, and Sand', which became the first section of her novel *Dreamsnake*.

What Sargent's first volume shows is that there were some, if only a few, women writers who did try to deal with the personal and the erotic. In her second volume, *More Women of Wonder*, the only pre-1970s stories are C.L. Moore's 'Jirel Meets Magic' and Leigh Brackett's 'The Lake of the Gone Forever'. Neither of these do much to challenge the 'space opera' conventions of much of the writing of the 1930s and 1940s; in which the protagonist may be a woman, but, as Joanna Russ points out in the same article, 'the he-man ethos of the world does not change, nor do the stereotyped personalities assigned to the secondary characters, particularly the female ones.'[6]

The weakness of these collections lies perhaps in the editor's self-limiting goal of reprinting stories with female protagonists. As she says in her introduction she decided on a historical approach for this and the previous anthology so as to show the development of the role of women in science fiction.

C.L. Moore's first published story, 'Shambleau', thus does not fall within the definition, as its protagonist is the pale-eyed, steely-jawed Northwest Smith. This retelling of the Medusa myth has a quite extraordinary erotic power. Most contemporary depictions of sexual passion in science fiction pale by comparison. And while in her later story 'No Woman Born' the depiction of the reconstituted heroine, Deirdre, is mediated through the eyes of two male characters, their reactions of unease to her lack of female flesh and blood (Deirdre's brain is housed within a glorious golden metal body) are clear indications of her powerfully autonomous sexuality. Deirdre no longer needs men. This provides an interesting contrast to Anne McCaffrey's 'The Ship Who Sang', in which Helva is almost pathetically dependent on a man for a sense of her existence *per se*.

In her collection *The Best of C.L. Moore*, C.L. Moore provides an 'Afterword: Footnote to "Shambleau" . . . and Others', in which she gives a delightful account of how she started 'Shambleau' while practising her typing so as to keep her first job (this was during the Depression, and she had had to leave the state university to learn shorthand and typing in a business school).

. . . this is where 'Shambleau' began, halfway down a sheet of yellow paper otherwise filled up with boring quick-brown-foxes, alphabets, and things like 'The White Knight is sliding down the poker. He balances very badly,' to lighten the practice.

Midway down that yellow page I began fragments remembered from sophomore English at the university. All the choices were made at random. Keats, Browning, Byron – you name it. In the middle of this exercise a line from a poem (by William Morris?) worked itself to the front and I discovered myself typing something about a 'red, running figure'. I looked at it a while, my mind a perfect blank, and then shifted mental gears without even adding punctuation to mark the spot, swinging with idiot confidence into the first lines of the story which ended up as 'Shambleau'.

She goes on to describe the genesis of Northwest Smith and Yarol, and the logical work needed for the development of the plot. But what is striking is her insistence on the importance of the unconscious as a means of providing the writer with the wealth of fiction she has herself read and enjoyed. It seems to me that the power of many of her stories, and in particular 'Shambleau' and 'No Woman Born', perhaps resides in this openness to the processes of the unconscious.

Female protagonists are not a *sine qua non* of feminist science fiction. As Joanna Russ has said, 'Women in disguise as aliens or in disguise as "women" turn up in SF written by women quite interestingly.'[7] Nor do female protagonists a feminist story make. Indeed Pamela Sargent does not consider either of her anthologies to be feminist – her aims are otherwise – and points the reader instead to the collection edited by Vonda N. McIntyre and Susan Janice Anderson, *Aurora: Beyond Equality*.

This is a fascinating collection: it includes a story by James Tiptree Jr *and* one by Raccoona Sheldon ('Houston, Houston, Do You Read?' and 'Your Faces, O My Sisters! Your Faces Filled of Light!') before she revealed herself as one and the same person; it includes an extract from Marge Piercy's *Woman on the Edge of Time* when it was still a novel-in-progress, and Ursula K. Le Guin's thought-provoking article on feminism and her own work, 'Is Gender Necessary?'

Pamela Sargent's third anthology, *The New Women of Wonder*, is an excellent introduction to the women writing in the field in the 1970s. It includes James Tiptree Jr's 'The Women Men Don't See', which I will be looking at in some detail in Chapter 11, and Pamela Zoline's very interesting 1967 *New Worlds* story, 'The Heat Death of the Universe'.

The 1970s did see a great change in the representation of women in science fiction. However the response to Russ's article in *Vertex* showed that while the representations of women, particularly by women, may change, the attitudes of men do not necessarily change with them. Poul Anderson wrote a 'Reply to a Lady' (it might be unfair to hold him responsible for the title of his article) responding to Russ's concern over the lack of women in science fiction with the somewhat contradictory claims that 'women have not been relevant' and 'the frequent absence of women characters [in SF] has no great significance, perhaps none whatsoever.' His extraordinarily patronising article ends by accusing Russ of letting her 'fervor in a cause run away with her'.[8] Women speaking out for women's rights have long been accused of 'fervour', i.e. hysteria and exaggeration.

Philip K. Dick's response to Anderson was that Russ was right, and that around the lack of women in science fiction there is 'a conspiracy of silence' which needs to be shattered. Although Philip K. Dick appeared to agree intellectually with Russ's arguments, he accused her of seeming 'to feel the need of attacking us on a personal level', while his own accusation that Russ had 'shrilled at me in print' shows how very impartial he can be . . .[9]

In her brilliant and witty anatomy of women, men and language, *Thinking About Women*, the incomparable Mary Ellmann discusses the 'shrillness' of women in terms of their physical appearance and presentation. For where the male body 'lends credence to assertions', the female 'takes it away . . . The subliminal assumption is that from weight must come weight: men's shoes alone seem a promise of truth.' It is not just the look, but the sound too: 'Women's voices also diminish their plausibility . . . The knowledge of this sound has permeated the intellectual conception of women, even of those who do not make public speeches.' She goes on most pertinently, 'In the criticism of women's writing, not even the word *hysterical* recurs as regularly as *shrill*. The working rule: blame something written by a woman as *shrill*, praise something as *not shrill*.'[10]

In her novel *The Female Man* Joanna Russ includes a section of brief extracts from (fictional) reviews of *The Female Man* itself. They illustrate a wide spectrum of response to the speaking, or writing, woman, their very variety showing the absurd and ludicrous position into which women are forced, one in which they can *never* be plausible. 'Shrill . . . vituperative . . . no concern for the future of society . . . maunderings of antiquated feminism . . . some truth buried in a largely hysterical . . . trivial topics like housework and the predictable screams of . . .'[11] Amusing though these invented comments may be, they demonstrate that Joanna Russ, more than any other writer of SF, seems to arouse the ire of her contemporaries. And, as we will see in more detail later, the accusations made against her are often couched in terms of what she 'can't' do; i.e. 'she can't write science fiction', or 'she can't create a proper narrative', accusations that are patently absurd and yet continue to be made.

In 1978 many of the ideas in Russ's essay were further explored and expanded by Susan Wood. 'Women and Science Fiction' offers a subtle examination and re-examination of stories and novels by women and men, pointing to the recent changes that allowed writers to experiment with 'the separation of social role from gender'. What most concerns Wood is what she calls the 'compelling' nature of stereotypes which abound in science fiction. She wishes to reclaim the archetypes that lie behind them, with their 'marvellously rich material for the imagination'. Susan Wood's analysis of women in science fiction is linked to her analysis of SF as popular writing. 'Many of the images of women in science fiction, as in any Western popular art form, seem to be distortions of archetypes we have barely begun to understand, much less reject.'[12] Such a refusal to reject out of hand mere stereotypes allows for a complex reading of the stories that does not counterpose 'real' women to 'images' of women.

Susan Wood is able to point to the appearance in science fiction of more 'adventurous, strong-minded women' than Joanna Russ was able to earlier, her first example being Russ's own Alyx of *Picnic on Paradise* and, later, *The Adventures of Alyx*. She links this, correctly I think, to an ideological change, to the change in 'our ideas of what constitutes appropriate "feminine" and human behaviour'. The images of women that Wood finds predominant in science fiction are those of woman as hero, as heroine and as alien. These images do not come from nowhere, nor are they simple opposites of old stereotypes. They demonstrate how science fiction and feminism can engage in a fruitful interplay that releases the writers' imaginations to explore new relations between ideas of inside and outside, self and world.

2
Science Fiction Narratives

What is science fiction? Many definitions have been offered, from the narrowly exclusive to the all-encompassing, and including the incomprehensible; from the academic definitions of critics like Robert Scholes and Darko Suvin to the more workaday ones of SF editors such as John Campbell (the founding editor of *Astounding Stories*). One must conclude there will never be agreement. In *The Encyclopedia of Science Fiction* the editors, Peter Nicholls and John Clute, introduce their survey of definitions of SF with the observation that '"Science fiction" is a label applied to a publishing category and its application is subject to the whims of editors and publishers'.[1] I would suggest that its application is also subject to the whims of readers and writers, who hold passionate views on what is or is not science fiction (irrespective. in many instances of under what label the work is published). These views depend, naturally enough, on the concerns of the interested party: science or society? Satire or speculation? Credibility or critique? It depends on what your priorities are.

A useful way to begin might be to see what science fiction *allows*.

By borrowing from other literary forms it lets writers defamiliarise the familiar, and make familiar the new and strange. These twin possibilities, apparently contradictory (but SF is full of contradictions), offer enormous scope to women writers who are thus released from the constraints of realism. The social and sexual hierarchies of the contemporary world can be examined through the process of 'estrangement', thus challenging normative ideas of gender roles; and visions of different worlds can be created, made familiar to the reader through the process of narrative. SF narrative can be used to break down, or to build up.

Joanna Russ suggests that science fiction expresses a tension between the possible and the impossible. To put it another way, science fiction can illuminate both what is, and what is not (yet, or in this world).

An illuminating analysis of the estranging powers of SF is offered by Rosemary Jackson in *Fantasy: The Literature of Subversion*, although problems with terminology arise. She stresses the subversive nature of fantasy, its interrogation of unitary ways of seeing, its tendency towards the dissolution of structures and its open-endedness. I would argue that such potentially radical aims can be claimed also for science fiction, although her view of science fiction as compensatory and transcendental, while pertinent to some writers (and I will later draw on her acute analysis of Ursula Le Guin) is unnecessarily restrictive.

Rosemary Jackson's 'fantasy', confusingly, is not the same as 'fantasy' as used commonly in the terminology of science fiction criticism: this latter usually denotes what she calls 'faery'. Fantasy, in science fictional terms, is used on the whole to describe a literature that is not open-ended, but is nostalgic, rather, for a past order; a literature of heroes and villains, dragons and demons, lords and villeins.

Modern fantastic literature, Rosemary Jackson suggests, is preoccupied with unconscious desire. Like Freud's concept of the force he called the uncanny, it 'uncovers what is hidden, and, by doing so, effects a disturbing transformation of the familiar into the unfamiliar'.[2] One of the defining characteristics of fantasy is that it moves towards an ideal of undifferentiation, with a tendency to dissolve structures. This, I would maintain, is precisely what can be found in the work of writers like Tanith Lee or Angela Carter, both of whom I see as science fiction writers, where metamorphoses abound and the dead walk in the land of the living.

It could be argued that both Lee and Carter are primarily writers of fantasy (in both senses of the term) rather than science fiction. But I would argue more generally that contemporary science fiction offers this subversive potential, based as it is on an Einsteinian model of the universe with entropy as a central trope. SF offers a language for the narration of dreams, for the dissolution of self and for the interrogation of cultural order.

While science fiction offers the means to break down certainties and to question notions both of femaleness and of character – and I would suggest that the possibilities opened up for the de-centring of a coherent self, as exemplified in the fiction of Joanna Russ, Monique Wittig and others, are not unrelated to ideas developed in feminist theory about the construction of a gendered subject through language and culture – it also offers the means to construct a subject. Much of science fiction is heavily indebted to traditions of romance fiction and there are writers, again such as Tanith Lee, who explore this aspect of the genre. Whereas in one discourse it may seem subversive to deconstruct, to replace presence with absence, in another, it may be subversive to explore the opposite, to replace absence (in this case the female subject) with presence. In other words to insert a female subject into a preponderantly male discourse.

Rosemary Jackson says of Mary Shelley's *Frankenstein: or the Modern Prometheus* and *The Last Man* that they are 'fantasies of absolute negation or dissolution of cultural order'.[3] Yet these works are claimed most convincingly by Brian Aldiss and David Wingrove as the first novels of science fiction. Their final comment on *Frankenstein* in the chapter on Mary Shelley in *Trillion Year Spree* in no way contradicts Jackson's thesis: 'It is appropriate that "darkness and distance" should be the closing words of *Frankenstein* just as "darkness" is almost its first word . . . SF is often haunted by that same sense of corruption and loss.'[4]

Rosemary Jackson's arguments, it seems to me, afford a valuable insight into the meanings and functions of fantastic narrative. Much of what she says, I believe, can be applied to science fiction, and in particular to the work of writers that I will be concentrating on in these pages. The fact that both she and Brian Aldiss afford Mary Shelley's *Frankenstein* a central place in their theses is significant. I would like to use this as a starting point for an exploration, in the next section, of the female Gothic tradition.

3
Travelling Heroinism

While I would not deny the importance of creating women as subjects in a field of literature so closely packed with men as is science fiction (a field in which, let us remember, 'women have not been relevant'), I feel that the virtues of strong role models can be overrated. We do not read simply to be instructed in appropriate or ideal behaviour, although there are some writers whose work tends towards this kind of classroom didacticism.

Of course it is great to have Anne McCaffrey's girls and women with their skills and strengths and emotions, or Le Guin's Odo, anarchist and feminist.[1] Vonda McIntyre's resourceful Misha in *The Exile Waiting* and serious, passionate Snake in *Dreamsnake* are encouraging, too; as are Sandi Hall's contemporary and future women in *The Godmothers*, Caroline Forbes' credible female protagonists in her collection *The Needle on Full* and Octavia Butler's tough, intelligent Alanna in *Survivor* and powerful Mary, who can heal as well as kill, in *Mind of My Mind*. These latter, like all Butler's heroines, are remarkable too for challenging the science fictional norm of hero by being Black as well as female and sexually autonomous. And it is a pleasure to come across complex female protagonists imagined by male writers, such as Delany's Rydra Wong in *Babel – 17* and Yaleen in Ian Watson's *The Book of the River* trilogy.

But women as protagonists do not necessarily interrogate the social and literary construction of women as gendered subjects. Creating a female protagonist simply seems to me an obvious stratagem a science fiction writer can adopt to offset the weight of books-by-men-for-men under which the reader sometimes feels herself squashed. My emphasis, then, is not on female characters as simple protagonists; but on the *how* and the *why* and the *to what end.*

First, I shall look at women as rebellious heroines in the tradition of those Gothic narratives claimed by Brian Aldiss as the antecedents of present-day science fiction. While the Gothic and fantastic modes of writing, with their beasts and monsters, their transformations and translocations, can be seen as precursors of science fiction in general, it is particularly interesting to look at the female Gothic tradition and to catch its resonances in contemporary science fiction written by women. For the female Gothic offers more than strong-minded heroines; it offers a means to women, as does science fiction, to challenge dominant literary conventions and to produce a literature that can be at once subversive and popular.

Of the women novelists who wrote in the Gothic mode Ann Radcliffe and Mary Shelley are probably the best known. The novels of Ann Radcliffe, one of the most popular writers of her day, are, as Ellen Moers says in *Literary Women*, a 'locus of heroinism'[2] which women have since turned to feminist purposes. Radcliffe's heroines are great travellers, both in geographical and in psychological terms. Moers calls this 'travelling heroinism' (heroinism, in her witty distinction, being 'literary feminism' as opposed to feminism) and draws a distinction between Radcliffe's heroines' outdoor travels (particularly to Italy, land of warmth, sensuality, rapture) and their indoor travels, through the twisting ill-lit corridors of castles where they are tested for courage and endurance and quick-wittedness. Whereas male writers of Gothic fantasies (such as Matthew Lewis, author of *The Monk*) tended to portray their heroines as trembling, passive and weak, Radcliffe's heroines, like Emily in *The Mysteries of Udolpho*, are tough, curious and self-interested. Unlike the women in Jacobean drama, from which Radcliffe borrows some of her props (grinning skulls, bodies in various stages of corruption either removed or discovered, and vice masquerading as virtue), where the wicked women are the most interesting and the virtuous ones dull, Radcliffe's heroines manage to be both virtuous and interesting. Emily's virtue is active rather than passive; by protecting her virtue she is keeping a hold on the property that her father has left her. Her chastity owes less to conventional notions of purity and honour than to an understanding of the importance to her future autonomy of acquiring independent means. In other words, a denial of her sexual availability promotes her, in her own right, to the ranks of the bourgeoisie.

Mrs Radcliffe's heroines, it seems, did not offer models to writers during the boom years of science fiction (the 1930s, 1940s and 1950s) – perhaps the prevailing ideologies around the position of women had so infiltrated the American unconscious that such strong female figures were ejected from the common pool of cultural and literary images. Texts from the period revert to dreary stereotypes: virtuous women, usually defined primarily as wives or daughters, are such dullards, while the evil, sexy alien queens are allowed all the fun – before, that is, being tamed by love or exterminated.

In her novels Ann Radcliffe shows us women doing everything they were not allowed to do in contemporary life, or could do only with difficulty and under the protection of a man. Her heroines evince a physical and moral courage that was generally denied expression by the restricted social circumstances of genteel nineteenth-century women. Moers suggests that, as early as the 1790s, Ann Radcliffe set the Gothic 'in one of the ways it would go ever after: a novel in which the central figure is a young woman who is simultaneously persecuted victim and courageous heroine'.[3]

Twenty years later, Mary Shelley's *Frankenstein, or the Modern Prometheus*, 'made the Gothic novel over into what today we call science fiction.'[4] Lacking both a heroine and an important female victim, it is none the less enormously important within the tradition of literary women as well as the Gothic. *Frankenstein* certainly profitably encourages interpretation. Ellen Moers finds it 'most interesting, most powerful and most feminine' in its motif of 'revulsion against newborn life, and the drama of guilt, dread and flight surrounding birth and its consequences.'[5] She sees it as a creation myth, as a story of birth and death, and relates it to Mary Shelley's own experiences of giving birth and of seeing her babies die. It is through Mary Shelley that birth entered fiction not as realism, but as Gothic fantasy. Rosemary Jackson emphasises the 'open-endedness' of the structure of *Frankenstein*, reading it as an early modernist text. I would say rather that it has a *tight* structure, built as it is of descriptions within descriptions, narrative voice within narrative voice, but all centring round the heart of darkness which is Frankenstein and his monster. Rosemary Jackson has more recently modified her interpretation to emphasise the absent mother in the text and the spiritual sub-text which she relates specifically to women's writing.[6]

The imaginations of Ann Radcliffe and Mary Shelley knew no geographical boundaries. The various narrators of *Frankenstein* move through Switzerland, Germany, England, Scotland, the Orkneys, Ireland, France and finally, in a scene powerfully echoed both in Ursula Le Guin's *The Left Hand of Darkness* and in Mary Gentle's *Golden Witchbreed*, across the ice and snow of the Antarctic. It is here, as remote from civilisation as is imaginable, that the distinction between Frankenstein and his creation is questioned: who is the pursuer and who the pursued? Who the murderer and who the victim? It is on the polar icecap of Gethen that Le Guin's envoy from earth, Genly Ai, is confronted with a dissolution of female and male in the figure of the androgyne Estraven, an escape from distinction and difference that is offered to him but which, unlike Frankenstein, he rejects.

Like Gothic fantasy, science fiction opens up a universe of possibilities for women. If women's lives are restricted on earth then travelling heroinism takes us off earth through time and space. Science fiction heroines like Russ's time-travelling secret agent Alyx take us not to Italy but to the planet of Paradise, another land of ice and snow. Diana, in Jane Palmer's *The Planet Dweller*, is a menopausal single mother who throws away her prescription of Valium, and the containment of women's lives that it implies, to pursue adventures beyond the galaxy. Another extra-galactic adventurer is Jade of the galaxy in Doris Piserchia's *Star Rider*. Jade escapes a fate worse than death – marriage and motherhood, that is – to lead a rag-bag collection of humanoid drop-outs and misfits, along with a planetful of ever-grinning varks, to fresh stars and galaxies new.

While the two latter novels are in the outdoor travel tradition, Josephine Saxton's stories and novels marvellously illustrate what Moers calls indoor travel. Saxton's female characters are Gothic heroines *par excellence*. They are constantly, if often comically, persecuted, while their courage is matched only by their cool.

The dark and twisting corridors of crumbling Gothic castles

through which an intrepid heroine stumbles become the different 'realities' or states of consciousness through which the revolution-seeking Jane Saint, in *The Travails of Jane Saint*, and Magdalen Hayward, in *Queen of the States*, pass. Anything is possible and, like Emily in *The Mysteries of Udolpho*, these heroines are constantly challenged to show qualities of courage, resourcefulness and intelligence. Nor, like Emily, are they found wanting.

The constraints against which Saxton's heroines strive are, quite specifically, those imposed upon women by men. Jane Saint sets off on her adventures in an 'other' world as a direct consequence of the 'total reprogramming' that has been prescribed to cure her of her revolutionary aims and desires. She is immersed in a sensory deprivation tank prior to being brainwashed. Magdalen, similarly, is confined in a mental hospital and, like Jane, is not entirely in control of her visits 'elsewhere', this being, in Magdalen's case, an alien spaceship. The travails and the travels result in a modern version of the nineteenth-century goal of property secured: an existential freedom that is the premise for a woman's autonomy. Saxton's work shows the influence of philosophers such as Marcuse and Sartre, but she scrutinises their thinking in the light of sexual politics. Jane and Magdalen achieve a personal freedom that represents the possiblility, no more, of freedom for women in general.

The Gothic antecedents of science fiction are apparent too in the wider structure of these novels. Both Jane and Magdalen are characters on a Quest, up against the rest of the world. Jane cannot remember at first what her Quest is for; she knows only that she is on one. The monsters she meets on the way – rather than the grasping relatives of Gothic romance, the evil witches and wizards of modern fantasy or the BEMs (Bug-Eyed Monsters) and alien intelligences of pulp science fiction – all materialise as men. (Jane does in fact meet a witch, Agatha Hardcastle, the witch of Heptonstall, who turns out to be a very cool cookie indeed.) They are not just the men she has had personal dealings with, such as her husband, but men from fiction, popular psychology and film; men she recognises as the wraiths and shadows of the Great Unconscious. Husbands get a rough ride in Saxton's work: poor pathetic Clive desperately trying to impress his female students in *Queen of the States*, and

Hugh Kolz the man who claims to be Jane's husband in *The Travails of Jane Saint*.

After Jane and the demon Zilp have been rescued from a flight through the void by a helicopter, Jane looks up to see 'a vaguely familiar face virtually drooling with sentimental recognition. It had a greying beard and moustache the texture of steel wool, unkempt hair in strands obviously meant to cover a high forehead and a shirt neither conventional nor Bohemian open at its neck. There was a coarseness in the skin texture indicating careless washing and heavy drinking, and the watery eyes in this face had a pathetic and yet sly expression.'[7] This apparition reveals himself as her loving husband, dedicated to protecting her. 'She stared into the eyes of the stranger quite bewildered and repelled. Husband? Surely not?' Tender reconciliations are avoided as at that moment there is a fearful scream and Zilp falls out of the helicopter as it banks.

Other monsters include the men who refuse to grow up, whom Jane comes across when she is inadvertently sucked into the Womb of the Great Earth Mother. She recognises them soon enough: 'She knew this kind; they had tremendous power in the world. They disguised themselves with well-cut jackets and rust-free cars. They had solved the secret of life with a wallet full of credit cards. They ran after younger and younger women the older they became. She had long ago decided not to be part of all that nor would her daughters.' The resourceful Jane forces the Womb of the Great Earth Mother into contractions: many drown, but, as she says philosophically, 'liberty does not suit all'.[8]

As Jane nears the end of her Quest, whose meaning she now knows but is not at all sanguine about, the forces of male domination gather against her. As her sidekick Merleau-Ponty explains to Dolores, one of Jane's daughters: ' "They will take all her life's thoughts and everything thought about her and put them in some obsolete sub-section, then construct yet another version of the Red-Haired Heroine, make it seem ludicrous, and pop it into the Occasional Archetypal Nightdream section. It's that simple, apparently it has been done before, for example with the Suffragettes. The method makes people forget that the movement was ever about something *real*." '[9] Merleau-Ponty is a long-haired dachshund ('it had very sympathetic eyes and she therefore deduced that it was a bitch') who is the brains behind the Quest; the necessary magical input comes from Zilp.

Finally, Saxton draws on another popular narrative genre, one that predates the Gothic and which, in simple form, turns up in much pulp science fiction: the morality tale. In title itself *The Travails of Jane Saint* points back to *Pilgrim's Progress*. Much of the energy of the writing comes from Saxton's enjoyment of the materialisation of metaphor and the narrative jokes that that allows, as abysses open beneath Jane's feet, as she toils up slippery slopes or is sucked into bottomless bogs (the jokes are further pointed up by the hints at their links with what is going on in the sensory deprivation tank in the other world – a trick that Saxton plays too in *Queen of the States*). When Jane first sees her three lost daughters, but fails to recognise them, they are clanking about in a cantina kitchen, chained to the sink. The barmaid, who sports a much finer chain, of gold, around her ankle, maintains that it is their, and her, own choice. '"What is the alternative?"' asks Jane. '"Starvation"' is the laconic reply.[10]

The Travails of Jane Saint is inventive, funny and fantastical. Jane meets the characters from the Tarot, who prove worse than useless, and Simone de Beauvoir, who is much the same. She meets a shaman from Finland and is rescued from her bog by Joan of Arc. The interplay of different disciplines in *The Travails of Jane Saint* – history, fiction, philosophy, psychology, films – with different states of consciousness is a direct precursor of *Queen of the States*.

Such concern with disparate states of perception and, by extension, being, have characterised Saxton's work from the beginning, as in the strange and haunting *The Hieros Gamos of Sam and An Smith* or the short story 'The Triumphant Head'. In this latter we see Man (Saxton's early work often features an isolated couple or small group of people – it seems quite sparse compared to the baroque nature of her later work) as existing in his physical attributes – his body that he builds, his clothes that he displays – while Woman is many possibilities, her appearance a chosen mask that can change from day to day.

The multi-media playfulness of the later novels, *Jane Saint* and *Queen of the States*, is predicated on an original distinction, which is then challenged in the course of the book, between the 'real' world and the 'other' world. In *Jane Saint* the 'real' world holds the sensory deprivation tank; in *Queen of the States* it holds the mental hospital. Both Jane and Magdalen are being punished for refusing to conform to a male view of how women should behave. Yet it is precisely their confinement that releases them into adventures that lead finally to the possibility of freedom. The movement between these two states – of a constraining patriarchal world and another one – marks a political development in Josephine Saxton's work which, perhaps, reflects the shift from the individual-based existentialism of the 1960s towards a philosophy that reflects a more collective sexual politics.

In what sense then are these books works of science fiction? They seem to have less to do with science fiction than many of the books under discussion, although Josephine Saxton's concern with consciousness and its vagaries is not unrelated to the move towards the exploration of 'inner space' taken by the 'New Wave' science fiction writers of the 1960s. Saxton herself has never been happy with the SF label, fearing its ghettoising qualities. As she puts it in an introductory note – A Plea to My Readers – in the later edition of *The Travails of Jane Saint* (The Women's Press, 1986): 'What I would really like is for *readers* to read my work, not only SF fans, who have, like rubber fetishists and gourmets, Special Tastes, and often cannot enjoy anything outside their label. Let me put in a plea, not just, as is sometimes necessary with Fantasy and Science Fiction, for a suspension of disbelief, but for a suspension of strictly labelled parameters . . .'[11]

Josephine Saxton's work is difficult to classify and while in an ideal world with a free interplay between the writer and reader classification should not be necessary, the point is that publishers, and others, do like to do it. The fact that it is SF editors, of books and magazines, who have consistently shown interest in Saxton's work is not without significance. While I would say that she produces works of political metaphor, I would also say that that definition places them within the wider genre of SF, for SF in particular allows this. For Saxton's eclecticism, her borrowing from a variety of other popular forms, is not unusual within science fiction. Indeed science fiction is positively elastic as regards rules of style, and encourages a playful self-reflectivity. In other words, it is ideally suited to the kinds of fractured consciousness and gleeful mêlées of fictions that mark Saxton's work. Jane Saint and Magdalen Hayward may be direct descendants of Mrs Radcliffe's tough, resourceful young women; but it is in science fictional worlds that they now find freedom from a dominant and constricting order.

4
Amazons: Feminist Heroines or Men in Disguise?

Amazons, too, are related to the female Gothic tradition, not just for the rebelliousness they show against a given social order, but in particular for their place in tales of sword-and-sorcery, that marvellously Gothic locus of mayhem and magic.

For many male writers of science fiction Amazons serve as symbol of all that is most feared and loathed as Other, the castrating mother wreaking vengeance for her condition on her male offspring. She must be denied through death, or forced into submission to a male-dominated heterosexual practice which then becomes the norm. As a general rule, as is well illustrated in the collection *When Women Rule*, Amazons must be punished, nominally perhaps for their presumption in assuming 'male' characteristics, such as strength, agency, power, but essentially for their declaration of Otherness.

Joanna Russ has analysed these types of stories – and with particular reference to the collection *When Women Rule* – in her essay '*Amor Vincit Fœminam*: The Battle of the Sexes in Science Fiction'. She points out that they posit the possession of the male genitalia, no more, as the guarantor of victory in the battle of the sexes. 'This victory is therefore a victory of nature, and so the battle may be won without intelligence, character, humanity, humility, foresight, courage, planning, sense, technology, or even responsibility. So "natural" is male victory that most of the stories cannot offer a plausible explanation of how the women could have rebelled in the first place . . . The conflict is resolved – either for all women or for an exemplary woman – by some form of phallic display, and the men's victory (which is identical with the women's defeat) is not a military or political event but a

34

quasi-religious conversion of the women.'[1]

It must be said, too, that it is not only male writers who are filled with such fear of women. Kit Reed's story, 'Songs of War', shows a group of women who take part in an armed uprising. The women are, variously, stupid, cruel, violent and crazy; the uprising is doomed to failure and the protagonist returns to her loving husband feeling satisfied with herself and the world. The story seems to me to express nothing so much as a terrible fear of separatism and an insecurity about the solace offered by men. In such a world lesbians are monsters lurking in the dark abyss outside the nuclear home.

Joanna Russ's response in fictional form to the barely concealed hatred of women in such Amazon stories can be found in the delightful story 'The Clichés from Outer Space'. Along with her marvellous version of 'The Weird-Ways-of-Getting-Pregnant Story' ('"*Eegh! Argh! Eegh! Argh!*"' cried Sheila Sue Hateman in uncontrollable ecstasy as the giant alien male orchid arched over her, pollinating her every orifice.'), 'The Talking-About-It Story' ('"Oh my, how I do love to live in an equal society," said Irving the physicist . . .') and 'The Noble Separatist Story', Russ gives us 'The Turnabout Story, or, I always knew what they wanted to do to me because I've been doing it to them for years, especially in the movies', which stars 'four ravaging, man-hating, vicious, hulking, Lesbian, sadistic, fetishistic Women's Libbers'[2] whose plans to wipe men from the face of the earth all come to naught for reasons that are purely hormonal.

Besides the satirical approach, there seem to be two responses to the male-defined Amazon. First there are a group of contemporary women writers who are trying to free the Amazon, as Susan Wood said, from the Amazon stereotype.[3] These writers include Marion Zimmer Bradley, with her Free Amazons of Darkover, particularly in *The Shattered Chain*, Suzy McKee Charnas with the Riding Women *and* the Free Fems in *Motherlines* and Joanna Russ with the women of Whileaway in 'When It Changed' and *The Female Man*. But what, then, is the definition of Amazon? Is an Amazon a woman who is independent of a man or men? The writers mentioned above are just some of the writers who represent women in their work as tough, resourceful and strong. Some, like Charnas, are particularly interested in showing them as loving and nurturing as well. In other words, Amazons are being freed from their stereotypes in order to appear as more fully human, in which case, perhaps, independence overrides Amazonness. That is, some writers find it useful to borrow aspects of the Amazon genre for their representations of independent women.

The second response is the feminist intervention into the sword-and-sorcery genre. Here, once again, we find Joanna Russ, that most protean of writers, and Tanith Lee, another writer of great versatility whose pleasure in the structural conventions of genre writing, in particular of fantasy and sword-and-sorcery, is a delight. Attempts have been made to reclaim Amazons for women if not for feminists by taking the heroes of sword-and-sorcery tales and giving them breasts. While they tend to be less mighty in the thews than their brothers they go in for the same sword-wielding dragon-taming behaviour. Some of these have been collected in two *Amazons!* anthologies edited by Jessica Amanda Salmonson. The problem with these role-reversal stories – as with role-reversal societies – is that they do not necessarily challenge the gender stereotypes that they have reversed. Salmonson claims in her introduction to *Amazons!* that 'the very act of women taking up sword and shield, to a society like our own which is ruled predominantly by men, is an act of revolution whether performed in fact or in art.'[4] I would question whether you can relate sword-and-sorcery so closely to 'fact'; such claims have little relevance to women taking up arms in national liberation struggles, where, anyway, a Kalashnikov rifle would undoubtedly be more efficacious than sword and shield. In literature, it seems to me, an act of revolution can be achieved only through a subversion of the narrative structure that holds the protagonist in place: a gender reversal is not enough.

Joanna Russ's Alyx of *The Adventures of Alyx*, which includes *Picnic on Paradise*, is, as well as a time-travelling secret agent, a thief, assassin and wise woman. The traditional tropes of sword-and-sworcery – wicked magicians, swashbuckling thickly-bearded pirates (although Russ manages to make hers sexy) and cities in which conspicuous consumption is set next to starvation and disease – are offset by Alyx's strong vein of rationalism and scepticism, which makes her a peculiarly modern heroine. Russ is a humorist, and much of the fun in the Alyx stories comes from her clever borrowing from different *redefining gender* genres. While Alyx shows all sorts of heroic qualities she is not a simple female version of a male hero. She is, in fact, strongly gendered, that is, her femaleness is shown to be quite specifically constructed within the parameters of difference. The self-knowledge that Russ allows her heroine infuses the adventures with a real sense of sexual politics; the relationships that Alyx has with women and with men are, as a result, both subtle and strong.

Tanith Lee's Jaisel in 'Northern Chess' is, like Alyx, as quick with her wits as she is swift with her sword, and as aware of the social construction of femininity that would, if it could, entrap her in the world of sword-and-sorcery. Elsewhere Tanith Lee goes in for the magical metamorphoses that fantasy and sword-and-sorcery allow; here these are subordinated to Jaisel's understanding of the arbitrary – or conventional – nature of the linguistic and cultural system that represents women as inferior beings to men. The result is Jaisel's triumph over the male-dominated world in which she is placed.

While Alyx and Jaisel are heroines in terms of their representation as tough, clever and independent, it is their place within a particular literary tradition of sword-and-sorcery and their subversion of that tradition that makes them what I would call 'feminist heroines'. So, too, with the 'travelling heroines' like Jane Saint, whose travels towards freedom and independence draw on a specifically female Gothic tradition that has allowed women to re-enter a field that for many years was closed to them.

5
When Women Write of Women's Rule

The female protagonists of Tanith Lee, Joanna Russ and Josephine Saxton are inscribed in and variously transform certain forms of narrative – the Gothic, the fantastic, sword-and-sorcery – that allow for a vigorous rewriting of male traditions. I would like to look now at some of the problems raised when women writers intervene in a particular form much exploited by male writers with dubious aims: the role reversal. In the previous section I was looking at the individual woman-in-a-male-role; here I would like to look at the depiction of societies in which women are given the attributes normally reserved for men, that is, economic, political and sexual dominance. Here, the central questions are: what is role reversal for, and can it be feminist?

I should like to explore two novels by two writers of science fiction, *The Ruins of Isis* by Marion Zimmer Bradley and *Leviathan's Deep* by Jayge Carr, to see how they deal with the weight of woman-hatred that, it seems to me, lies at the core of role-reversal stories. To see whether they can transform it, and whether, indeed, this science fictional form allows that transformation. By contrast, I will look at a novel that draws on a quite different literary tradition – that of satire – for its purposes: Esmé Dodderidge's *The New Gulliver, or The Adventures of Lemuel Gulliver Jr in Capovolta*. Finally, I shall consider the work of Gwyneth Jones, whose novels may be far removed from role reversal, but who takes as a premise of her science fictional worlds the political and social dominance of women.

The Ruins of Isis is an immensely readable book, and full of ideas that potentially challenge accepted sexual power relations. The structure is common enough in science fiction: an outside observer comes to an alien culture, misunderstandings arise from the ensuing clash of value systems, and both sides learn something, if only a little, from the encounter. (This too is the framework for *Leviathan's Deep*.)

The Ruins of Isis opens with the arrival on the planet Isis of Cendri Owain Malocq, researcher in xeno-anthropology, masquerading as a Scholar Dame in archaeology, with her husband Dal Malocq, who is the real, although as yet unqualified archaeologist, as her Companion. The women of Isis have invited Dal's superior, the Scholar Dame di Velo, to come and examine the ancient ruins on their world, which might, or might not, be of Builder origin – the Builders being an ancient and mysterious race in which the Scholar Dame di Velo has done particular research. When she is incapacitated by an accident, the women of Isis extend the invitation to her assistant instead, assuming that in the male-dominated world of the Unity a woman who had achieved Scholar Dame status would ensure that her assistants, too, were women. Cendri Owain comes originally from Beta Capella, where it is not customary for women to change their name on marriage. Dal, however, comes from the macho culture of Pioneer, and at his insistence she has taken his name. Anthropologists are forbidden on Isis; Cendri is thus deceiving the women on two counts.

On Isis the men live separately from the women, except for the favoured Companions who are petted and pampered. Men are seen as uncivilised, naturally inferior to women, flirtatious, untrustworthy and prone to fits of aggression which are channelled off through organised games. In general they are referred to as 'it', 'he' being used only when their sexual function is emphasised. Cendri's first encounter with the Isis women's view of men takes place on the shuttle just before landing. The pilot asks her how she is going to control Dal, referring to him as if he were a pet animal, suggesting, among other things, the implantation of a controlling electrode in one testicle. Cendri, the little woman who gave up both name and work on marriage, is horrified, but finally agrees to a collar with name tag being put around Dal's neck.

A major part of Bradley's critique of male dominance and female oppression is expressed in the relationship between

Cendri and Dal. Cendri believes in the possibility of equality between women and men without experiencing it in her own life. She is full of contradictory notions. She pays lip service to the notion of equality between the sexes on University, where she and Dal live, but to explain the preponderance of male over female scholars she admits some vague notion about women being less competitive than men. In some cases, she thinks, 'dominance [of a woman by a man] is not so bad'. This naivety about her own oppression points up the general acceptance of male dominance throughout the Unity; Cendri is so imbued with the liberal ideology of the planet University that she cannot see the oppression it masks, even when it affects her own life.

During the course of the book Cendri begins to question some of her received ideas on the glories of sexual equality and even, tentatively, on the naturalness of heterosexual love. But her glimmerings of self-doubt do not lead her very far. Most of the time she is too busy vacillating between being angry with Dal and trying to placate him. She becomes angry with him on a personal level because he constantly belittles her, sulks, makes demands, and is a drain on her energy; she is angry for professional reasons when he becomes involved in an attempted revolt by the men of Isis and thus breaks the laws of Unity against interference in another culture (a favourite law of science fiction writers, the lowest common denominator, it seems, of political consciousness: We All Know It's Wicked to Interfere).

So what is Dal like? Unfortunately he is so grossly unsympathetic that the reader soon loses patience with Cendri. It is hard to imagine why she married such a bully in the first place, let alone why she wishes to continue the relationship. The following is an example of the quality of their exchanges. Cendri has just discovered the lavish and luxurious bathroom they have been given, and is exclaiming that if cultures were to be judged by their plumbing techniques then Isis would rate high.

Dal looked dubious. He said, 'I'm not sure; societies which place too much value on luxurious body-care have usually been decadent, historically speaking. Viable and vigorous societies tend to be more spartan in emphasis; but the overemphasis on physical comfort is what I would expect of a society where females define the major priorities.'[1]

He continues in this vein for some paragraphs, concluding with,

'Of course you wouldn't be interested in historical perspective, would you, Cendri? Women aren't – it's excusable, of course, probably necessary for biological reasons, but women always tend to live in the present, and leave historical perspectives for men. And women never seem even to define this as a fault!'[2]

The message of *The Ruins of Isis*, and it does indeed have a message, is that the women of Isis are wrong to view and to treat their men in the way they do. The unusual (for Isis) relationship between Cendri and Dal affords a lesson to some of the women; to Laurina, who is an aspiring scholar, and who is intellectually persuaded that men can be the equals of women after working with Cendri and Dal in the Ruins. And to Miranda, the daughter of one of the pro-Matriarchs, who believes that her love for her mother's Companion is deviant and shameful, and who thus sees Cendri's life amongst men on University, and her relationship with Dal, to be a vindication of her own feelings and a state towards which she aspires. The problem is that the reader – this reader, at least – feels both these young women to be sadly mistaken, for Dal shows little intellectual or sexual respect for Cendri. If Dal were the touchstone, then one might be forced to conclude that, authorial intentions to the contrary, the women of Isis were right, and separatism would be vindicated.

It must be said that Cendri does, to a certain extent, respond to the new values she meets on Isis and begins to show a little self-awareness. Her movement towards autonomy – alas, never fully realised – is punctuated by a series of sexual encounters. The first is a stagey 'seduction' of Cendri by Dal, when he suggests they spend the night together in the rather grossly named 'Amusement Corner' in their room:

Cendri laughed, putting her arms up around his neck. 'Don't you be arrogant with me, love, on this world I could have you put out at night like a puppy dog!' But she let him scoop her up in his arms and carry her to the padded alcove. It was considerably more comfortable than that high, narrow bed!

'This seems to be my only proper function on this world,'

Dal murmured against her lips, 'I might as well take advantage of it!'

Don't be ridiculous, darling,' she whispered, drawing him down to her. 'We'll call it a second honeymoon.'

Dal had made a joke of it. And yet there was a trace of bitterness behind the words which told Cendri that in Dal's heart it was very far from being a joke.[3]

The second encounter takes place on the seashore, and reveals to Cendri how the women on Isis become pregnant. It is a thrice-yearly ritual, when the men come, in disguise, out of the water and make love with any number of women:

'She had expected, feared, something cold and impersonal, a ritual brutality like rape, had braced herself to endure that. Her preconceptions melted away before the gentleness of the man whose face she never saw. His hands on her were clumsy, yet tender; his body on hers warm and inviting. Her dread melted away; she welcomed him into herself, giving herself over to the night and to the soft sounds all around her.[4]

The two passages mirror each other in the coyness of their language and in their imprecision of detail. The stereotypical steps of seduction in the first scene are described in appropriately vague terms: Cendri is 'scooped up' just like the aforementioned 'puppy dog', she is obliged by the conventions to 'draw him down to her' even though only a second before he was 'murmuring against her lips', surely one of the least efficient means of communication. The second passage is the stuff of the softest of soft pornography: hands that are clumsy yet tender, unknown bodies that are warm and inviting. But Cendri's reflections on this latter encounter anticipate the wider lesson she learns on Isis, for she decides that it is not about sex alone, but that it is 'for some kind of togetherness, some way of reuniting the sundered halves of the society.'[5]

Cendri's participation in the ritual by the sea, in which she discerns a 'genuineness' of 'communication', although the reader may well not, is the first step away from Dal's possessiveness, but it is what happens *after* she has had sex with eleven, twelve or thirteen strange men (she loses count), that really threatens the relationship, for, apparently unexhausted, she turns to her friend Laurina, just as all the other women are turning to each other once the men have gone.

She did not protest when she felt herself drawn into a close embrace, felt Laurina's kiss like a lover's on her mouth. She had been too shaken, too surprised by the strangeness of this ritual mating on the sand, to find the sort of pleasure she normally took in sex; surprised, shocked at herself, she discovered that the woman's touch was bringing her to the release which tension and uncertainty had denied her before. In a surge of tenderness she found herself reciprocating, felt a curious shaken delight as the other woman trembled and cried out under her caresses.[6]

There is something for everyone here: single sex, group sex, lesbian sex. It is this last, sex with Laurina, that prompts the rebellious thought in Cendri's head. 'Why should I care what any man thinks?' About time, you might say, but again the scene is unconvincing, lacking in the emotional weight that detail might give it. The predictability of 'the other woman trembled and cried out under her caresses' (the fictional formula for good sex) is as dreary as those familiar clumsy yet tender hands and the murmuring against the lips.

Still, this is at least a step in the right direction, away from a pathetic dependence on Dal. But Marion Zimmer Bradley does not develop it. Cendri's relationship with Dal continues in the same old cycle of irritation and guilt until, at the end, miraculously it seems, she discovers Dal's 'true' feelings about her. They are standing together in the presence of the Beings in the Ruins, with everybody's thoughts open to each other, and Cendri feels coming from Dal 'an acceptance, a respect, a tenderness, which had nothing, or very little, to do with sex; it came from caring, from shared work, from their long time of learning about one another.'[7] This, after so much has appeared to the contrary in the narrative, seems totally arbitrary.

The privileging of heterosexual love between presumed equals, as exemplified in the relationship between Cendri and Dal, is given the seal of approval by the mysterious Beings. This is the dénouement of the story, the transformation of the wider political arena within which Cendri and Dal have been playing their parts. For the ultimate sign of the women's mistaken attitude towards men comes from the Beings, and Dal plays only a minor role as the agent of that revelation. The structure of the matriarchate on Isis rests on the assumed blessing of the Beings in the Ruins, who appear to dictate the succession of High Matriarchs (over which there is a squabble when Cendri arrives) and who have always, it seems, supported the women with strong emanations (telepathic) of love and approval. But their apparent support for the status quo is revealed, finally, to have been based upon a misapprehension. The Beings have never spoken to the men on Isis simply because they have always seen them through the eyes of the women, as an inferior species, not fully human. When they recognise the men's humanness, they say ' " . . . now we know that the women and the men are very much alike, we shall speak to both . . . " '[8]

And so another matriarchy bites the dust. The final humiliation for the women is not simply the discovery that they are not favoured above men and thus not innately superior, but comes when the genuinely important powers of the Beings – that they can forewarn of the destructive tidal waves that so frequently threaten the lives of the inhabitants of Isis – are finally revealed. For the women had never been aware of this; it is as a result of questions put to them by a man that the Beings admit to this power.

The majority of matriarchies portrayed in science fiction, as Susan Wood pointed out in 'Women and Science Fiction' are vicious, static, crumbling from within, or a mixture of all three.[9] *The Ruins of Isis* is no exception. A vicious power struggle is taking place between the two pro-Matriarchs, the stasis of the society is exemplified both in its isolation from the wider world of the Unity and in the women's apparently half-witted inability to secure themselves against the constant threats of destruction, and, as we have seen, the matriarchy finally crumbles at a few words from a man. So what are the author's intentions? Why has she chosen this science fictional form?

It does allow for an attempt at satirising some of the grosser aspects of women's oppression in the contemporary world. The women of Isis see men as creatures programmed by their biology, recognisable only in terms of their natural, physical functions. So, for example, intellectual work is considered bad for them as it spoils them for their sexual and reproductive uses. Playmates, drudges and reproductive organs in human form, excluded from positions of power 'for their own good': the parallels between this and a patriarchal society's view of women are obvious. Perhaps this is why Zimmer Bradley has achieved a reputation as a feminist writer.

But this is only a minor aspect of the novel. Bradley's wider intention does not appear to be satirical: the female-supremacist society on Isis is not a mirror image of any contemporary male-supremacist society. Nor, conversely, is it set up as a viable alternative. Imagined alternatives belong to a different tradition, the utopian one, and, as we shall see, are separatist rather than supremacist. The intention, rather, seems didactic. Cendri learns a lesson, that 'tyranny is tyranny, be it the tyranny of the man over the woman, or of the woman over the man'.[10] Complementarity, the reader is meant to conclude, is the ideal solution; but it is a complementarity that does not take into consideration the complex history of sexual inequality, and one that, finally, leaves women disprivileged. In *The Ruins of Isis* it is the women who have to make all the sacrifices, admitting the error of their ways. A familiar story, perhaps, but an odd resolution for this particular one that sets out, or so it seems, to investigate sexual relations of power and powerlessness.

Finally, then, *The Ruins of Isis* is an anti-feminist book, just like the role-reversal stories written by men that preceded it. Where men use this form of narrative simply to restore the status quo (which in some sense they must feel is threatened), Bradley's intention seems to be to forgive men for their unkindnesses towards women by showing that women can be just as bad as men. What we need, this book suggests, is balance; but because she seems unable to imagine a truly egalitarian society, instead she gives women power and then takes it away from them. Men, meanwhile, are waiting to regain the power that is rightfully theirs; the weakness of women, one must conclude, resides in their sex. What is expressed most strongly is a fear of powerful, strong women: their downfall must be engineered, and what more welcome downfall than love for a man?

The final scene of *The Ruins of Isis* shows women and men working alongside each other in equality on Isis. Cendri is a Scholar Dame at last, but she is pregnant. In Bradley's vision women are intimately connected with their biological role: they must always choose, and a price must always be paid. If they are mothers, they must forgo a public life; if, as in the *Darkover* series, they are telepaths, they must be chaste. Bradley shows *in Bradley:*

that women *can* do anything – and this perhaps is why she is hailed as a feminist – but they can't do *everything*. And while women must choose, men just exist. It is enough, for men, to be.

The dualistic structure of role-reversal stories excludes the possibility that they might be claimed for feminist ends. It allows only two options: that one group retains or regains power over the other; or that some kind of balance is achieved. It is this latter that is expressed in the work of Marion Zimmer Bradley, at the cost of her female characters. Inscribed in all her novels (including *The Shattered Chain,* the reputedly feminist novel of her *Darkover* series) is a warning to women: avoid too much power or you will sacrifice the love of men; and a plea to men for love and understanding. She forces her female characters into submissive roles towards male characters who are obviously their emotional and intellectual inferiors. And then suggests that that is as it should be.

This is not satirical but prescriptive writing. For Bradley does not portray female characters who act just like men (hers is quite unlike the satire of George Orwell's *Animal Farm*, where the animals reflect on the human behaviour they ape); nor is she saying that women in power are better than men in power. She is suggesting that women are different, but should be equal: in other words, she attempts to portray harmonious social relations based on different spheres for women and men. Political analysis of women's oppression is eschewed along with the satirical possibilities that role reversal seems to hold out. The difference finally comes down to biology, although it is disguised behind an apparent liberal concern with the question of individual choice. Bradley, for whatever reason, seems incapable of creating a credible male character. Yet her female characters, on whom her reputation as a feminist writer rests, all knuckle under to the notional Man. And it is precisely this idea of biological difference that is foregrounded in another science fictional role reversal by a woman, Jayge Carr's *Leviathan's Deep*.

Leviathan's Deep is another culture-clash story. Set on the largely ocean-world of Delyafam, it concerns a confrontation between its female-supremacist society and that of potential colonisers from the male-dominated world of Terra. Although the women of Delyafam are the ruling class, they are constrained by a hierarchical social order that precludes intimate personal relationships and by a rigid religious tradition that allows little personal freedom. A power struggle is in progress between two of the 'Nobleladies'. But Jayge Carr is more generous to her matriarchy than Marion Zimmer Bradley is to hers, for the forces of progress are allowed to come from within, through her protagonist, the Kimassu Lady, who learns both how to protect and safeguard her planet for the future against Terre greed, and how to restructure her society to ensure greater personal and political freedom for all its citizens – including the men, who have previously always been disenfranchised.

The role reversal of Delye society allows a critique of human – male-dominated – society through the process of estrangement. In this story the visitors from Terra, the men, are the aliens. It is as an alien form of behaviour that we view their greed, their rapaciousness and the sadism that fuels their lust. The reader is invited to identify with the women of Delyafam, despite their non-human aspects: their bright orange colouring and their webbed feet. To be female is the norm, to be male is to be 'other', inevitably defined in terms of sex. Throughout the book the female pronoun is used generically, 'she' to mean a person (as seemingly natural as Marge Piercy's gender-free 'per' in *Woman on the Edge of Time*). In a neat reversal of our linguistic conventions, boats – the most important artefacts on Delyafam – are given masculine nomenclature because they are guided, controlled and driven by women. The sea, too, is masculine, being 'as capricious as a male'.

The Kimassu Lady is, herself, an outsider: the rigid conventions of her society ensure that her physical deviation from the norm – she has a noticeably pale skin – results in social ostracism. Forced to prove her merit somehow, she takes on the unpopular job of dealing with the Terrene. She is uniquely placed to appreciate both the advantages and the dangers of their systems and ideas. She learns the strengths of their weapons, which include 'guile and lies and deceitful smiles . . .'[11] She becomes more critical of the weaknesses of her own society, realising that an unquestioning belief in the sanctity of tradition, whether religious or secular, is wide open to manipulation.

The narrative structure works well on two counts. The strange

– the female figure as central and normative – is familiarised; the mundane – male attitudes towards women in a sexist society – is brought into sharp focus through defamiliarisation. At the same time, the society which allows the expression of female as norm is not shown uncritically; while the alienating quality of the male role is tempered by the introduction of a male character who offers some hope of progress. And at the centre stands a protagonist who is herself an outsider.

But the book embodies, and cannot resolve, a political and aesthetic problem. What is striking about the sexual organisation of society on Delyafam is that the dominance of women has not come about as the successful result of a struggle waged by women against men, nor is it ascribed vaguely to religious tradition as in *The Ruins of Isis*, although it is, necessarily, corroborated by religious ideology. It is based on an important biological distinction between women and men. Delyafam is a world on which women cannot be raped. Women are the initiators, controllers and choosers in all sexual matters: men are sexually vulnerable and sexually available.

And again, as in *The Ruins of Isis*, because the book's purpose is not primarily satirical (although there are satirical or absurdist elements in the portrayal of one sex being defined solely by their genitals), a narrative conclusion must somehow be reached. Both books, finally, are romances, with a happy ending based on compromise. Carr offers this through the rather ambiguous figure of the Terren Neill, who represents a healthy and basically progressive scepticism towards the static and rigidified Delye society. He becomes Kimassu's 'dear, loving comrade', and although he is killed by her to protect the secret of Delye reproduction, his ideas live on.

This romantic resolution is completely at odds with the book's description of a cultural premise of gender differentiation based on anatomical sexual difference, which although not necessarily 'untrue', reduces everything to the level of genital structure. The societies of both Delyafam and Terra are shown as falling far short of an ideal, precisely because both are based on the power wielded by the threat of potential sexual violence. But the conventional narrative structure requires a conventional resolution.

This confusion is what finally distinguishes these role-reversal stories from the ones written by men. In the latter the narrative drive leads towards a pre-ordained conclusion: male power is reinstated whether it be through love or arms. But here the conclusions, or dénouements, are at odds with the preceding narrative. Bradley's men are insupportable. The reader can be sure that with only one of them around there will be little chance of a fair deal for women, while Carr suggests that anatomical difference leads inevitably to a social imbalance of power. Perhaps part of the problem lies in what it is that the female characters are meant to represent. The female characters are women, but women with the attributes of men, that is, women with power and the capacity to abuse it. They must, finally, be shown to be at fault. Yet the fault seems as much to lie in their womanness (otherwise why invent them as women?) as in their position of power. Powerful women are seen as biological monsters. Biology is muddled up with social structures. Both authors are then forced to fall back on the commendable, but vague, notion of equality for everyone; the potential critique of a male-dominated society gets lost along the way.

While the idea may be to give women a fairer deal than they have had in previous role reversals, the dualistic structure of the parameters within which the authors are working does not allow it.

It is interesting that male writers who are seriously concerned to explore the oppression of women have eschewed role reversal and have instead chosen to use the fiction of separatism. As early as 1951 Phillip Wylie set up parallel worlds in *The Disappearance*, a lengthy discursive novel in which, at an instant, all men disappear from the world and, to men, all women disappear from it. As the two stories develop, the women fare quite well, although disadvantaged by their lack of scientific and technical knowledge (denied them in the ordinary world), and set up co-operative forms of social organisation that work with credible and creditable efficiency. The all-male world soon degenerates into chaos and barbarism, equally credibly. It is rather more than the 'slightly old-fashioned but well-meaning attack on the double standard', which is how it is described in *The Encyclopedia of Science Fiction*.

In the search for early works of science fiction Jonathan Swift's *Travels into Several Remote Nations of the World by Lemuel Gulliver, first a Surgeon, and then a Captain of Several Ships*, more commonly known as *Gulliver's Travels*, is outstanding. Whether it is seen as proto SF, ur-SF or whatever, its influence on the development of science fiction is unmistakable. Full homage is paid in the work of a British writer, otherwise unknown in the science fiction field, Esmé Dodderidge, with her novel *The New Gulliver, or The Adventures of Lemuel Gulliver Jr in Capovolta.* Esmé Dodderidge takes her junior Gulliver into, as her title suggests, a world turned upside down, where women are in male roles and men in female ones, which reflects and reveals the absurdities and iniquities of a sexist society.

Lemuel is on an obscure mission in some kind of airship when he is suddenly snatched from the sky and finds himself in Capovolta, where he remains sick and unconscious for a long period and is tended back to health by a family whose daughter, Vrailbran, he eventually marries. Capovolta is run by women; all of them have careers and are breadwinners for their families. Men assume all the domestic responsibilities. Klemo, as Lemuel is now called, is first puzzled and then astounded by the gross injustices he sees around him. Vrailbran's aged father does all the heavy work around the house and is never consulted for his opinion. On the streets Klemo, like all men, is subject to constant sexual harrassment; he brings it upon himself by wearing the sexually revealing clothes – insisted upon by Vrailbran – that all men are expected to wear. When he gets a job in the national transport company he finds there are few opportunities open to men for advancement, while women are promoted irrespective of merit. Male employees are constantly exposed to the sexual advances of their superiors, and suffer accordingly if they do not acquiesce. When Vrailbran gives birth to twins, Klemo gives up his job to look after them and to run the household. Vrailbran soon becomes bored with his dreary domesticity and looks for fun elsewhere. She abandons her family and Klemo is left to reflect bitterly on the double oppression suffered by men.

The arguments put forward by the Capovoltans to justify the inferior social position held by men rest on the assumption of a natural order in which women are on top. Men cannot succeed in public life because their first responsibility is to the family. Klemo feels that his abilities (proven in his earlier life when he was a member of the ruling sex) are wasted, but is told that if he were really able then he would succeed. As a single parent he comes to appreciate the illogicality of the system: men are considered useless and dependent creatures but when deserted by their wives have the full responsibility of childcare and of earning thrust upon them. When Vrailbran files a claim for custody of the children she asserts that Klemo is irresponsible because, having to earn a living, he cannot look after the children full time.

In our terms, Klemo lives down among the women. He can appreciate the underdog's view of a 'natural' order of being, where one sex is allowed all the opportunities and the other sex is blamed for its position in the pile. He vows that if he ever returns to his own country he will 'never again be so insensitive to the subtle bias I had so casually accepted as the natural, predetermined order of things.'[13]

The New Gulliver is complex and subtle. Its effectiveness as a critique of the sexual status quo is attained partly through the consistency of the humour of its satire – the absurdity of the situation is never less than pertinent to our own society – and partly through Dodderidge's faithfulness to the original in the character of Lemuel Gulliver Jr. Despite his pridefulness he is an innocent; injustice is heaped upon injustice and it is almost too much for the reader to bear.

A rather more schematic satire using role reversal as its strategy can be found in Gerd Brantenburg's *The Daughters of Egalia*. Again, a male character is outraged and insulted by the afflictions forced upon him because of his sex, but Brantenburg tends to target the grosser forms of sexual exploitation and oppression, and does little to offer an internalised view. The result is depressing rather than enraging, whereas Dodderidge manages to arouse a sympathetic passion.

These two works have as the object of their satire male-dominated societies. Their authors write of women ruling as a specific strategy for writing about men ruling. In the work of the young British writer Gwyneth Jones, women rule, but not necessarily over men. Men are peripheralised; politically of no account in the depiction of shifting allegiances and hidden sources of power in *Divine Endurance*; absent except as an occasional bunch of noisy extras, or as a parodic 'man interest' in *Escape Plans*.

Gwyneth Jones has said that she sees writing as rehearsal; a rehearsal in the imagination for what might be in the world. Political power is an important theme in her work; power held by women.

Divine Endurance is set on a peninsula where the ruling house of Garuda the Eagle has long been deposed and where people are kept in order by agents of the Rulers, who come, it is suspected, from an ancient and perhaps decaying race, and who inhabit shining islands off the coast. It is still the women who maintain power, as has always been the case: the Dapur behind their high walls, in the recesses of their garden, where all is stillness and silence. It is they who say to the population: you must not resist; you must not risk lives. But the dark-skinned Derveet, of the house of the Eagle, rebels, wanting to choose life over the slow sliding of the world into chaos and death. She looks for allies amongst the tough, practical Samsui women, and amongst outcast bands of mutants and cripples, the Pulowljo. Into the peninsula from the poisoned desert to the east comes a beautiful girl child Cho – Chosen Among the Beautiful – with a cat, Divine Endurance, in search of her centuries-lost twin brother, Wo – Worthy to be Beloved – and ready to fulfil a mission that she does not yet understand. Cho is a Wayang Legong, an angel doll, a meta-genetic gynoid, fashioned aeons before. In Cho's relationship with Derveet Gwyneth Jones explores the complexity of human desire.

In *Escape Plans* the earth has been made clean again and is now a nature reserve, a tourist resort for visiting members of the ruling class, who live offworld. The masses, or numbers, have been tidied away below the surface; all works smoothly as part of the system SERVE, zero-variation process control. Some of the numbers are literally plugged into the system, with sockets burned into their brains. But, apparently dehumanised, machine-interfaced, they are still human, despite their enforced cultural poverty. But into this world comes an anomaly, a messenger with a message that is open to multiple readings: a call to revolution, perhaps, or a symbol of hope, or the promise of salvation, or, finally, none of these things. In pursuit of this anomaly comes ALIC, a member of the ruling class, who plunges after her into the underworld. ALIC fancies slumming it in hell, and with a nifty piece of computer work covers her tracks. Only she covers them too well, becomes, herself, permanently misplaced data and then permanently wired in. Stripped of name, identity, meaning, she discovers the humanity of the numbers, and in the process her own humanity.

This is science fiction in its 'hardest' form, and at the same time a quite remarkable reworking of Christian mythology, just as *Divine Endurance* recreates Hindu mythology. Both are mythopoeic inventions of worlds of women in which the complex relationship between the wider world of politics and the passions and desires of the human heart are explored with subtlety and wit. Gwyneth Jones has said that feminist science fiction can offer a different view of events. This is certainly borne out in these two novels, which take an imaginative leap out of the constraints imposed by the dualistic structure of women/men, and open up worlds in which such constraints are no longer relevant.

6
The Dream of Elsewhere: Feminist Utopias

The word utopia is generally taken to refer to the fictional representation of an ideal place, somewhere that is 'better' than the society or the world in which we actually live. Originally the word meant 'no place', deriving from the Greek ου τοπος, later assimilating to itself an additional meaning from the Greek ευ, 'good'. While the feminist utopias I want to discuss here all present 'better' worlds than our own, I think that the original meaning of utopia is an especially fruitful one: utopia as an imaginary place, a nowhere land, a realm like the unconscious, where dreams may flourish and desires be realised.

This is not to say that feminist utopias do not spring out of a concern with phenomena in the real world. On the contrary, it is precisely that engagement with the here and now that fuels the desire for something else, for something 'elsewhere'. Modern feminist utopias are intimately connected with the modern women's liberation movement. Joanna Russ, in her excellent article 'Recent Feminist Utopias' makes a causal connection: 'It seems to me reasonable to assume that, just as Gilman and Lane [Charlotte Perkins Gilman's *Herland* and Mary Bradley Lane's *Mizora*] were responding to the women's movement of their time, so the works I discuss here are not only contemporaneous with the modern feminist movement but made possible by it.'[1]

Russ also refers to an article by Carol Pearson, 'Women's Fantasies and Feminist Utopias' and its revised version, 'Coming Home: Four Feminist Utopias and Patriarchal Experience' which appears in the same collection as the Russ article.

Carol Pearson discusses the 'surprisingly numerous areas of consensus among such seemingly divergent works'[2] as Gilman's

Herland, Lane's *Mizora: A Prophesy*, Dorothy Bryant's *The Kin of Ata are Waiting for You* and Mary Staton's *From the Legend of Biel*. She looks at growth and process, at the importance of mothering, at the rejection in all these works of 'a dualistic pattern of ownership, denial and repression'.[3] Her term, 'coming home', signifies both coming home to the self and coming home to mother, finding unity and integration, and a respect for the individual which she sees as an 'integral aspect of the feminist utopian vision';[4] the liberation of self and society. This interpretation posits a notion of an essential self revealed once the distorting and mutilating effects of patriarchal order have been removed.

Such a notion is not without its problems, denying as it does the social and ideological construction of the self, and falling back on the idea of a 'natural' woman. But these arguments drawn from structuralist or post-structuralist criticism fail to incorporate a feminist viewpoint: while deconstructing the bourgeois narrative, they often fail to deconstruct the patriarchal one. The point is that 'woman' in conventional contemporary science fiction is an absence, at best a pale imitation of 'man', if not actually the feared castrating m/other. So to imagine a woman as having a self that can be liberated from the strictures of male dominance, of narrative form as well as of the real world, as these feminist utopias do, is in itself a liberating experience.

Joanna Russ both expands Carol Pearson's paper to cover a wider range of works and offers a thematic analysis that is invaluable for understanding the feminist concerns that fuel these utopian visions. She points to the remarkable similarity of these concerns: these works 'not only ask the same questions and point to the same abuses; they provide similar answers and remedies'.[5] She notes these themes: the communal, quasi-tribal nature of the societies; the lack of central or indeed of any very formal government; the concern for ecology and the natural world; the rural or at least non-urban and non-industrial setting; the peripheral nature of war and violence (reflecting women's relation to war in the real world); and sexual permissiveness. The point of this last is, she says, 'not to break taboos but to separate sexuality from questions of ownership, reproduction and social structure.'[6]

In many of these utopias, as indeed in the utopias of the first wave of feminism, such as *Herland*, separatism is of prime importance, indeed is a prerequisite for any other form of social change. As Russ says, ' . . . if men are kept out of these societies, it is because men are dangerous. They also hog the good things of this world.'[7] A separatist world allows women physical freedom, access to the public world, and the freedom to express love for other women. All these are felt as a lack by women in the real world. 'Sexually', Russ says, 'this amounts to the insistence that women are erotic integers and not fractions waiting for completion.'[8]

Finally, Russ picks out the theme of the 'rescue of the female child', which offers an alternative model of female puberty, one that opens the way to 'a full and free adulthood'.[9] This is a theme which appears in non-utopian novels too, such as Joanna Russ's own *The Two of Them* and Vonda McIntyre's *Dreamsnake*.

I think it is worth raising the question of Russ's inclusion of a male author, Samuel Delany, in her list of feminist writers of utopias. She states at the outset of her article that while 'utopia' may be a 'misnomer' for some of the works, presenting as they do societies that are not perfect but simply better (rejecting, by the way, the definition of utopia as 'no place'), 'feminist', she says, is *not* a misnomer.[10] She defines Delany's work as 'feminist'; yet in almost every example of a theme that she draws out we find that his *Triton* is the exception. He deals with the same themes but . . . differently. Her comment that a comparison between *Triton* and the others is 'instructive' appears at first ingenuous. But she goes on with her customary honesty to say: 'it seems to me that for better or worse the one male author in the group is writing from an implicit level of freedom that allows him to turn his attention, subtly but persistently, away from many of the questions which occupy the other writers.'[11]

Some might question the inclusion of this 'one male author' in the first place, thinking that the 'level of freedom' he enjoys, and which Russ recognises, should debar him from such a grouping. Russ's 'for better or worse' is perhaps over casual in a context where questions of power and privilege are central.

Joanna Russ's article both offers insights into the connection between feminist beliefs and their expression in utopian fiction, and provides a context for a discussion of Marge Piercy's *Woman on the Edge of Time* and Sally Miller Gearhart's *The*

Wanderground. (I shall be looking at some of the other utopian texts later – those by Charnas, Sheldon and Russ – in the context of the authors' other works.)

The feminist utopias of the 1970s did not have much of a tradition to draw on. In *Demand the Impossible: Science Fiction and the Utopian Imagination* Tom Moylan suggests a definitive break in tradition occurred partly as a result of the liberation politics of the 1960s, and names the utopias of the 1970s 'critical utopias'; 'critical' not just for their critical reflection on previous utopian writing, but critical in the sense of being potentially explosive. Unlike earlier utopias, he maintains, these ones prioritise process over system; moreover, he argues for their political effectivity as texts. The latter half of the nineteenth century saw a large amount of utopian writing, but even women writers tended not to address the specific position of women. As Ann J. Lane says in her introduction to Charlotte Perkins Gilman's *Herland*, Mary Bradley Lane's *Mizora*, published in 1890, was the 'only self-consciously feminist utopia'[12] published previous to *Herland* she was able to find. And *Mizora*, with its well-bred beautiful blonde women, has its flaws, as Ann Lane points out. 'The author's claim that this world is without class privilege, that intellect is the only standard of excellence . . . is something less than convincing, even as an imaginative creation.'[13]

While there were many women involved in the utopian movements of the mid and latter nineteenth century, such as Anna Wheeler, who was involved with the Saint-Simonians, and the Owenites Emma Martin and Frances Morrison, all of them militant feminists, all suffering social ostracism and material hardship for their beliefs, the literary utopias continued to be the domain of men.[14] And it is these that have been passed down to us, works such as Samuel Butler's *Erewhon* and *Erewhon Revisited* (1872 and 1901), Edward Bellamy's *Looking Backward* (1888) and William Morris's *News from Nowhere* (1890).

Charlotte Perkins Gilman wrote three utopian novels, *Moving the Mountain* (1911), *Herland* (1915) and its sequel *With Her in Ourland* (1916), of which *Herland* is the wittiest and liveliest and most looks forward to contemporary feminist utopias. She was a friend of Edward Bellamy and with him a contributing editor to the magazine *The American Fabian*, but where his

Looking Backward, set in Boston in the year 2000, posits the advance of technology as the prime mover of social change, Charlotte Perkins Gilman centralises human agency, and in particular, that of women. *Looking Backward*, which was enormously popular, and translated into several languages, was severely criticised by William Morris for its disregard of human agency, for the attitudes expressed in it towards work, art, leisure, for its depiction of a regimented life as a utopian one. A critical review of it by Morris appeared in *The Commonweal* on 22 January 1889, and is quoted at length by A.L. Morton in *The English Utopia*, who goes on to suggest that *News from Nowhere* was written as a response to, or at least stimulated by, *Looking Backward*. Where Bellamy ignored class struggle, Morris insisted on it, and Gilman eschewed it. As Ann Lane says, 'In her vision, the peaceful collective action of women replaced Marx's class struggle.'[15]

In Gilman's work the transformation of the private mother/ child relationship (and she was reviled for 'abandoning' her own child and for the unorthodoxy of her personal relationships) into a vision of a community of women and children anticipates a central theme of the feminist utopias of the 1970s.

Also influential, and particularly of interest in terms of science fiction because of her emphasis on the liberating potentialities of technology – although her vision is rather more fierce than Bellamy's – is Shulamith Firestone.

'We haven't even a literary image of this future society; there is not even a *utopian* feminist literature yet in existence.'[16]

So wrote Shulamith Firestone in *The Dialectic of Sex: The Case for Feminist Revolution*, one of the early texts of the second wave of feminism. Shulamith Firestone herself furnished many of the ideas that were incorporated into the feminist utopias written over the next ten years. Indeed, without her pioneering work of analysis and vision, the utopias of Charnas, Gearhart, Piercy and Russ would have been quite different. For Firestone gave primacy of place to the question of reproduction, seeing the oppression of women as inextricably related to their work as child-rearers as well as child-bearers. And it is this insistence on that central question, 'who looks after the children in our brave new world?', that is the hallmark of the feminist incursion into science fiction.

1970

Firestone's minimal demands for the feminist revolution are: that women should be freed from the tyranny of reproduction through the use of technology and that the rearing of children should be the responsibility of society as a whole, men as well as women; that through 'cybernetic communism', that is, the use of machines for all drudgery work and the elimination of wage labour, there should be economic independence and self-determination for all, including children; that women and children should be completely integrated into the larger society; that with the elimination of the nuclear family's stranglehold on the individual, and thus the end of the Oedipus complex and the incest taboo, there should be sexual freedom for all untramelled by unequal relations of power and freed from the primacy of genital sex; and that sex should be allowed expression as Freud's 'polymorphous perversity'. Last, and absolutely not least, Firestone demands the possibility of love.

These demands are made within a wider context of libertarian politics inspired by the social utopianism of Charles Fourier and the Owenites and by Simone de Beauvoir's analysis of the oppression of women in *The Second Sex*. They are informed by, although not totally uncritical of, the development of race politics in the Black Power movement of the 1960s and the theories of the family as developed by Ronald Laing.

Firestone's ideal living unit is the loosely constructed house-hold; she is committed to a collectivist politics that, on the Left, is now less of an accepted ideal than formerly. Her fierce denunciations of schools as prison-houses for children also place her within a no longer fashionable libertarian trend. She has been strongly criticised for the centrality she gives in her analysis to the psychology of power and for her insistence that class is based on biological sex. But many of her ideas were formative for the developing women's liberation movement in the late 1960s: that there would be no revolution without the liberation of women, for example; that the rhetoric of the sexual revolution, 'if it brought no improvements for women, proved to have great value for men';[17] that the confusion of sexuality with individuality – the romantic pretence that it is in their sexuality that women differ – is precisely what binds women to their generality as a sex class; that women are a subject class because of the privatisation of the family and the home and the denial of the political nature of women's oppression there.

While many writers took up Shulamith Firestone's challenge and did create a utopian feminist literature in the 1970s, very few accepted her vision of nature – 'pregnancy is barbaric' – as itself oppressive of women, and of liberation's achievement through the technological control of reproduction and cybernation. Such a negative attitude towards nature has remained unpopular within feminist ideology; and Firestone's enthusiasm for technology and the scientific method, with the aim of realising 'the conceivable in the actual'[18] seems positively heretical today. Indeed she is praised by Dale Spender in *For the Record* for her denunciation of 'the absurdity of empiricism'[19] which I think is a misreading for, according to Firestone, it is only through empirical science that the real laws of nature will be uncovered; the empirical method pushes forward the progress of technology, whose ultimate goal is the building of the ideal in the real world.[20] The question of who controls technology is inherent in all her analyses. I find her vision an inspiring one: 'The double curse that man should till the soil by the sweat of his brow and that woman should bear in pain and travail would be lifted through technology to make humane living for the first time a possibility.'[21]

The above is perhaps a wishful dream, but it is out of dream-wishes that utopias are made. More than any other utopian writer Marge Piercy has engaged with Firestone's ideas on technology. In the future community of Mattapoisett in *Woman on the Edge of Time* babies gestate in tanks and are 'born' into the community at carefully planned times. The sexual difference between women and men is totally divorced from reproduction and child-rearing. There is no wage labour, no drudgery, no social, political or sexual hierarchies. Where writers like Sally Miller Gearhart reject all traditional science and technology as being impossibly male-tainted; where Vonda McIntyre and Joan Slonczewski concern themselves with the more traditionally female-interest life sciences; Marge Piercy, rather, grapples with the potentialities of technology. And she also takes on the wider political implications that Firestone explores: the inevitably oppressive relationship between mother and child in a traditional nuclear family; the freeing of sexuality from its narrow expression in genital sex. While Firestone continues to be sniped at for her apparent desire to eliminate all difference, Piercy is praised for exploring precisely that in

Woman on the Edge of Time. Most unusually in feminist science fiction Marge Piercy shows passionate and convincing sexual love in a world where bisexuality is the norm and there are no sexual differences based on gender role.

Both Piercy and Gearhart are writers whose incursion into science fiction consists of one novel only. Gearhart's utopia is separatist, Piercy's posits sexual equality. Joanna Russ describes _Woman on the Edge of Time_ as 'a splendid book in the tradition of nineteenth-century utopias, with all the wealth of realistic detail that tradition implies.'[22] What makes _Woman on the Edge_ unusual, and I think particularly powerful, is its portrayal of the real world with the same wealth of realistic detail. The two worlds reflect on each other to highlight their differences; the comparison illumines the horrors of the present day as well as the liberating potentialities of the future. And the present day _is_ horrific. Connie, Piercy's protagonist, is Mexican, female, poor; in terms of the values of contemporary capitalism she is the wrong colour, the wrong sex and the wrong class. She is abused by all those in power over her: the state authorities who have taken away her daughter 'into care', the medical authorities who have kept her drugged in mental hospitals and who killed her lover Claud in a medical 'experiment', her brother Luis who charts his struggle up the social scale with a succession of increasingly pale-skinned women, and the brutal Geraldo, pimp of her favourite niece, Dolly. At the beginning of the book Connie finds herself back in mental hospital, put there by Luis and Geraldo. She says, 'A bargain had been struck. Some truce had been negotiated between the two men over the bodies of their women.'[23] In this world men control, exploit and abuse women for their own ends. Women such as Connie are not abused directly by the ruling class of white educated males but by their lackeys, upwardly aspiring and desirous of power over others. Gentle, loving men, like Claud her lover, blind and Black and earning a living as a pickpocket, or homosexual Skip put away in a mental hospital, do not survive.

Connie's own narrative is enough to condemn the world we live in, but we are given additional evidence. First, we get the viewpoint of Connie's visitor from Mattapoisett, Luciente, through whose eyes we see some of the more unpleasant aspects of twentieth-century urban life: pollution, dirt, noise, traffic. Luciente is baffled by what is happening to Connie in the state mental hospital. Then we see Mattapoisett through Connie's eyes: the difference is telling. Connie is a complex character. In her twentieth-century world she is no victim, but a fighter, and she enters Mattapoisett in 2137 not as a passive observer but with opinions and, importantly, prejudices of her own. Piercy convinces her readers with skill: objections that the reader might have to the society portrayed – that it is too good to be true, for example – are raised by Connie herself and answered by the people there. This device makes possible the gradual revelation of this complex new society, and it also offers a means of charting Connie's development. As life gets worse for her in the twentieth century, as she gets increasingly swallowed up in the bland cruelty of a system that treats her and the other inmates of the hospitals as sub- or even non-human, she becomes more open to the potentialities of Mattapoisett, and as she becomes more involved in the life of its inhabitants, so her understanding of what is happening to her in the twentieth century deepens too. At the beginning of the book Connie is a powerless victim, but by the end she has become an agent for the future. She has come to believe that the Mattapoisett community, which at first she criticised for being as primitive and backward as the rural Mexico she knew as a child, with its grinding poverty that enslaved women above all others, is worth fighting for. She has learnt from its people a political lesson that she would not have discovered on her own: that revolutions are made by the weak and the oppressed, not by the powerful.

In Mattapoisett the village-based society is run by consensus; there is no work that is exploitative of other people – jobs that involve ordering other people around have been abolished, as have jobs that involve shifting around piles of money; there is no hierarchy or status; no violence. Both privacy and communality are respected; child-rearing is a communal endeavour; there are no distinctions of race or class and, central to the depiction of this society, no sexual distinction. Women and men live together and work together at all tasks including mothering. Women no longer bear and bring forth children; the creation of new life is socially planned; conception and gestation occur in machines. When a new baby is released it enters a family of three co-mothers, of both sexes, who suckle it as a baby and share responsibility for its welfare until it is old enough to choose a name for itself and strike out on its own. After an early adolescent rite of passage, when the child spends time on its own in the wilderness, the co-mothers are forbidden to speak to the child for three months, like the ban on communication between bloodmother and child in Suzy McKee Charnas' *Motherlines*. The similar concerns expressed in these two feminist utopias are nowhere more striking than in the depiction of child-rearing and mother/child relationships, where a deep dissatisfaction with the status, or significance, of such relationships in the real world is being expressed.

Connie's first reaction is one of horror. She is revolted by the foetuses in the machine which she sees as 'bland bottleborn monsters of the future, born without pain, multi-coloured like a litter of puppies without the stigmata of race and sex'.[24] Connie, who has been declared an unfit mother, whose own child Angelina has been snatched from her by the State, who will never again conceive a child since her womb was removed as 'practice' for young doctors, hangs on desperately to the memory of suckling a baby. When she sees a man nursing she first feels sick, and then angry. 'How dare any man share that pleasure,' she thinks. 'These women thought they had won, but they had abandoned to men the last refuge of women. What was special about being a woman here? They had given it all up, they had let men steal from them the last remnants of ancient power, those sealed in blood and in milk.'[25]

She is shocked at the thought of a child being left to fend for itself in the wilderness, shocked too at the way young children are allowed to experiment sexually with each other. But always she is brought back to the twentieth century, where children are abandoned, abused, removed into institutions; despite all her misgivings about Mattapoisett she knows that it represents a life worth living. As Joanna Russ says, 'Connie's longing for and assent to utopia states eloquently the suffering that lies under the utopian impulse and the sufferer's simultaneous facing of and defiance of pain.'[26] Connie knows that she will never live in Mattapoisett, but she yearns for it and grasps it for her own lost child:

> Suddenly she assented with all her soul to Angelina in Mattapoisett . . . Yes, you can have my child, you can keep my child. She will be strong there, well fed, well housed, well taught, she will grow up much better and stronger and smarter

63

than I. I assent, I give you my battered body as recompense and my rotten heart. Take her, keep her! . . . She will never be broken as I was. She will be strange, but she will be glad and strong and she will not be afraid. She will have enough. She will have pride. She will love her own brown skin and be loved for her strength and her good work. She will walk in strength like a man and never sell her body and she will nurse her babies like a woman and live in love like a garden, like that children's house of many colours. People of the rainbow with its end fixed in earth, I give her to you![27]

Connie assents to a world in which no sex, class or race oppresses another. Every community contains people of different colours, as the genetic mix for each new child is chosen by that community. There is a fluidity around sex that initially makes it difficult to distinguish between female and male and finally makes that distinction irrelevant. Language in Mattapoisett reflects this revolution: no gender is ascribed to a person in speech; instead, 'per' is used as a universal personal pronoun, thus demonstrating the interconnection of language and politics. Mattapoisett speech is vivid, racy and economical. It is remarkable how quickly, as a reader, one becomes accustomed to its lack of gendered pronouns, and begins to enjoy this.

At the heart of Woman on the Edge of Time is a tension of possibility. The novel does not simply present one form of society as superior to another: it offers Mattapoisett as a choice, as a future that must be struggled for. Towards the end of the book we get a glimpse of another possible future that Connie slips into by mistake, a grim world in which humans are commodities to be bought and sold or specialised in their functions to such an extent that they approximate machinery. Connie, out of anger and hope, chooses Mattapoisett. What makes Woman on the Edge of Time so powerful is the presentation of a utopia alongside a realistic portrayal of contemporary life. For Connie's life in the twentieth century is not science fictional: the brain surgery she is about to have inflicted on her at the end of the book to 'cure' her deviancy is not something 'out of science fiction'. Control is a necessary part of the patriarchal order. For one moment Connie seizes control and acts so as to bring the future into being before she herself sinks under the weight of oppression and is effectively wiped out.

Sally Miller Gearhart's _The Wanderground: Stories of the Hill
Women_ is a utopian vision of an all-female society in which
women are free to develop qualities presented as essentially
feminine, in order to create a self-sufficient women's culture.
This is a magical and a mystical world, not only in harmony with
nature but also in receipt of nature's active blessing. Women,
animals, plants and the earth itself live in a glorious communion
of spirit, from which men are necessarily excluded. Men are
confined to the Cities; outside the City walls men are sexually
impotent; technology does not work for them and the earth
itself rejects them.

In the opening story of the book, called simply 'Opening',
young Jacqua introduces us to many of the themes that will
recur in later stories: the development in the women of the
Wanderground of all five senses – their increasing keenness of
hearing, taste, smell, etc. – and their sixth sense of telepathy;
the women's negative attitude to men, and their justification for
it. Jacqua recites to herself: 'It is too simple to condemn them all
or to praise all of us. But for the sake of earth and all she holds,
that simplicity must be our creed.'[28] She muses on the Gentles,
men who, 'knowing that maleness touched women only with the
accumulated hatred of centuries, touched no women at all.
Ever.'[29] She introduces us to the women's rejection of possessiveness: 'There are no words more obscene than "I can't live
without you." Count them the deepest affront to the person.'[30]
Through Jacqua's eyes we see in action their principles of
non-aggression: she watches from a distance, nervously, as Seja
lays herself down, closes her eyes and bares her throat in front
of an armed and armoured stranger. This stranger heralds the
change that threatens the Wanderground, for it transpires that
she has been raped outside the City walls.

This opening statement of themes exemplifies the tension that
lies at the heart of _The Wanderground_, a tension between
pedagogical intent (how women could and indeed should live)
and dream vision (not the 'what if . . . ?' of mainstream science
fiction but the impassioned 'if only . . .' of feminist science
fiction). Put another way, it can be seen as a tension between a
political hard line of feminist separatism, in which anatomy is
destiny, and a powerful wish-fulfilment fantasy that is nothing if
not romantic. For 'the essential fundamental knowledge', we

are told, is that women and men 'are no longer of the same species'.[31] The impossibility of inter-species sex is a common theme in science fiction, as, for example, in Ursula Le Guin's *Planet of Exile*, where adaptation overcomes this natural law; or in Octavia Butler's *Survivor*, where, again, it is overruled and thus makes a point about the 'humanness' of the humans. Here, it is politicised: male violence towards women, inseparable from the expression of male sexuality, makes them a different species, unfit to be considered human.

Apart from the underlying threat from men there is no real danger in the Wanderground. It is a snug, happy, loving world, strangely comfortable considering the lack of modern technological conveniences. Seja's 'thick pine-needle bed', for instance, is shared cosily with chipmunks, squirrels, lizards and a black bear cub. There is no sense at all of the discomforts of the natural life, of fleas, mosquitoes, sudden drenching downpours. Carnivorous animals and poisonous snakes are included in this life-affirming vision; harmony is achieved through sweet co-operation.

Death hardly disturbs the tranquillity. Death among the animals is harmonious: in 'Krueva and the Pony', a dying pony eventually gives itself, bequeathes itself one might say, to a hungry mountain lion, in a manner that is right and fitting. When one of the Wanderground women dies, her life and her memories are incorporated into a body of knowledge that is transmitted through songs and stories and rememberings to all the other women: she becomes a part of the Wanderground women's culture. Indeed the women are only differentiated from each other in terms of what happens to them, not in terms of who they are or how they act. As in life, so in death. Individual foibles are presented, but only in so far as they serve to illustrate a theme. They are anyway subsumed in the higher synthesis. *The Wanderground* is a portrait of a culture rather than of individuals.

Within this never-never land, where death and danger lurk only on the periphery, women are free to develop and to strengthen their creative potency. Most important are their telepathic and telekinetic powers, the stuff of childhood fantasies. The women can communicate without speaking, even over long distances; they can fly; they can make objects move; they can think things into existence. By refusing to abuse power, as men did with their technology, they become, in fact, all-powerful, able to enter into the consciousness of the animate and the inanimate, and in turn to gain their help and protection. The girl-child Clana gets energy from a fern she has willed into existence. Diana enters the consciousness of a bush and 'they knew each other instantly by an exchange of old forgotten rhythms'.[32] The same bush then acts with a passing cloud to become 'a warm shade to cover the sleeping Diana'.[33] The women have developed a kind of automatic pilot in their bodies, called Ionth, somewhere deep in the abdomen, which can take over functions such as breathing.

Gearhart's. is a vision *par excellence* of the unity of mind and body. Each feeds into the other; emotions, desires, states of knowledge affect the body and give a physical materiality to the experience. At times this is expressed with remarkable power. Here, in 'Voki at the Welling Place', Voki learns that Artilidea, an older woman whom she much admires, is about to die:

First there would be an edginess in her belly, the bare suggestion of something rough and uncomfortable. Then it would intensify and creep upwards through her body, gathering strength like a tidal wave and sharpness like some inverse intestinal pain. The first time earlier that afternoon she had been staggered with astonishment but now she knew the pattern, knew how each wave would rise from the depths, swirl upward to crash against the high cliffs of her skull and there wash all contentment from the corners of her mind. It would pulse through all the convolutions of her memory and over all the crevices of her awareness; it would pull every surface taut and suck it dry.

Only when she groaned aloud would the wave subside, leaving her empty and barren, hollow and utterly deprived. This time standing at the welling rocks, she sent her cries into the cleft itself, into the lining of the stone faces, into the interstices where in some restless shift of the earth ten thousand years ago they came together first. Voki felt the rocks moving. They parted ever so little yet so vastly to receive her pain; with sudden vulnerability they gave way before her face, separating to receive her cries, to enfold and welcome the vulnerability she brought to them.[34]

This sense of communion with nature, when the rocks

themselves move in response to human anguish, then becomes an illustration of the moral precepts that govern life in the Wanderground. Not, indeed, that there is any mealy-mouthed moralising. Gearhart, it seems to me, manages to fuse her teaching and her dreaming into powerful parabolic form. Voki's despair at the approaching death takes her back to the impotent anger of babyhood, screaming, slobbering and helpless. She cries out in her mind:

'What is it Artilidea? What's happening to me? Why can't I control this?'

Artilidea seemed to be remembering. 'It's called grief. Named as one of the obsoletes. It used to be quite common among us. Some of us still occasionally feel it, but it's counted a product of possessiveness.'

'What do I do with it?'

'It's yours. Claim it.'

'Possessive.' Voki felt stunned.

'I'm not sure of that.' Artilidea's doubt coloured her mindstretch. 'Often I think we may have lost a good thing when we left off grieving . . .'[35]

Here and elsewhere the physicality of emotions is convincingly portrayed, yet overall there is no sense of the materiality of the women's lives. Unlike the societies depicted by Marge Piercy, Suzy McKee Charnas and Joanna Russ, questions about the production of food, clothing, building materials are left vague. And although there is a whole story about it, 'The Deep Cella', conception and childbirth too remain strangely out of focus. Yet perhaps it is not so strange, for the elements of realism in this book are confined, like the men, to the City, where there is an attempt, even if only sketchy, to show the history of a social and political process, that is, the undermining by men of women's autonomy. The Wanderground is a dream world, a world with its past named only through what it has rejected, a world without history or future, a world in which the questions 'how?' or 'by what process?' are irrelevant.

The women of the Wanderground are all Dianas, strong, virginal, youthful, in spite of the superficial characteristics of old age with which some are endowed. Perhaps it is because the actuality of birth-giving is too close to danger and death that it is not allowed a place in this world of synthesis and harmony.

There are no dark angels here.

When Gearhart describes the way the women live and interact she uses, or invents, verbs that describe traditionally 'feminine' powers: to enwomb, to enfold, to encircle, to enwrap, to soothe and caress. Some of these verbs become nouns as well: warmths and soothes can be given and taken, a softtouch can be exchanged. It is all gentle, loving, caring, non-invasive. Communication means merging, not penetrating.

Telepathy is the women's preferred mode of communication. Speaking aloud is 'a discipline they frequently used for the refining of present images and the generation of new ones. Still it created a far less vulnerable state, even a less honest one, than their usual stretch-communication.'[36] The implication here of a residue of truth, lying underneath the problematics of language, is the corollary of the notion of an essential femaleness. Language is seen as a barrier between thought and thing; remove it and thoughts become material. Womanness exists independently of, and before, the construct of language.

While telepathy does leave the women vulnerable to the painful memories and experiences of other women, so that they actually relive physically the suffering undergone, the original pain is always instigated by men. The women never inflict pain on each other; their world is one of mutual consent, with no room for contradiction. As the refrain to their retelling of the myth of Hecate, transformed from Hek, a 'gentle manchild', into a woman by the violent patriarch Dis, Lord of the Underworld, puts it: 'Never can I take her if she does not choose to go . . . Never can I bring her if she does not choose to come.'[37]

The novel pits this strong unified society of women, celebratory of female virtues and blessed by mother nature, against that of the men, who are essentially rapists, not only of women but of the earth itself. In 'The Remember Rooms' Rhynna explains to Clana how men view the world. ' "Just because it was possible," ' she says, ' "they thought it had to be done." '[38] In 'The Telling of the Days of Artilidea', the women intone the men's 'invasion litany':

    If it moves: shoot it down
    If it grows: cut it
    It is wild: tame it, claim it

If it flows: a harness
It shines or burns: gouge it out
It is female: rape it[39]

Men must be forced to change, and if they won't change then they must die. The women's memories and stories portray men as unmitigatedly evil; all of them, except for the Gentles, driven by a desire for violent domination. And it is the Gentles who threaten the fabric of consent, who sow dissent among the women.

The Wanderground is, I think, a difficult book for men to read, since it appears to stress only feminist separatism. But to read it only in those terms is to ignore what makes *The Wanderground* powerful and gives it its creative tension. In many ways the novel represents an imaginative recreation of an unthreatening childhood world, one that exists before the complexities and dangers of language and sexuality come into being. Its very structure is dream-like and, on another level, deliberately 'feminine' (the women of the Wanderground are not constructed out of sexual difference; if their world is pre-sexual it is at the same time female, however contradictory that may seem). But it is transformed by that deliberation from feminine into feminist; it is illustrative, discursive, non-developmental. Its linked stories seem to wind round and down, like the downwards spiral towards the deep cella in the story of that name, at the heart of which conception takes place and the hot breath of the earth wells out of the depths. *The Wanderground* takes us back to an earlier self, ignorant of the strictures and limitations concomitant with being female in a male-dominated world, a self whose imagination and desire are strong enough and clear enough to create a vision of the 'if only . . .' world that sweeps aside those limitations and explores instead the endless realm of potential.

In structure, then, these two books are very different, one with a strong linear narrative form, the other discursive, non-individualised. But, as we have seen, they share explicit feminist concerns and feminist aims.

Feminist utopias are sometimes criticised for being too bland and lacking in conflict, but that I think is to confuse them with realistic, or mimetic, fiction. With reference to this, Russ says, 'I believe that utopias are not embodiments of universal human values, but are reactive; that is, they supply in fiction what their authors believe society . . . and/or women, lack in the here and now.'[40] While these utopias do fill up gaps, they do not offer a picture of completion. These worlds are in a 'no place' as well as a good place; they express potentiality rather than achievement. They could perhaps be seen as messages from the unconscious, translated through the authors' imaginative powers from the language of dreams into the language of materiality, for without dreams we cannot hope to change the world.

As utopias reflect on a present by imagining a future, so, in a different way, do their corollaries, the dystopias. The dystopian tradition has a particular potency for women, related perhaps to one of its first practitioners, the impassioned Cassandra whose prodromic utterances were fated to be ignored. Cassandra spoke out of and into silence. In the next chapter I will look at some of the women writers whose dystopian works explore that nightmare land of silence in which the struggle for subjecthood and autonomous speech is paramount.

7

The Reduction of Women: Dystopias

The foregrounding of women's sexual autonomy in feminist utopias and the particular portrayal of lesbianism and bisexuality, connects sexuality to a wider politics. The illusion of a private contract between two individuals, magically separate from their surroundings, is challenged. Sexuality is seen as constructed by, or predicated on, other social relations. Feminist SF challenges the notion of a natural heterosexuality, a notion common to much SF written by men, despite the strange absence of female characters. In this sense perhaps, feminist SF reflects mainstream SF more than is at first apparent: where the latter peripheralises women, the former peripheralises men. But where the peripheralisation of women by male writers merely reflects the dominant ideology within which they write, the peripheralisation of men by women writers challenges that same ideology. (How many times do we hear, 'Why can't we have a Men's Press?' or Men's Studies, or whatever it is men feel excluded from, as if they haven't shored up exclusive privileges for themselves since the beginning of recorded history?)

Women's dystopias foreground the precise opposite: the denial of women's sexual autonomy. They show women trapped by their sex, by their femaleness, and reduced from subjecthood to function. This theme is central to the dystopian novels of Katharine Burdekin, Suzy McKee Charnas, Margaret Atwood and Zoë Fairbairns, of whom the two last, like Marge Piercy and Sally Miller Gearhart, are not primarily science fiction writers, but find the form of the dystopian novel ideally suited for their exploration of sexual politics. Where these novels differ most tellingly from those by male writers is in the interrelation they expose between gender hierarchy and class structure.

Katharine Burdekin's *Swastika Night* was first published in 1937 under the name Murray Constantine. This was the second of her future dystopias (*Proud Man* was published in 1934), and she wrote, too, in a variety of other forms. The setting is Europe after seven centuries of Nazi domination. The Jews have been wiped out, Christians are Untouchable and Hitler is revered as a god. There has been a 'Reduction of Women': women are kept solely for their breeding functions. They lack control over their own bodies, being denied the right of rejection of sexual advances, and over their children. Male children are removed from their mothers at the age of eighteen months so that they are not corrupted by femaleness. While *Swastika Night* is a fierce critique of Nazism and militarism, what distinguishes it from other anti-fascist novels of the period is Burdekin's location of this ideology within a 'cult of masculinity'. As Daphne Patai points out: 'Burdekin's special insight was to join the various elements of Nazi policy into one ideological whole. She saw that it is but a small step from the male apotheosis of women as mothers to their degradation to mere breeding animals. In both cases women are reduced to a biological function out of which is constructed an entire social identity. And she linked this reduction to the routine practices of patriarchal society.'[1]

Daphne Patai comments on the remarkable internal similarities between *Swastika Night* and George Orwell's *Nineteen Eighty Four*, published twelve years later. Although there is no direct evidence that Orwell had read *Swastika Night*, the details of similarities that Patai lists do suggest this. Particularly curious, as she says, is the scene in both books in which the protagonist (Alfred, Winston) reads aloud, from a secret book given to him by his mentor or mediator (von Hess, O'Brien), to his friend/lover (Hermann, Julia) who falls asleep during the reading. Burdekin recognises and analyses the preoccupation of the ruling class of men with domination, power and violence: she names it the 'cult of masculinity'. Orwell fails to do this: he uses males as models for the human species, imagining that he is describing innate human characteristics. This is perhaps why *Nineteen Eighty Four* is so hopelessly gloomy, whereas *Swastika Night*, because of Burdekin's understanding of sexual politics and the social construction of gender, allows room for hope.[2]

As Katharine Burdekin extrapolated from the growth of fascism in the 1930s, so Margaret Atwood in *The Handmaid's Tale* extrapolates from the social and political forces, including the growth of moral conservatism, in the USA in the 1980s. Gilead is a military religious state in a near future North America in which women are totally controlled and reduced to their separate functions: as wives, servants and handmaids. The function of the handmaids is to open their legs and become impregnated by the Commanders. They are not allowed to read, barely to speak. They are allowed no individuality, stripped even of their names. The Handmaid of the title is called Offred, denoting her status as possession of the Commander Fred. Failure of function is punished by death.

In haunting images of suppression, subjugation and fear, Margaret Atwood explores the terror aroused in men by women's autonomous sexuality. As well as analysing the forms of control imposed by the law of the Father, *The Handmaid's Tale* depicts a search for the absent Mother. Offred's portrait of her own lost mother, a feminist of the 1970s and 1980s, is ironic, exasperated and affectionate. It is partly through that search that Offred manages to construct a subjecthood for herself.

Dystopian visions are in a sense mythopoeic: depicting a creation myth in a future world of darkness and silence. It is perhaps not surprising that a writer like Michèle Roberts, who is fundamentally concerned with the significance of myth in a secular world and the psychological power wielded by male mythologies, should explore the mythopoeic elements of dystopias. In *The Book of Mrs Noah* one of the many stories within the story – and the novel is about the telling of stories – is set in a future world similar to Atwood's Gilead. Again, women's bodies are used to enclose women; function is used to eliminate desire; and again order is broken by the demands of the unconscious.

Less concerned with questions of desire and the unconscious than Margaret Atwood and Michèle Roberts, Zoë Fairbairns concentrates her narrative skills in *Benefits* on dramatising the contradictions between biological function and social being. Her story is set in Britain in a near future (although it begins in 1976) and investigates the oppression of women by focusing on the economics of reproduction and the relationship between the family unit and the government.

The novel was born out of a debate within the women's movement over the question of wages for housework. This is also the name of a group: the phrase 'wages for housework' interprets housework as all the servicing work done, unpaid, by women for men, including the bearing and rearing of children. In an article called 'On Writing *Benefits*' Zoë Fairbairns describes her confrontation with this debate and how she found herself in complete agreement with both sides of it: that to pay housewives would free them from their dependence on individual men, and that to pay housewives would institutionalise their inferior status and keep them in the home. She wrote:

> It's not very comfortable holding opinions that are mutually contradictory, but that is the sort of niggling mental discomfort that gives birth to novels. The best stories are those that ask a question (what will happen to her? will they fall in love and live happily ever after? whodunnit?), and the question that I wrote *Benefits* to examine (though perhaps not answer) was this: what would actually happen, to you, me and the woman next door if a British government introduced a wage for mothers? Inevitably, because I did not want to avoid the challenge of asking how such a thing might come to be, in what circumstances might a British government do it?[3]

What Zoë Fairbairns has done is not just to use the science fictional convention of extrapolation (her united Europe and her 'welfare' state are grim warnings of bureaucratic overgrowth); she has allowed the nature of her enquiry to be informed by an unresolved political conflict. This tension between contradictory opinions runs through all Fairbairns' work: she is at pains to express in her fiction the differences that exist within the women's movement, or movements, and so to challenge the 'monolithic' view of feminism so dear to antifeminists. She is not primarily a science fiction writer, but writes in a variety of popular forms (*Stand We At Last* borrows from the epic romance, *Here Today* from the whodunnit) although she returned briefly to science fiction with the short story 'Relics' in 1985. This witty story, set in Greenham Common before and after a nuclear explosion, deals with the trials and tribulations of a heterosexual feminist in a world where it has been *shown* that men are pretty much to blame for everything; in other words, it treats of the vicissitudes of a liberal who would like to remain a liberal in a world where, when all is said and done, radical answers seem to be required.

The dystopian tradition, as we have seen, draws on and extrapolates from contemporary political forces, and in particular the expression of class and gender hierarchies. We have seen female characters taking tentative steps out of darkness and silence, towards finding a speech for themselves. For there is a hidden utopian streak in these dystopian novels by women. They contain an element of hopefulness that rests on a belief in the power and efficacy of women's speech.

In the next chapter I will look at the depiction of the sexually autonomous subject, in fictional worlds further removed than these dystopias from present circumstances, in worlds more fantastical, or perhaps closer to traditional science fictional worlds. I will look at love, and the expression of desire through the language of the unconscious.

8
The Vicissitudes of Love

For women, SF can be seen as allowing the expression of wish fulfilment; a means of picturing an erotic relationship, with woman as subject, in a variety of ways. What I want to talk about here is love, and how it might be imagined in the space between the impossibility of its achievement now and the conditions for its achievement in some distant otherworld. In *The Dialectic of Sex*, that bizarre and powerful mixture of analysis and vision produced in the early days of the women's liberation movement, Shulamith Firestone shows love as firstly, a means of oppression and subsequently, transformed, as an ideal towards which we must strive. Where other feminists have stepped around these shifting sands and directed their analyses elsewhere, not so brave Firestone, who states unflinchingly: 'A book on radical feminism that did not deal with love would be a political failure. For love, perhaps even more than childbearing, is the pivot of women's oppression today.'[1] In brief, Firestone sees the privatisation of love and sex as one of the main instruments in male control of women; she envisions technological developments that will help eliminate sexual repression, class privilege, drudge work and biological parenting so that 'love can flow unimpeded'.

Such a vision of love unimpeded is expressed nowhere more clearly than in the positivistic feminist utopias of the 1970s. Sexual love is depicted there as non-exploitative, non-possessive, non-monogamous, and strongly combined with friendship. The feminist utopias affirm the joys of bonding between women. Except for Marge Piercy's bisexual world of Mattapoisett, these are separatist, lesbian worlds.

If a traditional concern of novels has been love and its vicissitudes then let us see what happens in non-utopian science fiction when women are allowed to be the agents of their own desire.

In science fictional romances written by women the object of the heroine's love or lust tends not to be a common or garden man; instead, women writers conjure up creatures quite alien, or creatures that are not exactly men: robots or cyborgs. Playing around with such fantasies we find writers like Naomi Mitchison, Tanith Lee in her lighter moments, Joan Vinge. James Tiptree Jr's work swarms with aliens, but they function as complex, shifting metaphors in her explorations of sexual difference and desire. I shall devote the whole of a later chapter to Tiptree. Here, firstly, I will look at some of these romances.

Naomi Mitchison's *Memoirs of a Spacewoman* provides a gentle analysis of sexual ethics and mores. Her protagonist, Mary, is a communications expert. She and her colleagues meet, tangle with and learn from a variety of attractive and not so attractive alien life forms. Mitchison and Mary, the author and her protagonist are both fascinated by the processes of reproduction – unusually in science fiction – and Mary volunteers for a course of experiments involving grafts of other life forms on to her own body. Mitchison's interest in biology, and in particular matters of reproduction, along with the empathetic sensitivity she gives to the female characters in this novel (including the female animals), have led to criticisms of biological determinism. (One doesn't hear male authors being criticised for biological determinism when their male characters are engaged in conventionally masculine activities, such as thrusting through the boundaries of space in their long sleek rockets. For a delightfully over-the-top depiction of rocket as phallus see Tiptree's 'A Momentary Taste of Being'.)

But as much as anything, *Memoirs* is about cultural relativism. One of its most memorable sequences involves Mary's shy friend Vly, a Martian hermaphrodite, and his attempts to comfort and console her, after a disastrous expedition, in the way that he knows best – through genital communication. This leads, accidentally, to the activation of an egg and Mary's delivery of a haploid child. Apart from this accidental sexual encounter with Vly, it must be said that Mary and all her colleagues practise a normative and fairly unthinking heterosexuality.

In the world of Tanith Lee's *The Silver Metal Lover* the men are all too old, too evil or too interested in other men to function as suitable objects of desire for Lee's young heroine Jane. Then she sees the man of her dreams: he is young, handsome, sexy. His name is Silver: he is a Silver Ionised Locomotive Electronic Robot, one of the 'Sophisticated Format' range from Electronic Metals Ltd. Jane buys him.

Silver fulfils Jane's every dream, and as she blossoms under his care – for he is ideal father as well as lover – so he grows into humanness, without losing any of the qualities for which he was originally programmed. The jealous world, however, will not allow a happy-ever-after.

Such an ending is possible in Joan Vinge's story 'Tin Soldier', but it is at a cost. In this science fictional fairy tale the tin soldier is a half-plastic cyborg, a bartender called Maris, whose ballerina is a space traveller and poet called Brandy. Brandy survives a near-fatal crash in her spaceship, and she herself becomes a cyborg, unable to travel again, but with the consolation of centuries of love ahead of her.

One might say that science fiction opens up a space for the portrayal of romantic relationships that are free from the exigencies of contemporary sex-polarised society. Life, perhaps, is easier with aliens and robots than with 'real men'. But the conclusions are not entirely satisfactory. We have been left with a dead robot and a crippled cyborg. Perhaps the problem lies in the object of the search: romantic love.

Joanna Russ in *The Female Man* lets Jael concentrate on the sex. Without the quivering of a heartstring Jael turns off Davy ('The original germ-plasm was chimpanzee, I think, but none of the behavior is organically controlled any more'[2]) after he has pleasured her (and done the housework, the hard underbelly of sexual slavery). This to the consternation, or discomfiture at least, of her not entirely liberated otherselves. A later chapter is devoted to Joanna Russ's work, but I will just say here that her male characters do not fare well, particularly if they are loved by her women. Machine dies in *Picnic on Paradise*; Ernst Neumann in *The Two of Them* is killed by Irene herself, his loving partner.

Fairy tales do not have to affirm romantic love. Rather, they can be turned, or returned into fantastic narratives, dealing with sexuality, desire and death, drawing on the language of the unconscious with its ellipses, metamorphoses and reversals of meaning. Both Tanith Lee and Angela Carter explore this sinister side of fairy tales.

Lee's work is thronged with vampires, demons and the undead. Simmu, in *Death's Master*, changes from female to male: worlds shift and distinctions break down. In *Sabella, or The Blood Stone* death is denied: Sabella and Jason can feed off each other's blood for ever in a constant renewal of desire. Feeding and sucking play a large part in the perversion of life forces. In the bizarre and sinister 'Sirriamnis' a young slave girl, worshipper of Tanit the Phoenician goddess of the moon and night, becomes a hare and sucks the semen of her lover/master Lysias.

Angela Carter is a writer that science fiction fans can boast of for taking SF out of the ghetto and revealing its seriousness to a sceptical world. As with Tanith Lee, metamorphoses abound in her work. In *The Passion of New Eve* Evelyn is changed from man to woman. The wolves, lions and tigers of her fairy tales beckon young girls on to sexual knowledge and transgression. Social codes fall before the imperative of desire. Sexuality, in all of Carter's work, is presented in terms of fragmentation and chaos. Her work is gloriously protean, counterposing realism with counter-realism, modern myth with ancient magic.

I think it is worth looking in some detail at Angela Carter's novel *Heroes and Villains*, which powerfully uses the science fictional trope of a devastated world in order to explore sexuality. The premise: nuclear war or radiation has destroyed most of civilisation, leaving only the enclave of the Professors as a memory of the past. That too is destroyed, by wandering Barbarians, who capture and take with them Marianne, the daughter of one of the Professors.

Heroes and Villains can be read in a variety of ways, just as on a narrative level Angela Carter plays with a variety of forms.

As a fairy tale, echoing the stories of Beauty and the Beast and The Sleeping Princess, the novel is resplendent with magical and luscious imagery. But it is also modern and post-Freudian. This story does not end with marriage: the death of the virgin or individual separate being, and her entry into contingency, or wifehood.

Marianne's story, in *Heroes and Villains*, in a sense *begins* with her marriage; although it is precisely then that her coherence as an individual begins to fragment. Her marriage awakens her to sexuality, but more importantly it allows her to become an agent of that sexuality. The consummation of her marriage is more significant to her than Jewel's rape of her, which she experiences as painful and humiliating. But with agency she grasps sexual pleasure, accepting the knowledge of the 'extreme intimations of pleasure or despair'.[3] It is Marianne's desire that makes her adult, and her understanding of its necessity. She can dismiss the slogan of her rival Donally: 'Our needs bear no relation to our desires'.[4] Marianne becomes powerful. She denies Jewel an existence outside their sexual life: in light – with daylight and firelight – she sees him 'in two dimensions: flat and effectless.'[5] Jewel slowly loses materiality, until, that is, Marianne's autonomy is threatened by the possibility of her conceiving.

As in a fairy tale the characters are ciphers, images with no substantiality. Jewel is the 'sign of an idea of a hero',[6] while Marianne, in her 'palpable white infection'[7] of a wedding dress, at her wedding that is a grotesque parody of a fairy-tale wedding, is a 'sign of a memory of a bride'.[8] Meaning accrues only through reference to a culture and literature of the past.

On another level *Heroes and Villains* is not a fairy tale. Carter uses the conventions of mainstream novels to describe an interior journey, an investigation of moral character. Marianne's search for meaning after the death of her father – which reverberates throughout the book – is a flight from loneliness and an attempt to make a connection with society, even although that society is one she despises. It is for her a journey into 'a perilous and irresistible landscape, a terra incognita',[9] which is how she describes Jewel's tattooed back. It is a journey, too, into her own imagination; one that leads inevitably to fragmentation and chaos.

The Barbarians travel along 'roads [which] were arteries, which no longer sprang from a heart.'[10] Travelling with them Marianne's 'consciousness of reason' withers away, as malign magical chance takes over. She sees herself in Donally's dark glasses: 'The cracked mirrors of his dark glasses revealed all manner of potentialities for Marianne, modes of being to which she might aspire just as soon as she threw away her reason as of no further use to her, since it scarcely helped her to construe the enigmas all about her.'[11] Their journey takes them to the ultimate chaos of the sea, where form and language and artifice are all destroyed.

There, out of the forest that stretches down to the seashore, comes a lion that looks exactly like the pictures of itself that Marianne has seen. For this is a literary journey: the images of chaos and unreason are constantly referred back to language and literature, as the lion is to pictures in a book, and the flora of the sea to the terminology of classification.

Questions of order and disorder are explored, too, through the book's obsession with time. The opening and the closing images are of clocks: a clock which carves the hours into sculptures of ice in Marianne's father's house, and a clock emerging from the sea at the end which echoes the image of the Statue of Liberty at the end of the film *Planet of the Apes*: a sign, at once simple and banal, of aeons passing.

Time seems to exist separate from experience. In the Professors' enclaves the measurements of time are used, unsuccessfully, as a means of ordering experience: 'The time-scale of the community stretched out years forever and also somehow cancelled them out, so an event could have as well taken place yesterday or ten years before.'[12] Marianne feels as if the ticking of the clock is a private message, as if time is a secret between the clock, her father and herself. When her father is killed she buries the clock, and with the Barbarians loses time altogether:

If time was frozen among the Professors, here she lost the very idea of time, for the Barbarians did not segment their existence into hours nor even morning, afternoon and evening but left it raw in original shapes of light and darkness so the day was a featureless block of action and night of oblivion.[13]

Only Donally amongst the Barbarians has a sense of time: for him it is running backwards, back towards a pre-historical time of myth.

Time has collapsed with the collapse of civilisation; it no longer serves humans but marks instead only the natural processes of growth and decay, expressed, for example, in the squirrel Marianne sees in the forest, which is 'a biological timepiece of flesh and blood which did not tell the hours'.[14] Time is swallowed up in the ceaseless churning of the sea. But the movement of time in *Heroes and Villains* also marks a progress: towards death. Marianne and Jewel re-enact in secular terms the story of Eve and Adam; sexual knowledge is knowledge of mortality.

If Jewel is the instrument of Marianne's sexual initiation, then she is the instrument of his death. The occasions when she saves his life only delay his final submission to mortality. But while she is instrument, or agent, she is also victim, for Marianne is an icon like Jewel, and she waits, like Mariana of the Moated Grange, outside time.

Through *Heroes and Villains* Angela Carter offers a meditation on form, artifice and art. The distinction between the Professors and the Barbarians is not one of simple opposition; reason and unreason, art and nature are not clearly distinguished in Carter's riot of imagery. This perhaps explains the ambiguity in Marianne's movements. The natural state of the Barbarians is even more of an artifice than the world of books and reasoned language that the Professors inhabit. The riot of growth and decay has resulted from a human apocalypse, an all-engulfing war, that has left behind it a state of uncivilisation in which mutants roam. The Barbarians, with their beads and necklaces and tattoos, see their humanity as linked to artifice. They are a mixture of the archaic and the modern, but they have no future and no past. They stand outside history. Marianne sees Jewel as 'a fantastic dandy of the void';[15] Donally, obsessed with myth-making, sees him as a potential prince of darkness. Jewel himself sometimes dreams that he is an invention of the Professors. Jewel is a *tabula rasa* on which can be inscribed the fears and longings of the world. He is at once empty and full of meaning.

A redemptive vision is offered by the Barbarians, but only through the innocence, or simplicity, of children. Marianne watches Precious water his horse and is struck by his grace; Donally's wild boy offers grass stalks and rose petals as a wedding present and later intuits that Marianne is pregnant. Neither needs to speak: language precludes such harmony with nature.

Like all the images in this book, these are presented as symbols or representations of a culture; writing about dissolution and decay Angela Carter is using images that have a cultural history; she joins the grotesque to the mundane, the archaic to the modern, the intellectual to the emotional. Just as Marianne moves from alienation to emotional involvement and back, so the reader is both involved and distanced. As a meditation on dissolution the novel is, of course, a highly formalised artefact; the levels of knowingness in which the reader is implicated, combined with the visual intensity of Angela Carter's writing, make this for me a book that beckons, like the tattoo on Jewel's back, towards a 'perilous and irresistible landscape'.

Angela Carter can be compared with Joanna Russ in her complete vindication of female sexual desire and her exploration of the world that sexual desire opens up. As Irene kills God the Father in *The Two of Them* in order to take her place as an autonomous sexual being in the world, so Marianne kills her Adam. Both demand a life beyond virginity; both reject contingency.

But such a demand and such a rejection open up frightening possibilities. It is possible to see in contemporary science fiction a return to the Gothic as a means of representing them. The vampire, for example, a powerful image for the Victorians, has now reappeared in the work of writers such as Suzy McKee Charnas (*The Vampire Tapestry*), Chelsea Quinn Yarbro (*Hotel Transylvania, A Flame in Byzantium*), Anne Rice (*Interview with the Vampire* and *The Vampire Lestat*) and Jody Scott (*I, Vampire* and *Passing for Human*). The image of the vampire represents transgression, the breaking of social codes, a denial of death. It is interesting that so many women writers are attracted by this image for the vampire is traditionally a male figure, active over his female victims' passivity; a barely concealed symbol of phallic penetration.

It is perhaps that identification with the vampire figure allows a claim to be made for a libertarian sexuality for women, a transgression – no longer the prerogative of men – from the constraints of social order.

The desire to transgress also lies behind another common premise of science fiction: the ability to communicate telepathically. It is as if the boundaries and distinctions set up by the spoken word can be overcome. The results can be interesting, not least in the almost universal failure of writers to persuade us that telepathically communicated thoughts come from the unconscious. In Octavia Butler's *Patternist* series, for example, the telepathic ability is, despite all the problems it creates, above all extraordinarily convenient. Unspoken thoughts are codified within a consciously recognisable speech: what is fascinating is the emergence of chaos and violence elsewhere in the novels. Dana, in *Clay's Ark*, goes out in such a blaze of sex (of which she is the agent) and violence (of which she is the victim), that it suggests that the force of repression that one might expect to find revealed through the central notion of telepathy has been transferred.

A similar tension is apparent in Kate Wilhelm's *Margaret and I*, although here the unconscious is a much more stated presence than in Butler's works. As with Butler, the unconscious speaks in a strangely familiar way: both writers create a kind of cosiness in their secret languages (telepathy in Butler, the two selves in Wilhelm's *Margaret and I*). This is perhaps not unrelated to the development of Freudian theory in the USA into ego-psychology; the unconscious is a less problematic concept than in European post-Freudianism. But again, what is repressed breaks through elsewhere; *Margaret and I* contains scenes of quite startlingly active sexuality.

Autonomy brings with it fear, guilt and a sense of loss. The creation of a desirous female subject – outside of utopias – necessitates contradictions.

Metamorphoses and transgressions are common themes in the work of Lisa Tuttle, who is a writer of horror stories as well as of fantasy and science fiction. Like Tanith Lee she explores in her horror stories the paradigms set up by the polarities of animate and inanimate, of human and animal (her sinister carnivorous horses go well with Lee's sinister carnivorous sheep), of dead and alive: but her setting is not fantasy. The power of these stories lies in the tension between the 'ordinary' world (often the central character is a woman whose everyday concerns are work, marriage, relationships, children) and the breakdown of these seeming polarities. Lisa Tuttle's science fiction stories, too, are often set in a secure everyday world, but, as with Lee, nothing is what it seems. Her story 'A Spaceship Built of Stone' explores the unease behind such certainties (in this case the making of histories) in traditional science fictional style; while stories like 'Mrs T' and 'The Wound', both of which depict a change of sex in the main character, are particularly concerned with questioning the certainties of sexual difference. Christa Wolf has explored this theme in 'Self-Experiment: Appendix to a Report'; in all these stories the central concern is the relationship of mind to body and its construction of a gendered sense of self inserted in a social and political order.

It seems as if the subject-object paradigm of love is not a particular concern of women writers of science fiction. The portrayal of sexual desire in science fiction – except in the feminist utopias and in certain romances – leads us to a deconstruction of the female self. What then is the concern of women writing science fiction? Is there, indeed, a distinct women's science fiction, and if so, what is it 'about'? And how does it differ from men's science fiction? And how, if at all, does it differ from feminist science fiction? In the next two chapters I hope to suggest some answers to these questions.

9
Authority and Sentiment: Is There a Women's Science Fiction?

Virginia Woolf believed in the existence of a 'woman's sentence', saying, of Dorothy Richardson, that she 'has invented, or, if she has not invented, developed and applied to her own uses, a sentence which we might call the psychological sentence of the feminine gender.'[1] Yet, as Mary Ellmann points out in *Thinking About Women*, the only certain femininity in the sentences Woolf is analysing lies in their subject matter.[2] Ellmann looks at contemporary women writers in terms of their relationship to authority and power, suggesting that their best writing comes from an anti-authoritarian position, writing from the sidelines as it were, using the tools of irony, rashness, modesty. As she puts it:

> Writing now involves a subterranean embarrassment, which we commonly associate with feminine rather than masculine statement; and this embarrassment issues in the cultivation, on the part of the talented, of either modesty or rashness – again both, in the past, conventional aspects of femininity . . .[3]

This kind of writing is possible nowadays, Ellmann contends; hesitant times demand hesitant writing. Women are thus able to forge their own relationship to literature, without having to borrow a cloak of (male) authority. Her comments on Simone de Beauvoir are telling on this point: she goes on to talk about the avoidance of sentiment as well as authority:

> . . . I hope to define the way in which it is now possible for women to write well. Quite simply, having not had physical or intellectual authority before, they have no reason to resist a

literature at odds with authority. There are, of course, those who prefer instead to wear hand-me-downs, to borrow now the certitude of the nineteenth century. One might say that the defect of Simone de Beauvoir is the authority of her prose: the absence of hesitation in hesitant times amounts to a presence, a tangible deficiency, a sense of obtuseness.

In better work by women now, while sentiment is avoided as stigmatic (as the inimical mark of their sex in others' minds) authority too is skirted – again, as in Mailer and Svevo, by deliberate rashness or by ironic constraint.[4]

The presence of women writers within science fiction raises rather different questions, for science fiction itself is not a literature of authority. It is able to break through the parameters of realism: in literary terms to enjoy the freedom of the fantastic mode, or to employ modernist techniques to challenge the hegemony of the mainstream novel, or again, importantly, to centralise the short story as a literary form that is both viable and popular. In social, or political terms, it is able to extrapolate from, to comment on, to satirise the real (although science fiction is not *necessarily* progressive). But at the same time it has always reflected and continues to reflect a particular type of authority, that of men over women. The absence of women from much science fiction before the 1970s is only one expression of this: the presence of women within science fiction since the early 1970s does not necessarily undermine it.

How then do women position themselves in relation to this literature that is at once authoritarian and anti-authoritarian? Some writers take upon themselves, and bestow upon their female characters, the mantle of authority that until now has been reserved for heroes and their male authors. Some might call this 'post-feminism' – we can all be heroes now – but I would not. Other writers eschew the hierarchies of authority in favour of what, in Mary Ellmann's terms, could be called sentiment: the writers of 'soft' rather than 'hard' science fiction. In my opinion the best women writers of science fiction – that is, those who exploit to the full both its literary and its political possibilities – are those who reject both authority and sentiment, and speak, as it were, from a position of relativism, questioning not just an apparent reality but its very construction.

a) "mainstrean" w/ ♀ protagonist

An example of the first group is the British writer Mary Gentle, in whose *Golden Witchbreed* Lynne de Lisle Christie is an envoy from earth entrusted with the delicate mission of persuading the Ortheans into a relationship with humans. Christie's unproblematic femaleness begs various questions (as indeed does the maleness of Le Guin's envoy Genly Ai in *The Left Hand of Darkness*); not lessened by the Ortheans' remarkable and sudden assumption of sex, after a childhood in which they are neither female nor male, at puberty. This echoes the Gethenians' state of *kemmer*; neither Le Guin nor Gentle confront the social construction of gender and sexuality. Like Le Guin, Gentle is a powerful and lyrical writer; and, like Le Guin, her simplifying view of sexuality is strangely at odds with her interest in portraying a society varied enough to sustain different levels of political and moral complexity. Within the trope of envoy in a strange land, Christie assumes the cloak of authority.

Mary Gentle uses a traditional science fiction narrative framework, as do other women writers such as C.J. Cherryh, Octavia Butler, Cecelia Holland. All of them, importantly, are concerned to undermine sexual and racial stereotypes, which, as Jenny Wolmark says, are 'still found distressingly often in SF'.[5] For example, Cherryh's female *hani* pilot and crew the spaceships while the males remain planetbound. Despite their glamour I must admit to finding the leonine *hani* just a bit *cuddly*: they approximate to Margaret Atwood's criticism in *Survival* of animals in British literature (although Cherryh is an American), as people zipped into furry suits pretending to be animals pretending to be people. At least the *hani* don't wear aprons over their fur.

Jenny Wolmark suggests that such stories – in which certain stereotypes are undermined within a traditional science fiction narrative – prompt in the reader more of a sense of dislocation than stories in which the narrative conventions are rewritten from a feminist viewpoint. Yet while these works doubtless have a wider readership because of their place within 'mainstream' science fiction, I think it is questionable to what extent readers might feel dislocated. After all, SF fans will, notoriously, swallow anything. Wolmark goes on to say:

> . . . the conventional narrative frameworks of rival inter-
> planetary ambitions, warring political factions and alien races

rest on taken-for-granted assumptions about the social and economic structures of patriarchal, capitalist society which are incorporated wholesale into the stories.[6]

The undermining of sexual and racial stereotypes exists in an uneasy tension with these unquestioned assumptions. At the same time, the tone of authority remains, but it is a woman who speaks with it rather than a man.

The writers of 'soft' science fiction can also be placed within the mainstream of SF: Ursula Le Guin and Vonda McIntyre have earned themselves a place there for their continuing output in the genre (unlike, say, Gearhart or Piercy), as well as for their seriousness of intent and the quality of their prose. In the late 1970s and early 1980s these two writers in particular were seen as representative of a progressive (in political terms) shift in SF away from ideas and hardware towards people and politics. They seemed to be breaking down rigid definitions of science with their emphasis on the 'soft' sciences of ecology, psychology and anthropology (in her fiction McIntyre draws on her work as a geneticist as well); they emphasised, concomitantly, both the subjective and the political aspects of these sciences and of science in general. And, importantly, they emphasised characterisation.

There was, and is, a bit of a muddle as to whether these qualities in the writing are related, as stigma, to the writer's sex (like Ellmann's stigma of sentiment) or whether they spring from the writer's political position as a woman within patriarchal science fiction.

Vonda McIntyre's *Dreamsnake*, for example, is set in a world laid waste by nuclear devastation: a common science fiction convention that opens up for treatment a variety of interrelated themes. These include the uses and abuses of technology, the more or less fatal consequences of human overreaching, interaction between post-radiation mutant forms and non-mutant forms (the 'other' rears its head again). Women writers have used the disaster convention as a means of criticising patriarchal society and imagining something different, often separatist. The disaster convention offers a clean sweep; the question of transformation from one kind of society to another is avoided. In other words, the science fiction writer does not have to be a political analyst (although Firestone tried to be

90

both); Russ takes us straight to Whileaway, where there haven't
been men for hundreds of years; in Gearhart's Wanderground
the earth has rebelled against the domination of men some time
before; and in *Dreamsnake* Snake the healer picks her way
through the debris of a past unspecified disaster. Perhaps this
convention is more than just a literary convenience: perhaps in
the 1970s, if not in the gloomy 1980s, it reflected a real belief in
the possibilities of a brave new world.

Central to the feminist utopian tendency in SF of the 1970s is
a concern with ecology, with the relationship between humans
and the world they inhabit. The disaster convention may
provide a convenient background, or it may be read as a dire
warning. In the work of Vonda McIntyre and of Ursula Le Guin
this concern appears as part of a generally holistic vision that is
expressed not only thematically but also in terms of narrative
structure: a story based around the development of, and
accretion of experience around, a central character. This is quite
different from the disintegrationist nature of the narrative in
Suzy McKee Charnas' *Walk to the End of the World* and
Motherlines, or the episodic nature of the narrative in Sally
Miller Gearhart's *The Wanderground: Stories of the Hill
Women*. All these writers, however, deal thematically with the
dichotomy between ecology and technology; indeed Charnas
and Gearhart go further than McIntyre and Le Guin in setting
up man and nature as the dichotomy rather than human and
nature.

Dreamsnake is Vonda McIntyre's second novel. Her first, *The
Exile Waiting*, is set in what seems to be the one remaining city
on earth, called Center, which appears in *Dreamsnake* as the
antithesis to life outside and representative of a challenge to the
protagonist Snake. The protagonist of *The Exile Waiting* is a
resourceful young woman called Mischa. Center is dominated
by its ruling families and is a cruel, decadent society; the
mutants who are the casualties of nuclear radiation are hounded
out of the city streets and live deep underground. The qualities
of loyalty and compassion shown by those underground, who
are united through suffering, are contrasted with the viciousness
of the slave society up above. After various trials and
tribulations, including the death of her brother, with whom she
has telepathic links, Mischa makes her escape offworld.

Snake, of *Dreamsnake*, can be seen as an older and wiser

version of Mischa. As a healer Snake is very powerful, although crippled in her work by the loss of her dreamsnake. The short story 'Of Mist, and Grass, and Sand' concerns this loss and forms the opening sequence of the novel. The novel, which shows Snake's attempts to obtain another of the death-easing dreamsnakes and her eventual discovery of the secret of their breeding, which allows her reintegration as a full healer, becomes more politically wide-ranging than might be guessed at from the original short story (or 'novelette'). It allows for an exploration of lifestyles that are different from, indeed set up in opposition to, the patriarchal norm.

Snake is brave, loyal and intelligent. She is sexually active; she is kind-hearted and filled with the desire to see justice done. While there is no overt dramatisation of sexual politics – the abuse of the girl-child Melissa by Ras is as much an illustration of the intolerance of the people of the idyllic-seeming Mountainside towards physical deformity and an illustration of control through violence, as it is of sexual oppression – McIntyre is quietly making the point that it is possible both to be a woman and to be fully human, at least in her future world.

At first sight the different societies that inhabit the post-disaster world of *Dreamsnake* appear primitive: nomadic groups that move with the seasons; the placid archaic village-world of Mountainside. Technology seems to be a thing of the past, visible only in Center with its visitors and traders from offworld, or in its remnants – the mysterious apparently indestructible domes. But the societies outside Center are not unsophisticated. Biological sciences are practised: people control their own fertility through biocontrol; and while snake fangs may seem more primitive than syringes, the end result – immunisation – is just as effective.

Writers like McIntyre and Le Guin prioritise certain sciences – biological and natural sciences – over others; more importantly, they relate them to the social structures of which they are a part. Joan Slonczewski, in *A Door Into Ocean*, shows a similar concern – the biogenetic engineering practised by the Sharers of Shora (who are all female) is dialectically related to their political philosophy of pacifism, and is presented in opposition to the death-dealing technology of the neighbouring world and the patriarchal empire of which it is a part. This shows, I think, a successful attempt to expand the frontiers of science fiction and to claim new priorities in terms of theme. Rather than single female figures assuming an authority that was previously reserved for men, social relations are placed in the foreground. In a sense, this becomes a literature of feeling rather than action, although it is feeling with a political edge.

While an emphasis on traditionally feminine values – embodied in the wise woman rather than the commander – does challenge science fictional norms, there is a danger that this SF might slip too much into sentiment, and become ghettoised precisely as 'women's SF'. An anomaly here is Doris Lessing, who is not primarily a science fiction writer but who has, over the years, incorporated science fictional settings into her novels and, more recently, has produced a series of five science fiction novels, _Canopus in Argos_. It is in these that she seems to me to express the worst of both tendencies described above: the stories unfold against a background of imperialistic domination that is nowhere challenged while they treat with some of the more mystical aspects of the 'woman's viewpoint', extra-intuitive horses and perfect complementary marriages being just two examples. Lessing somehow manages to come over as an authoritarian sentimentalist, which is perhaps explained by the religious instruction which is the barely concealed sub-text of the quintet. SF has never taken kindly to religion, although pedagogues continue to try to exploit it – the late L. Ron Hubbard being another instance.

Science fiction seems to me most at ease when it deploys a sceptical rationalism as its sub-text. Indeed, that is perhaps another reason why feminist ideas are able to flourish within SF despite reader resistance – for feminism is based upon a profound scepticism: of the 'naturalness' of the patriarchal world and the belief in male superiority on which it is founded.

I would say that writers like McIntyre and Slonczewski function within the paradigm of woman writer and patriarchal tradition: their concerns come from a sense of the exclusion and peripheralisation of women. So too with Le Guin, although her attitude to the 'woman question' is subsumed within her interest in anarchic social forms and the philosophy of Tao. But the response of McIntyre and Slonczewski to their position, like that of other writers already mentioned, is to set up in their work another paradigm, that of woman and man. This is an essentialist position: it accepts, somehow, the naturalness – even

4)

the god-givenness – of sexual difference. While it runs counter to prevailing ideology by prioritising women over men, and feminine over masculine, and thus challenges the end result of that ideology, it does not interrogate its construction.

Yet science fiction is a literature with the universe for its field and relativity for its philosophy. Feminist writers like Vonda McIntyre, or Marge Piercy, or Mary Gentle, have indeed in their work rewritten some of the narrative conventions of SF and have, I think, had a permanent and important influence on its development. But, perhaps surprisingly, it is amongst those writers who turn to the more traditional 'science' aspects of science fiction that we find some of those who have been able to create a feminist rather than a feminised body of work.

10
Feminism and Science Fiction

[handwritten annotation: a) - accept form & basic content; just change protagonist]

[handwritten annotation: a), b), c)] I would like to look now at some of those writers who speak neither from a position of (transformed) authority nor from a position of (newly validated) sentiment but who deconstruct notions of essentialism from a relativistic position: Pamela Zoline, Rhoda Lerman, Monique Wittig, Angela Carter, Joanna Russ and James Tiptree Jr.

Unlike many of the women mentioned so far, Tiptree is a prolific short story writer, favouring that form above all others. Her story 'The Women Men Don't See' exemplifies the notion of woman constructed as 'other', with its play on ideas of visibility and invisibility, alienness and non-alienness. It is written in a convincing pastiche of the Hemingway/Heinlein school, which further dislocates a straightforward reading. Tiptree uses the alien and human paradigm to powerful effect in her treatment of sexual difference. As Susan Wood said: 'As is common in much contemporary SF, the fictional situation serves as a metaphor for the author's vision of contemporary society, in which the cultural differences between men and women seem insurmountable.'[1]

Joanna Russ's novels and short stories show a similar playfulness of form. They are all, in different ways, 'about' the oppression of women in a patriarchal world: in perhaps her best-known novel, *The Female Man*, she uses the metaphor of parallel universes, with a concomitantly fragmented narrator, to question the status quo of women and men not just in the contemporary western world but in the various other worlds that might or might not exist.

Where writers like McIntyre and Le Guin bring the tradition

of the mainstream 'bourgeois' novel – with its emphasis on characterisation, its notion of a coherent self – into science fiction, with far-reaching, positive consequences; where more avowedly feminist writers like Sally Miller Gearhart, while eschewing the individualism inherent in the 'bourgeois' tradition, nonetheless subscribe to its essentialism, albeit a female one; the writers mentioned above use the metaphors of science fiction to subvert it from within, without making compromises with another literary tradition – that of the 'bourgeois' novel – that, too, glosses over the construction of sexual difference.

I am not trying to construct here a hierarchy of feminism, to measure one writer against another and find one lacking. I want to show the ways in which science fiction is feminism-friendly. With its metaphors of space and time travel, of parallel universes, of contradictions co-existing, of black holes and event horizons, science fiction is ideally placed for interrogative functions. The unities of 'self', whether in terms of bourgeois individualism or biological reductionism, can be subverted.

The goal of absolute unity between self and other, or subject and object, that is, the point of maximum entropy, is indeed exemplified by Pamela Zoline's short story, 'The Heat Death of the Universe' and Rhoda Lerman's *The Book of the Night*, both of which have as their sub-text the Second Law of Thermodynamics. As Lerman puts it in an epigraph: ' . . . the world will eventually die, decay, fall into drift, come to a hopeless end, burn out, slide into disorder.'[2] The potential implications of this in *The Book of the Night* are held in tension by a contrary proposition, namely that in certain instances the Second Law fails; that there is within matter an anti-entropy drive. Or as Zoline puts it in paragraph 19 of her 54-paragraphed story:

'The second law of thermodynamics can be interpreted to mean that the ENTROPY of a closed system tends toward a maximum and that its available ENERGY tends toward a minimum. It has been held that the Universe constitutes a thermodynamically closed system, and if this were true it would mean that a time must finally come when the Universe "unwinds" itself, no energy being available for use. This state is referred to as the "heat death of the Universe". It is by no means certain, however, that the Universe can be considered as a closed system in this sense.'[3]

The 'subject' of 'The Heat Death of the Universe' is a housewife and mother, the archetypal figure who brings order out of disorder, life out of death, meaning out of chaos. But, here, housework is a closed system, tending towards maximum entropy. The story describes a day in Sarah Boyle's life, from the dishing out of Sugar Frosted Flakes to her children at breakfast time to clearing up after a birthday party in the afternoon. The paragraphs are numbered; seven of them including the one above, are 'inserts': on entropy, heat death, light, Dada, love, Weiner on entropy, and turtles.

Sarah Boyle's life is a struggle against disorder. Death and chaos are held at bay by cleaning, ordering, measuring and naming. The numbered paragraphs fulfil the same function, as do the 'factual' or scientific inserts, and the careful precision of Zoline's language. But order seeps away, the I tends towards not-I. Sarah has 32 lines on her face (charted in an image on the wall) but isn't sure how many children she has; cancer lurks, perhaps, in the Sugar Frosted Flakes; the turtle is dying.

The wealth of metaphor and meaning that make up language, literature and art becomes irrelevant. The touchstone of nature has been replaced as a source of meaning by value-free, culture-free synthetic creations. On the colour of Sarah's eyes, for example:

> 24. Sarah Boyle's blue eyes, how blue? Bluer far and of a different quality than the Nature metaphors which were both engine and fuel to so much of precedent literature. A fine, modern, acid, synthetic blue; the shiny cerulean of the skies on postcards sent from lush subtropics, the natives grinning ivory ambivalent grins in their dark faces; the promising, fat, unnatural blue of the heavy tranquillizer capsule; the cool, mean blue of that fake kitchen sponge; the deepest most unbelievable azure of the tiled and mossless interiors of California swimming pools. The chemists in their kitchens cooked, cooled and distilled this blue from thousands of colourless and wonderfully constructed crystals, each one unique and nonpareil; and now that colour hisses, bubbles, burns in Sarah's eyes.

As natural order is displaced so hierarchies of value tumble. The meaning acquired through weight of cultural accretion is wiped out. So, on the Sugar Frosted Flakes packet are squandered 'wealths of richest colours, virgin blues, crimsons, dense ochres, precious pigments once reserved for sacred paintings and as cosmetics for the blind faces of marble gods.'[5] As signifiers slip from signifieds, the sign becomes arbitrary. Sarah incorporates this arbitrariness into her ordering activities: 'Sometimes she labels objects with their names, or with false names; thus on her bureau the hair brush is labelled HAIR BRUSH, the cologne, COLOGNE, the hand cream, CAT.'[6]

The housewife's struggle for order is renewed each day. Dust creeps in and settles on all surfaces. As with dust, so with death. With the resigned irony with which she accepts the arbitrariness of signs, Sarah Boyle allows death and dust into her fantasies. 'The plants would grow wild and wind into a jungle around the house, splitting plaster, tearing shingles, the garden would enter in at the door. The goldfish would die, the birds would die, we'd have them stuffed; the dog would die from lack of care, and probably the children – all stuffed and sitting around the house, covered with dust.'[7] As the conventions that join signifiers to signified are shattered, so the conventions of sentimentality are broken apart. Children are the 'too often disappointing vegetables of one's own womb', or, in a reversion to a time of pre-culture, apparently edible.

Sarah herself is a construct, she 'muses or is mused'. Here is no quest for wholeness, rather a doomed struggle against the slipping of self into other, a struggle to set up difference in the face of undifferentiation. Chaos is kept at bay and the elements of dissolution are separated out, paragraph by paragraph, until there is no available energy left. The turtle is dead. The floor is covered with smashed eggs and broken shards of bunny bowls. The stove bleeds, the particles in the universe attain complete disorder, time runs backwards and Sarah Boyle opens her mouth again and again and repeatedly begins to cry.

'The Heat Death of the Universe' was first published in the magazine *New Worlds* in 1967 and is one of those SF stories that has achieved a small cult status, reappearing every so often in anthologies. It reappears in a *New Worlds* anthology edited by Michael Moorcock (Flamingo, 1983) where it is one of two stories by women (the other is Hilary Bailey's 'Dr Gelabius') out of a total of 29. I mention this merely to point out the rarity of women participants in the 'progressive' New Wave. While 'Heat Death' is obviously a part of the entropy-orientation of *New*

Worlds, its meditation on entropy is grounded in the organisation of a woman's life.[8]

'Heat Death' achieves two apparently contradictory goals: it deconstructs the notion of woman as stable centre of family life, subverting the conventional values that are attached to that concept; while at the same time it also subverts accepted notions of what is a suitable 'subject' for a story by focusing on a housewife and housework. It at once centralises and deconstructs 'woman'. This, I think, exemplifies a problem that structuralist and post-structuralist criticism poses for feminists: the radical, or transgressive aspects of the structuralist subversion of the subject do not allow for an analysis that shows 'woman' never to have been the subject in the first place. 'Heat Death' is one of my favourite of all science fiction stories, expressing as it does with such elegance and wit the vistas of emptiness hidden behind the slogan 'a woman's work is never done'.

Interestingly enough, Pamela Zoline's most recent SF story, 'Instructions for Exiting this Building In Case of Fire', also centralises the experience of women and children, although, again, not in any conventional way, as it is about breaking, or undermining, the ties that hold together families and nations. I say interestingly as Zoline does not, I think, consider herself particularly feminist; where some writers, as I have mentioned, centralise women and questions of reproduction as a way of challenging the male-dominated concerns of SF, Zoline, it seems, finds the metaphors of science fiction speak to the fragmentation of a woman's life. Male writers do not, on the whole, write about female *experience*; but women writers, like Judith Merril and Pamela Zoline, use that experience, to remarkable effect, within a science fictional framework. So we have motherhood and nuclear radiation; and housework and entropy.

Rhoda Lerman (and Tanith Lee and Angela Carter, as mentioned earlier) is concerned with the body's interchangeability. In Lerman's *Call Me Ishtar* the movement is between goddess and mortal, the queen of the heavens and a middle-class American woman. In *The Book of the Night* a girl child, Celeste, is brought up as a boy and accepted into the monastery on Iona where she subsequently lives. At puberty she is transformed into a cow. While some of the tenth-century monks are attracted by the increasing power of Rome, for others ancient Seth still roars from the chaos. The forces of disorder and entropy are marshalled against the order of language, progress and rationalism. As in the Zoline story, language takes on a logic of its own that is unrelated to the objects to which it was formerly tied. From this follows a breakdown, not just of women's role in the order of human society, but of the very nature of femaleness. As with Zoline, it is not only culture that is interrogated but nature. But the pivot in Lerman's work is the powerful awakening of sexuality, which transgresses linguistic and cultural codes. So, too, with Angela Carter, who takes the anodyne out of fairy tales and re-equips her young girls with claws, teeth and a powerful desire. There is an element of violence in Lerman's work which is traditionally not a quality of 'feminine' writing: such an element appears in the work of other women, for example Octavia Butler and Chelsea Quinn Yarbro, as well as Carter, Lee and Tuttle. It too is transgressive; the construction of the inviolable body is a corollary of the construction of the coherent self. Woman as 'woman' is interrogated as well as woman as self.

Perhaps it is the position of science fiction on the periphery of mainstream fiction that makes it so open to borrowing from elsewhere, from physics and fairy tales, from philosophy, folklore and myth. And perhaps it is the position of women on the periphery of mainstream (patriarchal) culture that makes SF so suitable a genre for them to work in. For women have not had to bear the awful weight of the Great Tradition, and so have been free to experiment, to riffle through, stopping here and there to work in odd corners, as Tiptree's Ruth describes to Don how women live, 'by ones and twos in the chinks of your world-machine'.[9]

Monique Wittig's *Les Guérillères* is often included in discussions of feminist utopias of the 1970s (see for example Joanna Russ, 'Recent Feminist Utopias'), but I think it is more fruitful to read it in the context of the 'disintegrationist' writers. Like Carter, Lerman and Russ, Wittig questions the laws of language and difference that govern our place in the world. *Les Guérillères* gets included under the 'utopian' label because it shows a future, separatist, almost women-only world. But the guerrilla fighters of the title are not simply waging a war against men (who appear only peripherally anyway) but a war against the language that constructs them as women and then contains, or encloses them. They are trying to get back to point zero, denying even the names that women have given to themselves in defiance of men, and questioning in particular the metaphors that bind women to the processes of Nature. *Les Guérillères* does share a certain dream-like quality with Gearhart's *The Wanderground*: a similar circular structure with the story unfolding through many different voices; but its aims are quite different. Where Gearhart seeks harmony and synthesis with nature, Wittig questions the possibility of such a notion.

Monique Wittig's most recent novel, *Across the Acheron* is a fierce and witty re-enactment of Dante's journeyings through the circles of Hell. Wittig herself is the vengeful voyager, her anger, passion and contempt for sexual slavery held in check, not always successfully, by her guide Manastabal, and resting from her labours every so often in the lesbian bars of limbo.

None of these writers is concerned with the conventions of the 'feminine' in terms of construction, imagery or language, yet all of them, I think, are powerfully feminist. If we want to see what women writers of science fiction have to offer the reader, then we shouldn't be sidetracked by essentialist, and finally moralistic notions of 'feminine' and 'masculine', although the appearance of such a dichotomy is understandable, given the received view of science fiction as a male bastion. We should be looking instead at how science fiction, true to its tradition (not always exploited) of political as well as scientific speculation, can be grasped and used by women writers whose ideas are rooted in a feminist analysis of the world.

Different writers of course hold very different ideas of what feminist SF is. Unlike other forms of genre writing, such as detective stories and romances, which demand the reinstatement of order and thus can be described as 'closed' texts, science fiction is by its nature interrogative, open. Feminism questions a given order in political terms, while science fiction questions it in imaginative terms. I have tried to show the many ways in which contemporary women writers express this, and I hope that I have shown the political and aesthetic vitality of science fiction. If science fiction demands our acceptance of a relativistic universe, then feminism demands, no less, our acceptance of a relativistic social order. Nothing, in these terms, is natural, least of all the cultural notions of 'woman' and 'man'.

In this first section I have tried to show the breadth and variety of women's writing in the genre. In Part Two I am going to look in more detail at four writers whose work I think expresses, in different ways, the conjuncture of politics and the imagination: James Tiptree Jr, Ursula K. Le Guin, Suzy McKee Charnas and Joanna Russ.

PART TWO

11
Who is Tiptree, What is She?: James Tiptree Jr

. . . critics talked about my 'narrative drive' as being a male writing style, but narrative drive is simply intensity, and a desire not to bore. It has never been confined to men. Take one of the first women utterers that we know about: Cassandra. *She* was never accused of a lack of narrative drive. She was just a little before her time, which is often what women's crimes consist of.[1]

James Tiptree Jr published her first science fiction short story in 1968. For the next eight years her identity remained secret, while critics held forth about her masculine writing style, her feminine sensitivity to the portrayal of women and, in general, used Tiptree as a weapon, on one side or the other, in the debate that could be loosely called 'women and science fiction': can women write it, images of women in it, can men write about women in it, etc.

In 1975 she took part in a written symposium – published later as the double issue *Khatru 3 & 4* – precisely on this question, with nine women (Suzy McKee Charnas, Virginia Kidd, Ursula Le Guin, Vonda McIntyre, Raylyn Moore, Joanna Russ, Luise White, Kate Wilhelm and Chelsea Quinn Yarbro) and two – at that point two 'other' – men (Samuel Delany, and Jeffrey Smith, who initiated it). Tiptree was eventually asked to withdraw; the women found her male persona too irritating to deal with.

Khatru 3 & 4 is a fascinating document to read, not just for the wealth of ideas debated, on science fiction, feminism and women, but for the way the men, and Tiptree under a male persona, participated. Delany and Smith, well-meaning though they appear, do show a tendency to go on about themselves: their feminism and lack of it, their feelings of guilt, their role as male participants, etc. Tiptree's contributions provide what is, at times, the positively bizarre experience of reading the words of a woman, writing about the politics of being a woman, who is masquerading almost utterly convincingly as a man. Later, in an interview conducted by Charles Platt, she said, 'Everything I said to everybody was true, with the exception of the gender implied in the signature. I never *stated* I was a man.'[2] I think here Tiptree is leading us up the garden path, a game she seemed greatly to enjoy. For how is one meant to interpret this statement: 'The motive [for genital display, or 'flashing'] is an obscure and yet apparently potent one, which seems to have missed me or be buried deep . . . '?[3] This is protective coloration, at the very least, for 'the gender implied in the signature'.

In this symposium she talks at some length about her ideas of sexual patterning and mothering, and offers an analysis of power and privilege in a male-dominated world. I find reading her contribution with a double perspective quite an unnerving experience, and can sympathise with the suspicion, and at times hostility, that it aroused in the women participants. As with the fiction published before her identity was known, her contribution to the symposium challenges the notion of a neutral reader. The question of the writer's gender becomes enormously significant, much more significant to me than I would like to admit.

When Tiptree's cover was blown by Jeffrey Smith in 1976, and she was revealed as the woman Alice Sheldon and the writer Raccoona Sheldon, Ursula Le Guin's response was both generous and appreciative. She describes the 'joyous shock of revelation, recognition' she felt, and calls Tiptree a 'beautiful Jill-in-the-box'.[4] Such a revelation, Le Guin says, must surely make us question all the theories put forward about feminine and masculine writing. 'She fooled us. She fooled us good and proper. And we can only thank her for it.'[5]

Much of this successful fooling derives from the tough, cool, hard-boiled male narrators – one imagines them with half-closed eyelids, speaking out of the corners of their mouths – who feature in many of Tiptree's stories, from the first person narrator of the early 'Fault' (1968) through to the authorial narrative voice of the painful, pitiful 'With Delicate Mad Hands' (1981). Similarly, many of the descriptions of women, and their effect on men, correspond so convincingly with an objectifying macho view that it is hard to believe that they are written by a woman. Here is one of her world-weary male characters in 'I'm too big but I love to play', as he finds himself automatically giving the come-on to a drunken woman at a party:

> Christ but he was tired! Whacked out . . . Young cunt, old cunt, soft, sinewy, bouncy, bony, wriggly, lumpy, slimy, lathery, leathery cunt squeaking, shrieking, growling – all of them after him, his furry arms, his golden masculinity, his poor old never-failing poker – Oh Ches I've never oh Ches it's so it's oh Ches oh Darling darling darlingdarlingdarling – [6]

Tiptree's descriptions of hard-ons amongst the male of the species have a convincingly misogynist specificity. The first person narrator of 'And I awoke and found me here on the cold hill's side', a young journalist chasing stories about aliens, listens to his interviewee's description of a Sellice dancing in a sleazy nightclub:

> Her arms went up and those blazing lemon-coloured curves pulsed, waved, everted, contracted, throbbed, evolved unbelievingly welcoming, inciting permutations. *Come do it to me, do it, do it here and here and here and now.* You couldn't see the rest of her, only a wicked flash of mouth. Every human male in the room was aching to ram himself into that incredible body . . . [7]

But there is always an element of ridicule. In 'Houston, Houston, Do You Read?' one of the three male astronauts, who have discovered they are the only surviving men, fantasises all the women on earth queuing up for his favours. He attempts to rape in zero gravity one of the crew of the spaceship that has rescued them; his violence grows in proportion to his frustration as he struggles with his victim, quite unaware that it is a set-up job, that the scene is being filmed and that his 'victim' is intent on bagging a sample of his sperm.

Dave Lorimer, the narrator of this story, is a scientist, one of the three rescued men. As Lillian Heldreth has pointed out the narrative is so skilfully constructed that for much of the story the reader shares Lorimer's reactions to the society he has been thrust into. He is a sympathetic character who has never fitted in with the tough guy ethos expressed by the captain and the navigator (the would-be rapist), yet he is weak enough to admire them precisely for that. He watches Bud trying to rape, finding it both erotic and pitiful, and finally absurd.

Bud would be a figure of fun were it not for the fact that were he to be let loose on earth he would rape in earnest and with more success, probably, than in zero gravity. The conclusion is uncompromising: in a world of women there is no place for men with their innately aggressive sexual drive. The women of earth, it is revealed, are bred from a limited number of clone types. And while Lorimer sympathises with, and even likes, the ones he has met aboard the spaceship, he too, like the other men, grieves for the loss of competition and individualism. Having watched Bud's ludicrous performance, and having helped the crew overpower his own captain, who was on the verge of destroying them all, in the name of God, by shooting a hole through the ship's hull, Lorimer still tries to justify the ways of men to women. He talks of men's contribution to history, of the sacrifices men have made to protect women. The ship's captain, Lady Blue, remains unimpressed, saying, 'As I understand it, what you protected people from was largely other males, wasn't it? We've just had an extraordinary demonstration.'[8]

Earlier in the story, before the men are picked up and saved from a slow death as their air supply runs out, they listen in to the transmissions from base to the spaceship that will rescue them. ' "Maybe they're dead?" ', the men overhear. It goes on, ' "I think they're aliens." Are we not? Lorimer thinks.'[9] By the end of the story their alienness has been confirmed: it is the cloned women who are now the human race, humanity *in toto*.

'Houston, Houston, Do You Read?' explores some of Tiptree's most common themes. The question of the alienness of women to men and men to women is an important one in her work. The alienation of one sex from another stands as the paradigm, one to which she repeatedly returns, of other forms of difference, of the relation between self and Other; in the complex relationship of human and extra-terrestrial species, as in, 'And I awoke and found me here on the cold hill's side', or the exploration within a species as in 'Your Haploid Heart'. When this theme's tragic aspect is explored, the potential for cruelty, for inflicting pain, is Tiptree's central concern.

In 'Your Haploid Heart', an early story (1969), the 'mystery' of the planet Esthaa lies in the relationship of its apparently superior, human-looking species, the Esthaan, to the cowering oppressed Flenni. It is revealed that these two groups are alternating generations of one species, the Flenni being sexed and, after mating, giving birth to the neuter Esthaan before dying. The Esthaan hate the Flenni with a hatred that can be felt only for a part of oneself: they try to force the Flenni to mate earlier and earlier.

Rather oddly, Tiptree saw this story as an early attempt at the themes of 'A Momentary Taste of Being', which she says shows what 'seven years of sweat do to the presentation of a similar psychosexual theme'.[10] 'A Momentary Taste of Being' seems to me a much more overtly determinist tale: it starts with a dream of an enormous penis pushing out amongst the stars, with the spaceship *Centaur* at its tip. The dream becomes reality as all the humans aboard save for the dreamer himself, Dr Aaron Kaye, rush to 'mate' with an alien life form that is brought on board, then fall into a state of permanent catatonia. 'The infinite variety of us, all for nothing,' muses Dr Kaye.[11] Humans are only gametes; the development of space travel has a single goal, of which humans are blissfully unaware: that of increasing the motility of the sperms that we are. Our individual lives no longer have meaning even as vehicles for the selfish gene; we actually *are* the selfish gene.

Is Tiptree saying anything more here, albeit in a dramatic, nightmarish and, dare I say it, masculinist way (although undoubtedly original: earth as a 'planet-testicle' makes a change from earth as womb, egg, source of all nurturance), than that we exist only to mate and die? The earlier story dramatises the conflict that can arise from such a proposition; the later story concentrates on the gloomy inevitability of its consequences.

'Your Haploid Heart' and 'A Momentary Taste of Being' are not unusual in their concern with reproduction and death. Sex, death and violence are major themes in Tiptree's work. Lillian Heldreth describes a sample of Tiptree's stories:

The threads that thematically bind the stories are usually bloody. A survey of twenty-seven of them reveals scenes of physical violence or death in twelve, and a direct association of sex with death or violence (or both) occurs in eleven; six of them depict death as ultimately triumphant over the best human efforts. Of the twenty-seven stories, only seven are not in some way concerned with violence or death.[12]

It is not simply human sexuality, but specifically the male sexual drive, that Tiptree associates with violence and death; the stories that explore this theme are deeply pessimistic and have a deterministic slant that is not present throughout her work. One of the most powerful and disturbing treatments of this theme can be found in 'The Screwfly Solution' (1977).

In this story Alan Alstein, beloved husband of Anne and father of adolescent Amy, is in South America researching into the life cycle of the cane fly, an insect that deposits its larvae in the human nasal passages, causing terrible pain and hideous mutilation. Letters from his wife tell him of the spread of a sinister religious movement, the Sons of Adam, who, it seems, are murdering women and girl children. Anne also sends him reports on the work of his friend Barney, an ecologist who is looking for a way to control the spruce budworm, a wrecker of forests, without destroying other plant and animal life.

The work of Alan and Barney, the two scientists, forms the sub-text of the story, offering parallels and hints that can only be fully understood in the context of the main narrative. Both men are trying to manipulate the reproductive pattern of their respective insects in order to bring down population growth to zero. 'Look for the vulnerable link in the behavioural chain,' Alan tells himself.[13] This is the key to what is happening to the human population, the irony being that the work of Alan and Barney is essentially altruistic, for the good of humanity and of the planet, whereas what is happening to the human population benefits something else entirely.

Anne, as non-scientist and conventional wife and mother, bows to the superior knowledge of the men. Yet although the main narrative is told in the third person, with Alan as focus, it is through Anne's letters to him that the story becomes more horrifying and more complex. Anne is the emotional and moral centre of the story; the changes in her reactions draw in the reader. Her growing disquiet is shown alongside newspaper clippings sent from Barney that chart the spread of the Sons of Adam and underpin, in 'objective' language, her personal experiences of fear and horror. Alan at this stage is involved only as an observing outsider; it is the later shift in his position to, as it were, active participant, that increases the horror of the events.

The first newspaper clipping consists of a sinister eye-witness account by a Sergeant Willard Mews of a trip into one of the 'liberated zones' of the Sons of Adam with an investigative medical team, and the subsequent rape and murder of the woman team member by the mayor of the township. The Sergeant captures exactly the dangerously simplistic notions of fundamentalist religion. He is a picture of bewildered innocence, as he reports his conversation with the mayor:

He said some people raise the question of how can man reproduce without women but such people miss the point. The point is that as long as man depends on the old filthy animal way God won't help him. When man gets rid of his animal part which is woman, this is the signal God is awaiting. Then God will reveal the new true clean way, maybe angels will come bringing new souls, or maybe we will live forever, but it is not our place to speculate, only to obey . . . [14]

This might be laughable were it not a justification for the wholesale massacre of women. And in this story such a view of women is not restricted to the fundamentalist Sons of Adam. Other organisations such as the Pauline Purification cults within the Catholic church – on whom the Pope refuses to give an official comment – enthusiastically advocate the elimination of women 'as a means of justifying man to God'. In this case the rationale given is that nowhere in the Scriptures is woman defined as human, but merely as a 'temporary companion and instrument of man . . . a transitional expedient or state'.[15] Here Tiptree is pushing a familiar, mundane, ideology – the Catholic Church's Pauline tradition of hostility towards women – into the realm of the fantastic. The effectiveness of this 'horror story' rests on that close underpinning of the fantastical by the familiar.

Anne remains calm and brave, but the reports she sends show that the massacres are becoming increasingly widespread; Alan decides he must go home. He gets as far as Miami, then has a six-hour wait at the airport. For the first time he actually sees what is happening: women are trying to hide themselves, gathering in groups for protection. He falls into a daydream about his homecoming with Anne. Their sexual relationship is described powerfully and movingly, as an eroticism that has developed over the years, flowering into a mature and mutually satisfying sexuality after the birth of their daughter Amy. This relationship of sexual tenderness suddenly, without warning, turns into a violent, nightmarish fantasy. Alan breaks out of it to find that his clasp knife is open in his hand. He tries desperately to save his wife and daughter from himself but he hasn't taken into account the fact that Amy has an independent will. Amy's voice, that of a rebellious, but father-loving, sexually awakening girl, is heard for the first time in a diary extract, in which she writes down her plan to go and visit the father that her mother has apparently whimsically and cruelly banished from the home.

The dénouement is tragic and inevitable. The rest of the story is narrated by Anne, in hiding in the woods, thinking that perhaps she is the last woman left alive, and that she probably won't survive for long. She remains self-reflective and ironical to the end: 'Do you know [she writes] I never said "we" meaning women before? "We" was always me and Alan, and Amy of course. Being killed selectively encourages group identification.'[16]

'The Screwfly Solution' is a bleak story, whose pessimism is expressed in the scribbled quotation Barney sends to Alan with one of the news clippings: 'Man's religion and metaphysics are the voices of his glands. Schonweiser, 1878.' It explores the assertion that anatomy is destiny, an assertion usually considered anathema within feminist ideology because of its use in arguments about 'woman's place'.

Yet Tiptree is not interested in simple assertions about female and male. In the *Khatru* symposium she says, 'The problem is to try to understand real people, and to determine whether a handful of genes on one chromosome has any identifiable effects on their way of being human.'[17] She is rigorously opposed to a dualistic notion of the sexes, to the idea that 'they in some way mystically reflect and complement each other – on no greater evidence than that occasional men and women do get on well and that the race as a whole hasn't yet died out.'[18] Putting women on a pedestal and contrasting them with nasty hairy rough men, that is, imprisoning them within the parameters of a superior sex, is as oppressive as viewing and treating them as inferior. She expresses this form of oppression convincingly in

her disguise of male persona: '*I* think – therefore *they* emote . . .
Perhaps more perniciously, my superego whispers, *I* have selfish
and destructive drives – therefore *they* are altruistic, compas-
sionate and nurturant. (They better be.)'[19]

Rather, Tiptree plays with the idea of sexual patterns: a male
pattern that 'shares the neural pathways of aggression'[20] and a
maternal pattern she calls 'Mothering'. For this distinction, and
especially for her views on 'Mothering', Tiptree was properly
clobbered – her most vociferous antagonist being, perhaps not
surprisingly, one of the 'other' male contributors to the
symposium, Samuel Delany. She is, I think, perspicacious in
picking out an almost unspoken element of her previous
argument that has caused offence, one that recurs throughout
her work: 'And above all, I should never have advanced a view
of sex which violates the great sacred totem of our time: the
all-importance of copulation. My view of sex looks at the
reproduction of the race, and really trivialises intercourse. How
blasphemous can you get?'[21]

'The Screwfly Solution' explores the neural pathways shared
by both sexual and aggressive drives in the male of the human
species. Although one may disagree with its biological premise,
this nonetheless serves as a metaphor for the struggle between
women and men that Tiptree explores in other ways in other
stories. Here Tiptree offers a feminist version of a theme
common in science fiction, and whose comic possibilities she
exploits elsewhere: 'The Screwfly Solution' is a version of the
'earth as real estate' story.

The short story, the backbone of science fiction, is an ideal
vehicle for the display of Tiptree's versatility as a writer. She
takes great pleasure with the different modes in which a theme
can be worked. In this instance, I would suggest that 'The
Screwfly Solution' is a feminist (and pessimistic) reworking of a
theme that appears as serio-comedy in 'All the Kinds of Yes'
(1972), as knockabout comedy in 'Angel Fix' (1974) and tragedy
in 'Beaver Tears' (1976). Similarly, one of her most powerfully
feminist stories 'The Women Men Don't See' has echoes of the
comic early story (1968) 'Mama Come Home', although even
this latter has a feminist sub-text. Tillie, whose experiences of
men are not altogether happy, is warned by her colleague, the
male narrator of the story, of the possible danger from the
visiting alien Amazons, ' "*They're* dangerous?" ' asks Tillie.[22]

Tiptree sees herself as 'a frustrated comedian' and deserves a place, I think, within the comic science fiction tradition. As she says of her work, 'My own early stories, the shallow belly laughs, I esteem rather more than my critics do – a good laugh is rare. Not to be sneered at.'[23]

In 'All the Kinds of Yes' the human race is considered by other races in the galaxy to be lower than low, virtually worthless and only of interest because planet earth shows great potential for exploitation. This standard comic theme has been treated, for example, by such different writers as the Strugatsky brothers, Douglas Adams, Jody Scott; it can be seen as the opposite of (as indeed it is often a pastiche of) the human-achievement oriented science fiction of such luminaries as Asimov and Heinlein.

In this instance earth is recognised by one particular race of aliens as an ideal nursery for their offspring, who are born in huge numbers as crude energy. Not all survive 'babyhood'; no other species would survive either. Meanwhile advance agents from two other competing alien life forms are investigating future possibilities: one lot hoping to exploit an oxygen-free earth, the other hoping to install ants as the dominant species.

The human race is depicted as rushing headlong towards its own destruction, with no one to shed a tear for its demise. This is unlike the delightful 'Faithful to thee, Terra, in our fashion', which gently mocks but ultimately validates all that is left of earth: the legacy of the notion of fair play, now under threat from a whole variety of cross-galactic skulduggeries. The tone of 'All the Kinds of Yes' is tongue in cheek. Tiptree's loony but immensely likeable alien may signal the end of humanity as we know it, but he is also a joke directed not least against the army of science fictional aliens that have threatened the human race before him. What makes the story typically Tiptree is the generosity with which the humans are depicted. For Tiptree, for all her moments of pessimistic despair, is a humanist at heart. While we may be heading towards destruction, we are doing it in a wild, exuberant, open-hearted kind of way. Modern urban America may not have much to offer in terms of moral, political or ecological values, but as the alien says: 'Everybody never breathed quite so many kinds of yes.'[24]

In 'Angel Fix' the visiting alien gathers together a small group of 'good guy' humans, having tested them out with an Ethical

Vibesponder. He says he wants to offer his help to persons 'of altruistic temperament, of low dominance-submission orientation';[25] in fact he offers them paradise, which they can enter not through the needle's eye but through what is merely a 'technological convenience' that the alien happens to possess. The alien and his pals are not quite as altruistic as they appear at first. Earth is a potentially valuable piece of real estate; clear out the good guys and the bad guys will clobber each other to death. This 'angel' is in the same line of business as the one that reveals himself to Anne at the end of 'The Screwfly Solution'.

In 'Beaver Tears' it is specifically the white middle class, with their greed for land and property, whose actions are mirrored by those of the aliens. As indigenous animal life is gathered up and dumped elsewhere to make room for property development, so humans are scooped up by the aliens without a thought for the consequences. There will be, Tiptree hints at the end of the story, a degeneration into rape and murder amongst the mixed bag of humans so caught up.

The mad destruction of our home planet is a constant theme in Tiptree's work. In 'Time-Sharing Angel' (1977) the heroine Jolyone Schram has a hideous vision of the over-population of the earth:

> . . . a billion-headed monstrous wave . . . a great devouring mindless incubus that spread around the green ball of Earth – blotting out everything, eating everything, using everything, expanding and destroying without limit on a finite surface . . .[26]

The vision becomes nightmare:

> From under every foot rose the weak cries of the trampled and dying. Nowhere in all that panorama of strife was kindness, nowhere was anything she thought of as human – only the war of all against all raging on the despoiled earth.[27]

Jolyone's solution is marvellously simple: a single lifespan is divided out equally between all the siblings of one mother; while one is awake the others are in a kind of hibernation. The social consequences of this – such as the family skeletons that fall rattling out of cupboards, for this time-sharing scheme offers no respect for matters such as wedlock and legitimacy – are extremely funny. Poor Jolyone. The story ends with her working out the implications of the inevitable fall in population growth, musing aloud to a mysterious 'I' figure who has appeared – yet another of Tiptree's wicked angels.

This story is a fine example of Tiptree's light touch on weighty matters. She can be a mistress of black comedy, able to exploit to the full its possibilities in science fiction. Here is troubled Jolyone again:

> It was a fine sunny day. As she sailed up the ramp into the southbound lanes, she noticed something else she had missed the night before. The sea up north had a funny black-looking scum edge on it. An oil slick?
>
> 'It's the biggest one yet,' the girl at the Burgerchef rest stop told her, nodding proprietorially, 'They say it killed all those sea otters or whatever – hey, don't you want your Supercheese?'[28]

The science fiction short story is an ideal form for the constant reworking of themes. While the links between a writer's work and her life are never simple (and can be misleading if one tries to read too much autobiography into fiction), many of the themes that interest Tiptree – her obsessions, perhaps – do seem to have their roots in her bizarre life.

She spent much of her childhood exploring Africa with her parents, in the days when exploring meant walking: 2,700 miles to the Mountains of the Moon in Uganda in search of the black gorillas. Her parents were impressive: her mother wrote thirty-five books, and was the first Westerner to discover (what has since become popular knowledge) that the gorillas were gentle unaggressive creatures.

Alice was an only child, born after her mother had suffered nine miscarriages; as such she felt an enormous responsibility towards her parents' expectations. She says of her mother: 'She was a small, red-haired, blue-eyed person, the kind you help through doors, and then discover she can carry a Springfield rifle and walk forty-five miles hunting elephants, and do it again the next day while her first day's partner is resting up in bed, and then do it the next day, and the day after that. Even as a child, without meaning to, you compete.'[29] Her father, she discovered later, had always wanted a son: 'Every time I did anything boy-like, like going into the Army, Father approved deeply.'[30] At the age of twelve she tried to commit suicide. 'I didn't realise that my parents, in the name of love, had dumped their

accumulated nervous tensions onto me.'[31]
It is perhaps not surprising that Tiptree felt the need for disguises, for escape routes. She found it difficult to 'fit in' at school and at college. She was too smart, too accustomed to adult expectations and aspirations. It was while she was at college that she discovered the consolation of the stars – a discovery that I think more than anything is instrumental in making one a reader (or writer) of science fiction – the glorious indifference of the universe to the vicissitudes of human life.

I was a great one for running off from parties and finding a local cemetery or lawn, where I would lie down – even if there was snow on the ground – and look up at the stars. I'd think 'There's Sirius, and Sirius looks on all things, and *Sirius doesn't care.*' My life, my death – Sirius was utterly indifferent. And that was so comforting; the cold indifference of those stars . . . [32]

In 1942 Alice Bradley enlisted in the Army, and was the first woman to be trained in the Air Force Intelligence School at Harrisburg, 'with thirty-five men who had nothing better to do than watch me',[33] and became a photo-intelligence officer working in the Pentagon. In 1945 she joined the Air Staff Post-Hostilities Project, working under Colonel Huntington D. Sheldon, whom she soon married (an early unsuccessful marriage had ended in divorce). They left the military, but in the early 1950s were persuaded back to work in the newly formed CIA. She found its clandestine work was quite different in moral terms from her previous work in photo-intelligence. Once again, she felt the need to run: 'I used the techniques the CIA had taught me, and in half a day I had a false name, a false bank account, a false social security card, and had rented an apartment and moved in. I was somebody else.'[34]
Then in her late forties, Alice Sheldon worked for and gained a PhD in experimental psychology ('You can be young and stupid, or old and smart; I was old, so I had to be smart.'[35]), and went on to do four years of research in animal behaviour. This related back to an earlier interest of hers, dating from her days as a professional artist before the war, in problems of perception. Those four years were very important; she was finally doing what she really wanted to do; also they must have been influential on her science fiction, which she had just started

to write. 'There is no greater thrill I've ever had,' said Tiptree,

than to stand bare-faced in front of Nature and say, 'I think
this is the way your creations work; tell me, am I right?' And
Nature grumblingly and reluctantly makes you do – as I did –
thirteen different paradigms of the god damned experiment
before you get the thing without any uncontrolled variables,
and then finally says, in answer to your question, a clear-cut
'Yes'. That is the most thrilling moment I have ever had in my
whole life.[36]

This summary of Alice Sheldon's biography does, I hope, give
some indication of how her work in science fiction was
influenced by events in her life. Firstly, she explored her
scientific interests in science fictional form, and secondly, the
protean possibilities of that form allowed her to be as elusive a
writer as she at times felt the need to be in real life. It seems to
me that her work in experimental psychology serves as the basis
of her concern to explore, in fictional form, the notions of
nature and nurture, of free will and determinism, that recur in
her stories. Her psychological work also underpins her obsession, described above, with sex and death, which is given its
most chilling treatment in 'Love is the Plan, the Plan is Death'
(1973) and which appears in its most grotesque form in 'On the
Last Afternoon' (1972). In both these stories the practitioners/
victims of the sex/death drive are non-human, which is a relief.

Tiptree's love for the stars and the cold consolation they offer
is both emotional, rooted in her own experiences, and scientific,
in that the alien life forms with which she lovingly peoples her
distant galaxies offer a means of exploring the questions of
perceptual relativism that interested her for many years.
Tiptree's stars, and the vast disembodied beings she sets afloat
between them, represent for humanity an escape from the trap
of reproduction and death, an escape in fact from the *species*.
The vastnesses of space, in Tiptree's work, hold the promise of
immortality that her humans so often yearn for, but, and it is an
important contradiction, their attraction is held in tension by the
vitality of life on earth, precisely by the strictures of species-life.

To call Tiptree a pessimist is to deny this contradictory
element in her vision. While some of her more feminist stories
are deeply pessimistic, overall her work is imbued with a
humanist vision that allows her to explore both the comic and

the tragic.

Mysha, for example, in 'On the Last Afternoon', struggles to choose between the immortality that is offered him amongst the stars and certain final death if he stays faithful to his own species. The tiny human community that he has helped build up and preserve is threatened by the death-dealing mating rituals of vast sea-monsters. At first he chooses to sacrifice himself: 'The species lives, I die. The operative words. *I die*. Die, he thought, like a faithful ant whose nest lives on. Like those dying head-husks capering to the sea. Only that more may breed and die, breed and die. The building, the breeding, the towers raised and fallen, without end . . . '[37] His resolve fails, and he calls for help to the creature that offered him immortality, but it is too late: 'A vast impersonal tonnage fell upon him and the stars ravelled away from his brain.'[38] Even his death is rendered insignificant, for he has given up the stars for nothing.

In 'Slow Music' the beauties of earth are seen in opposition to the glories of immortal, non-human life. It seems as if the whole human race has chosen the latter, giving up its 'mortal dream' for transcendence, making of earth a shifting, sliding dream world. The young Jakko is not sure what he wants, but finds himself on his way to the River that leads offworld. He sees behind him 'dazzling cloud-cities . . . The vast imminence of sunrise'[39] and considers the attractions of the materiality of life on earth:

> He understood that all this demonstration of glory was nothing but the effects of dust and vapour in the thin skin of air around a small planet, whereon he crawled wingless. No vastness brooded; the planet was merely turning with him into the rays of its mediocre primary. His family, everyone, knew that on the River he would encounter the Galaxy itself in glory. Suns beyond count, magnificence to which this was nothing. And yet – and yet to him this was not nothing . . . [40]

Finally Jakko and the girl Peachthief – a heroine of *this* world, who wants babies and mortality – are both entrapped by the River. They are given immortality, but it is the immortality of the figures on a Grecian urn, bought at the expense of their humanity. Immortality, transcendence, but at what cost?

'Painwise' is a black comedy version of the same theme: the protagonist chooses pain and certain death on earth over an everlasting playfulness amongst the stars. Loneliness is as common a theme as violence: the loneliness of the light-distance being.

Over and again in the stories, counterposed to the figure of the human yearning away from species life on earth and towards the transcendence of the stars, there stands the figure of the human, or alien, or, like Enggi in 'Out of the Everywhere', both alien *and* human, turning away from the cold consolation of the stars towards the mysteries, however short-lived, of life on earth.

> Enggi was silent for a long distance. In him lived one aspect of a human mind that had been tormented by a hopeless longing for the stars. Now he had the stars; their glories and infinite spectacles were around him as pebbles had been underfoot for the beings on that far-off Earth. And now, paradoxically, in this same part of him another longing was being born, a shadowy nostalgia for the soft-coloured, organic intricacies, the growing things and tactile breezes and blue skies and racing waters – all the microlife he had loved as a human mind, or minds. Even for their strange mutual fevers and complexities, so intense, so meaningless to Enggi's kind, yet now not meaningless to him.[41]

Tiptree's characters, whether human or alien, long to be elsewhere. They find themselves trapped outside time, too, slipping away from a present into a past or future, desperately trying to get home for aeons, like the man in 'The Man who Walked Home', or hurrying towards death like Cory in *Brightness Falls from the Air*. In this, Tiptree's second novel (1985), Cory's fate is an echo of Mitch's fate in 'Fault': both men are pushed out of time as a punishment for a crime against an alien life form. Again, the grim picture Tiptree paints of the cruelties that humans inflict on one another is set against the horror of an eternity alone.

Tiptree's novels, *Up the Walls of the World*, *Brightness Falls from the Air* and *The Starry Rift*,[42] are set amidst scenes of cosmic glory, where time slips and eddies and singularities abound. Against this background, Tiptree explores political and moral questions.

In *Up the Walls of the World* she invents two groups of refugees, the Tyrrhenians who have escaped from their irradi-

Up the walls of the world

ated wind-planet Tyrrhee, and a bunch of misfits with telepathic powers from earth. On Tyrrhee the males raise and care for the young, while the females are footloose (if a winged creature can be – the Tyrrhenians are like enormous flying mantas), fancy free, but of low status. As Tiptree says in the *Khatru* symposium:

> Consider: If men alone had always raised infants, how monumental, how privileged a task it would be! We would have tons of conceptual literature on infant–father interaction, technical journals, research establishments devoted to it, a huge esoteric vocabulary. It would be as sacred as the Stock Exchange or football, and we would spend hours hearing of it. But because women do it, it is invisible and embarrassing.[43]

For one of the themes of *Brightness Falls from the Air* Tiptree returns to an earlier story, 'We Who Stole *The Dream*' (1978), in which the highly prized drink, Stars Tears, a fluid excreted under physical or mental torture by a race of winged, angelic-looking creatures, becomes the sign and reality of corruption of the Joilani, a race of small, gentle, pacifist creatures who have themselves suffered horribly, hideously (particularly the females) under human oppression.

Brightness is set on the planet Damiem, the home planet of the angel-like creatures that produce Stars Tears, the Damieii. Cory and her lover Kip are the wardens of the planet, determined that human sadism and savagery will never again be inflicted on the Damieii. But under the fallout from the wave-front of an exploded star, which a group of tourists has come to watch, levels of meaning and event shift, time moves (one might say) in a mysterious way, and questions of right and wrong prove more subtle than they at first appear to be. The Damieii, offstage and unquestioned in 'We Who Stole *The Dream*', are affected, like all the other characters, by the exploding star, and their status as romantic, beautiful victims is interrogated.

Why did Tiptree choose a male pseudonym to hide behind? 'A male name seemed like good camouflage,' she says. 'I had the feeling that a man would slip by less observed. I've had too many experiences in my life of being the first woman in some damned occupation; even when I wasn't the first woman, I was part of a group of first women.' Charles Platt, conducting the

interview, was not entirely happy, and pressed her further. 'I
simply saw the name on some jam pots. Ting [husband] was with
me; I said "James Tiptree" and he says – "Junior!" It was done
so quickly, without conscious thought; but I suppose I couldn't
have avoided having the thought – although I don't remember it
– that the editor would take my stories more seriously.'[44]

Tiptree's assumption of a male persona is at times utterly
convincing, although she says that '*trying* to write like a man'
was 'the last thing I was trying to do.'[45] As she explains, 'men
have so preempted the area of human experience that when you
write about universal motives, you are assumed to be writing
like a man.'[46] This political insight into ways of writing, into
what is *allowed* to women writers, does however mask a certain
disingenuousness. As we saw earlier, Tiptree writing in the first
person in the *Khatru* symposium was doing rather more than
just 'letting people think' she was a man because of the male
name. Her work cannot easily be divided into 'universal' –
written by James Tiptree Jr – and 'feminist' – written by
Raccoona Sheldon, despite her claim in her introduction to
'Morality Meat' in *Despatches from the Frontiers of the Female
Mind* that she used the latter when she 'felt the need to say some
things impossible to a male persona', producing 'a few overtly
feminist tales'.

Tiptree's feminist vision in fact appears at its most powerful
and complex in some of the stories that have a male narrator, or
where the authorial voice is mediated through a macho world
view, even though, or perhaps because, those stories, at least to
this woman reader, are the most disturbing.

I shall look first at 'The Women Men Don't See' (1973), not
least for the questions it raises about the nature of feminine and
feminist writing, and also for its treatment of the concept of 'the
alien', what Judith Hanna describes as 'a, if not *the*, dominant
theme in SF'.[47] In his introduction to the short story collection
Warm Worlds and Otherwise (1975), Robert Silverberg states:
'It has been suggested that Tiptree is female, a theory that I find
absurd, for there is to me something ineluctably masculine
about Tiptree's writing.'[48] He describes her stories as 'lean,
muscular, supple', and goes on to compare her with Heming-
way: 'And there is, too, that prevailing masculinity about both
of them – that preoccupation with questions of courage, with
absolute values, with the mysteries and passions of life and

death as revealed by extreme physical tests, by pain and suffering and loss.'[49]

While it seems to me there is something dangerous about seeing masculinity and femininity in such essentialist terms, with talk of absolute values – for we exist in relation to, and not separate from, that which is different from us – even more open to question are the parameters that Silverberg suggests for such a differentiation. Look at it another way: what is more of an 'extreme physical test' than giving birth, more imbued with pain and suffering and, in the case of miscarriage, stillbirth, or the death of a baby, with loss? Or does such a test, because it is undergone only by women, not reveal the absolute values of which he speaks? If, as I suspect, he is referring to the mysteries and passions of life and death in terms of killing, being killed or escaping being killed, then he is answered by James Tiptree Jr in 'The Women Men Don't See'.

Ruth Parsons has just shocked the narrator by revealing her vision of women in a man's world. He challenges her:

'Men and women aren't different species, Ruth. Women do everything men do.'

'Do they?' Our eyes meet, but she seems to be seeing ghosts between us in the rain. She mutters something that could be 'My Lai' and looks away. 'All the endless wars . . .' Her voice is a whisper. 'All the huge authoritarian organisations for doing unreal things. Men live to struggle against each other; we're just part of the battlefields. It'll never change unless you change the whole world. I dream sometimes of – of going away –' She checks and abruptly changes voice. 'Forgive me, Don, it's so stupid saying all this.'

'Men hate wars too, Ruth,' I say as gently as I can.

'I know.' She shrugs and climbs to her feet. 'But that's your problem, isn't it?'[50]

In a postscript to the introduction to *Warm Worlds*, added in 1978, Robert Silverberg says: 'She fooled me beautifully, along with everyone else, and called into question the entire notion of what is "masculine" or "feminine" in fiction.'[51] This is an important point, particularly in relation to what Silverberg said earlier about this story: 'It is a profoundly feminist story told in an entirely masculine manner . . . '[52] Both statements are correct. The notion of what is 'masculine' or 'feminine' fiction

124

must indeed be questioned; it is too simplistic to say that male writers of science fiction concern themselves only with technology or 'hard' science at the expense of development of character and the consequences in social terms of technological development. Such a distinction not only posits a crude sexual dualism – masculine is hard, feminine is soft – which anyway is anathema to Tiptree, but it also denies the connections between the different 'hard' and 'soft' sciences, connections that in good science fiction should be made. The fact that male writers all too often don't concern themselves with the personal or the private, but concentrate instead on so-called 'extreme physical tests', is nothing to do with an essential masculinity. It is to do with privilege, power and the division of labour between the sexes in the writer's own world, that is, now.

To say that this story has a masculine manner is to place it within a tradition in which machismo itself becomes the protagonist. Tiptree appears to allow this, and then subverts it: this is what makes it a feminist story, as much as what 'happens' in it.

'The Women Men Don't See' is a finely constructed story. A prologue describes how Don Fenton, the male narrator and would-be he-man, off on a fishing trip, meets and dismisses as of no interest to him two women, Ruth Parsons and her daughter Althea.

The story opens as the plane carrying the protagonists is approaching Cozumel airport, where they are going to change to different planes for the rest of their respective journeys. Fenton sets the tone with a distinctively 'masculine' voice: 'I see her first while the Mexicana 727 is barreling down to Cozumel Island, I come out of the can and lurch into her seat, saying, "Sorry," at a double female blur.'[53] The present tense is sustained throughout, heightening the sense of immediacy and physical involvement, those conventions of masculinity. The women are described only negatively, in terms of their sexual undesirability. They are 'small, plain and neutral-coloured.'[54] The girl has 'what could be an attractive body if there was any spark at all.'[55] Even when they don't behave quite as they should do – for example, they remain cool and unflustered when the second, smaller plane crashes – the narrator's assumptions about how women *should* behave override his observations of how these two *do* behave.

Women exist only in relation to himself, and only sexually, whether it's the 'little Mayan chicks' who are 'highly erotic', or the two women he's stranded with, who are 'in shorts, neat but definitely not sexy'.[56] His stock responses obscure the fact that the women themselves are concerned to present a negative, low-profile self-image. At first the mother gives only their surname, only later allowing him the use of their first names. Later, too, she says, 'I am not very memorable',[57] and it is only then that he begins to have an inkling that this self-reserve is deliberate.

He wants to think he has an effect on their behaviour. When the women sleep outside in the hammock, leaving him and the pilot Estéban to sleep in the crashed plane, he explains it in terms of his and Estéban's threatening maleness, although on another level he is aware that he doesn't pose that much of a threat. He is middle aged, tired. But to see Mrs Parsons as a mother hen fussing over her chick of a daughter is a convenient way to place her, and himself in relation to her. His honest perceptions are continually obscured by the habits of machismo. Fenton's relationship with the women develops, but he continues to misinterpret their actions and responses. This leads up to a night spent alone with Ruth Parsons in a mangrove swamp where they've gone to search for water; a classic scene of revelation in which, separated from the outside world, hostility between woman and man conventionally turns to love (or lust). There is revelation here but it is not of the kind the narrator/reader expects. Not only have the women refused Fenton's definition of them as sexual objects, they have objectified Estéban and himself solely in terms of their potential progenitive qualities; worse, it is Estéban who has been chosen and who is now, presumably, fulfilling this role back on the sand bar with daughter Althea, in a neat reversal of science fictional conventions.

Fenton is stuck within the parameters of 'I do want her' and 'I don't want her' and their corollaries, 'Does she want me?', 'Doesn't she want me?' Stock responses in a stock setting. So he is amazed to discover that he doesn't figure at all in her view of what is happening to them. At first he tries to relate it to a supposed hatred of men, for he would rather be hated than ignored. He cannot believe her response: 'That would be as silly as – as hating the weather.'[58] In his vision men must be central;

loved or hated, but significant above all.

Fenton's inability as narrator to grasp anything except as it affects or is affected by himself, now creates the gap that allows for the explanation of the woman's viewpoint to break through. First, he is relieved of his misperceptions about the women as sexual objects, as Ruth reveals that she deliberately accompanied him on a search for fresh water so as to allow Althea to become impregnated by Estéban the Mayan, one of a 'very fine type of people'.[59] Secondly, she tells him that equality between women and men is merely nominal:

> 'Women have no rights, Don, except what men allow us. Men are more aggressive and powerful, and they run the world. When the next real crisis upsets them, our so-called rights will vanish like – like that smoke. We'll be back where we always were: property. And whatever has gone wrong will be blamed on our freedom, like the fall of Rome was. You'll see.'[60]

Women are like oppossums, suggests Ruth, living secretly in the city. 'What women do is survive. We live by ones and twos in the chinks of your world-machine.'[61]

Finally, after the revelation comes the dénouement; the women go off with a boatload of aliens, whither we don't know, to escape men, the aliens of this world. Poor Fenton remains stuck in the conventions of male-dominated science fiction to the end. His response to the aliens, when they come, is to get out his gun. He is determined to try and stop the two women from leaving with them; but of course he fails. 'How could a woman choose to live among unknown monsters,' he muses once they have gone, 'to say good-bye to her home, her world?'[62] We are not told what kind of a choice the women have made; we don't even know whether they're heading for another world that is divided along sex lines. The ending reverberates with the echoes of decades of pulp science fiction; only this time the women are no man's property and have chosen to remain unrescued.

The 'masculine manner' of Tiptree's style is a cunning contrivance that reveals, first, the limitations of a machismo-oriented culture and the limitations of science fiction when that culture is incorporated unquestioningly into its fictive conventions. Fenton's responses, when he discovers that the women about whom he was so dismissive are, contrary to expectations, dismissive of him, are mocked for their predictability. Further, it allows a political argument to break through the gaps in the narrator's perceptions. The male narrator is swept from centre stage.

I think 'The Women Men Don't See' offers a strongly separatist vision, which is not to say that Tiptree is suggesting that women should take the next alien spaceship out. Rather, she offers an analysis of our own world, in which women and men, caught up in all the intricate relations of social, political and economic life, become aliens to each other, precisely because those relations are affected by the power that men exercise over women.

Aliens here, aliens there, aliens aliens everywhere. As Judith Hanna says, ' "The alien" is *difference* personified.'[63] Aliens are the Other, feared, loathed, longed for. In Tiptree's work aliens serve as a metaphor for women in relation to men and for men in relation to women; they are also a metaphor for the alienated part of the self and, in particular, the divided self forced on women by a male hegemony.

Finally, I would like to look at 'With Delicate Mad Hands' (1981), the story of a woman's determination to escape from the miseries of earth and find a home among the stars.

Carol Page, deformed by a snout-like nose, is considered grossly unattractive but uses this to her advantage. Unusually for a woman, she manages to get herself accepted as a crew member on a spaceship for, unlike other women, she offers no distractions to the important people, the men. Her first run is a success:

> She cleaned and dumped garbage and kept the capsule orderly and in repair at all times, she managed to make the food tastier than the men believed possible, she helped everybody do anything disagreeable, she nursed two men through space dysentery and massaged the pain out of another's sprained back; she kept her mouth strictly shut at all times, and performed her sexual duties as a 'human waste can' with competence, although she could not quite successfully simulate real desire. (It was after this trip that she began to be known as Cold Pig.) She provoked no personal tensions; in fact, two of the crew forgot even to say good-bye to her, although they gave her superior marks in their report forms.[64]

The tone of the narrative is cold and detached. The reader is distanced by the narrator's unemotional stance; it is as if the narrator refuses to pass judgment on the men who so abuse Carol Page, and this makes the abuse even more disturbing than if there were a stated sympathy between narrator and subject. It also serves as a measure of how Carol internalises her own oppression and, remarkably, transforms it. She is referred to in the story as Cold Pig or CP; but this is not just a term of abuse (the men call her 'Pig') for she builds a fantasy world around the 'Empire of the Pigs'. She retells her own life as 'The Adventures (or Reports) of the Pig Person on Terra', creating a narrative for herself in which she is subject.

The story of 'With Delicate Mad Hands' charts CP's journey alone into madness, to certain death, but before that to a vision of joy and love. She gains control of the spaceship *Calgary* after a successful fight with its mad captain, who has brutally raped and humiliated her; she sets the controls for outer space and heads away from Sol, to be 'alone and *free*, among her beloved stars.'[65] The level of ambiguity that Tiptree's characters feel towards the stars seems to depend upon their place within the hierarchies of human society. Here, and in 'The Women Men Don't See', the stars can only be good; they offer a possibility of freedom that doesn't exist for women on earth. In 'On the Last Afternoon', 'Slow Music', 'Out of the Everywhere', the stars offer both promise and loss. The difference lies in the fact, perhaps, that Tiptree's women usually have little to lose.

CP sacrifices the artificial gravity of *Calgary*, stopping it rotating so she can *see* all the stars. Then she turns off all the lights, to wipe out 'her own wretched reflection'.[66] Like that of pathetic P. Burke in 'The Girl Who Was Plugged In' (1973) her physical, female self, is cancelled, wiped out. This vision, though horrifying, is an extrapolation from a society in which women are expected to conform to a certain ideal of socially constructed beauty and sexuality, to a society in which, quite simply, 'ugly' women don't survive.

'Tiptree's women suffer', says Lillian Heldreth.[67] They do, but Tiptree uses the science fictional form to offer a vision of transcendence as well. Cold Pig/Carol Page meets death on an irradiated dark planet, but she also meets love in the form of an alien who is a misfit among its mutated companions. Is CP mad or not? Do the voices that call her come from herself or from outside? The point is that through an imaginative and literary effort CP recreates her own life and gives it a significance that was denied it on earth.

Tiptree's feminism does not constitute a simple unified vision. This is perhaps one of the reasons why she was attracted to science fiction, for its fluidity of form allows such a variety of approach. And while her novels are not without interest, it is in that most versatile of forms, the short story, that her strengths are most apparent.

The way Tiptree uses male personae to tell her stories is, finally, subversive both of a male-dominated world-view derived from unequal relations of power between the sexes and also of ideas of writing that divide experience, both lived and fictional, into separate spheres of masculine and feminine. Tiptree herself says that her so-called 'male writing style' is merely an expression of intensity, of narrative drive, and that such a style is not confined to men. I would go further and suggest that it is precisely her political vision that fuels her narrative drive, and that she has found the ideal form for its expression within the genre of science fiction. She is a writer who at once celebrates the possibilities that science fiction opens up, and challenges the way that men have claimed those possibilities for themselves.

In May 1987, when Alice Sheldon's beloved husband was in the advanced stages of Alzheimer's disease, she shot him dead and then turned the gun upon herself.

12
Inner Space and the Outer Lands: Ursula K. Le Guin

With its first issue in March 1972 the British magazine *Foundation: The Review of Science Fiction* began a series in which science fiction writers discussed their own beginnings in science fiction and their developing relationship to it. Writer number four in the series was Ursula K. Le Guin, with a piece entitled 'A Citizen of Mondath'. She describes herself at the age of about twelve coming across and opening Dunsany's *A Dreamer's Tales*:

. . . The moment is perfectly vivid to me now. I read:

'Toldees, Mondath, Arizim, these are the Inner Lands, the lands whose sentinels upon their borders do not behold the sea. Beyond them to the east there lies a desert, for ever untroubled by man; all yellow it is, and spotted with shadows of stones, and Death is in it, like a leopard lying in the sun. To the south they are bounded by magic, to the west by a mountain . . .'

. . . the moment was decisive. I had discovered my native country.[1]

Le Guin goes on to talk self-critically about her own work. Very interestingly, I think, she implies the existence of a conflict between her fantasy and her science fiction writing, which was resolved in 1967–8 when 'I finally got my pure fantasy vein separated off from my science fiction vein, by writing *A Wizard of Earthsea* and then *The Left Hand of Darkness*, and the separation marked a very large advance both in skill and content.' Since then, she says, she has gone on writing 'as it were, with both the left and the right hands; and it has been a matter of keeping on pushing out towards the limits – my own, and those of the medium.' Finally, she firmly refuses any suggestion or prediction that she will go mainstream. 'The limits, and the great spaces of fantasy and science fiction are precisely what my imagination needs. Outer Space, and the Inner Lands, are still, and always will be, my country.'[2]

In the same article Ursula Le Guin talks about the particular dangers facing a science fiction writer:

There is so little real criticism, that despite the very delightful and heartening feedback from and connection with the fans, the writer is almost his only critic. If he produces second-rate stuff, it will be bought just as fast, maybe faster sometimes, by the publishers, and the fans will buy it because it is science fiction. Only his own conscience remains to insist that he try *not* to be second-rate. Nobody else seems much to care.[3]

Writing, she goes on to say, is not only an originative act, but a responsive one. The reader should not be put off by Le Guin's use of the generic, or universal 'he'; what she is saying is important for an evaluation of her work. In her fiction and in her criticism, the fact that she cares about the craft of writing shines like an encouraging beacon to readers and to other writers, while the lucidity and grace that she strives for ensure the accessibility of her work (the same could not be said of a great deal of science fiction criticism). Le Guin's popularity is deserved. Her work is bought because it is good as well as because it is science fiction, and while she may not always achieve all she sets out to do, and while the works for which she is most widely known – *The Left Hand of Darkness* and *The Dispossessed* – are riddled with contradictions and unresolved tensions, she is never second-rate.

Since 'A Citizen of Mondath' was published there has been a mass of critical work published on Ursula Le Guin. She is firmly established as a leading writer of science fiction and fantasy. She is also one of the few writers of science fiction who has managed to reach out to a wider audience and one of the even fewer writers who is read by a large number of women who usually do not read science fiction at all. The wide interest in *The Left Hand of Darkness* and *The Dispossessed* shown by women who are not science fiction fans derives from the books' attempts to grapple with questions of a sexual-political nature. In this chapter I shall discuss these two works in particular, as well as indicating the range of the rest of her work and the reservations I have about some aspects of it.

There is a simple anomaly, or contradiction, at the heart of Le Guin's work. It features very few women; these are restricted either by biology – Rolery as childbearer in *Planet of Exile* – or by stereotype – Takver the prop and support in *The Dispossessed*. This is not unusual in science fiction; what is odd is that despite it, Ursula Le Guin should have such a feminist following and that she should be so committed to the 'characters' side of the debate ('What is science fiction?': scientific ideas explored in fictional form; or character-based fiction with parameters expanded in a scientific/futuristic setting?) rather than the 'ideas' side.

In the *Earthsea* trilogy women feature first as witches and enchantresses who are either wicked or ignorant – or, like Elfarran, dead (and still a bundle of trouble). Or they are absent: not a girl to be seen amongst the 'hundred or more boys and young men' of the wizard school. In *The Tombs of Atuan* girls get a rather better deal, even if they do need rescuing, but in the third novel of the trilogy, *The Farthest Shore*, they are relegated again to a minor role. As for the earlier books, there are no women in *Rocannon's World* except for princesses and the ladies of castles. In *Planet of Exile*, as mentioned above, the hilf (Higher Indigenous Life Form) Rolery is tough, rebellious and likeable, but her primary role is to mate with Agat Alterra, forming a political and social bond between humans and hilfs and offering hope to future generations. *City of Illusions* features the faithful woman who stays behind and the treacherous temptress. This latter reappears in both *The Left Hand of Darkness* (a society in which sex-role stereotyping really should not occur) and in *The Dispossessed* where she is part of the evils of capitalism.

There is certainly a big problem about women in *The Left Hand of Darkness*: Joanna Russ maintains that there are no women in it at all.[4] And in *The Dispossessed*, besides the sultry temptress Vea, Le Guin gives us a mother-figure who is cold, hard, rejecting and narrow-minded – which is a little unfair as they live in a society in which women are encouraged (or so we are told) to reject the one-to-one mother and child bond. And there is Takver. Oh dear, Takver.

It is only in *The Lathe of Heaven*, set outside the Hainish cycle ✓ of her other novels, that we find a strong, fully characterised woman, the Black lawyer Heather Lelache. Ian Watson questions whether this novel is anomalous, falling as it does between her left hand writing of *Earthsea* and her right hand writing of *The Left Hand of Darkness* and *The Dispossessed*, written with a third hand, he suggests rather neatly, attached to Palmer Eldritch's prosthetic arm.[5] Further, unlike the Hainish novels, it does not offer a way 'homeward', as a 'false' world is premised from the very start when George Orr dreams the nuclear holocaust out of existence. It is an odd book, resonating far beyond its central moral question of human overreaching. And Heather Lelache, despite inhabiting a 'false' world, has a solidity that seems to exist outside Orr's unconscious. She is morally dominant: a counterpoint to the powerful but hollow man Haber. And in contrast to most other Black characters in Le Guin's work, whose colour is given and is not discussed, racial politics are here articulated. (The casual portrayal of Black characters by White science fiction writers as a sign of future societies in which racial discrimination does not exist is perhaps an indication of how science fiction can, quite simply, jolt the reader's perception of the world – something not open to writers working in the 'realist' mode. But it runs the risk of depoliticising the question.) Elsewhere in the book racial politics are articulated less felicitously: in one of Orr's dream-worlds there is what purports to be a role reversal in South Africa, with Whites, unconvincingly, 'still' being 'massacred'.

For a clear and informative appraisal of Le Guin's first three novels, *Rocannon's World*, *Planet of Exile* and *City of Illusions*, there is no better critic to turn to than Le Guin herself. Her introductions to later editions of the works offer both a political and an aesthetic critique, are full of fascinating information on provenance, and engage intelligently with the debate on form and genre.[6] She describes *Rocannon's World* as having 'a lot of promiscuous mixing' of science fiction and fantasy, which, she says, have frequencies as different as red and blue; the result is purple.[7] *Rocannon's World* draws heavily on the images of Norse mythology: Le Guin admits she was too timid to make up her own, and chastises herself too for timidity in the peopling of her world. This is full of light-loving elves and cave-dwelling trolls, of feudal lords and trusty servants, of nice furry creatures and nasty insectoid ones. Rocannon, from the League of All Worlds with its faster than light ships and the ansible (the invention of which is portrayed in the later novel, *The Dispossessed*) feels that he has 'blundered through the corner of a legend . . . '[8]

Of *Planet of Exile*, in response to being asked why she writes so much about men, Le Guin explains that it was written in 1963–4, 'before the reawakening of feminism from its thirty-year paralysis.'[9] She was, she says, ' . . . self-confident, unexperimental, contentedly conventional . . . ' And, looking back on it, 'culpably careless' for letting the men in the story take over.[10] The story, 'this early easygoing adventure story',[11] concerns the abandoned colony of Rocannon's World and the tension and difference between two groups of its dwindling population, the human colonists with their powers of mind-speech and the indigenous hilfers, and the eventual reconciliation between the two groups, brought about by and symbolised by the union between the hilfer Rolery and the colonist Agat Alterra.

City of Illusions offered Ursula Le Guin 'the chance to take another journey.'[12] She goes on: 'Most of my stories are excuses for a journey. (We shall henceforth respectfully refer to this as the Quest Theme.) I never did care much about plots, all I want is to go from A to B – or, more often, from A to A – by the most difficult and circuitous route.'[13] Of the three books, Le Guin is most critical of this one. 'It has some good bits, but is only half thought out. I was getting vain and hasty.'[14] In particular, the book has 'villain trouble' in the Shing, who are 'the least convincing lot of people I ever wrote'.[15] They are indeed hard to visualise and hard to imagine, rather too shimmery round the edges.

The heroes of all three books have destinies; each has a mission that is inextricably, and satisfyingly, reflected in the personal crises of their lives. Each must find himself, and each does so at a certain cost. Each book represents a variation on the Quest Theme, and despite their flaws they are really very good. Each one is a romantic narrative of homecoming, prefiguring and illustrating the message that in Le Guin's later work *The Dispossessed* is spelled out: 'true voyage is return'.

The central struggle between, and final resolution of, self and other, is presented not so much in the human/alien binary structure as in the structure of protagonist and landscape; the journey is both through and around a landscape that is at once beautiful, hostile, frightening and fascinating. The moral and psychological development of the hero is secondary to his relationship to the terrain he crosses. There is an easy simplicity to these books that is lost in *The Left Hand of Darkness* and *The Dispossessed*, when Le Guin forces, as if against her heart's desire, the physical journey into second place. In *The Left Hand of Darkness* the tension is still there, and the journey across the icecap becomes the haunting central image of the book, but in *The Dispossessed* the landscape has been lost, battened down beneath what reads like Le Guin's feeling of obligation to show moral and psychological development.

Ursula Le Guin has described the genesis of *The Left Hand of Darkness*, comparing it to Angus Wilson's description of the 'very visual ironic picture' of two people, Mrs Curry and Bernard Sands, that became his novel *Hemlock and After*:

> Once, like Mr Wilson, I saw two of them. As my vision is not ironic, but romantic, they were small figures, remote, in a tremendous waste landscape of ice and snow. They were pulling a sledge or something over the ice, hauling together. That is all I saw. I didn't know who they were. I didn't even know what sex they were (I must say I was surprised when I found out). But that is how my novel *The Left Hand of Darkness* began, and when I think of the book, it is still that vision I see. All the rest of it, with all its strange rearrangements of human gender and its imagery of betrayal, loneliness, and cold, is my effort to catch up, to get nearer, to get there, where I had seen those two figures on the snow, isolated and together.[16]

This extract comes from a theoretical piece called 'Science Fiction and Mrs Brown' which is central to an understanding of Le Guin's view of literature and the aims she sets for her own writing, and, further, to the problematics of her work. It is an elaboration on Virginia Woolf's 'Mr Bennett and Mrs Brown' (1924) in which Woolf talks of the subject matter of the novel appearing to the novelist, calling 'Catch me if you can!'. Le Guin accepts as true Woolf's definition that 'all novels begin with an old lady in the corner opposite . . . The great novelists have brought us to see whatever they wish us to see through some character. Otherwise they would not be novelists, but poets, historians or pamphleteers.'[17]

Le Guin has two questions to ask: can a science fiction writer write a novel, and is it advisable or desirable that she/he should do so? The answer to the second question must be yes, for Le Guin tries to answer the first in her own work. The quotation above, then, is a description of the genesis of a novel; and *The Dispossessed* functions as a novel because at the centre of it is 'a person'. Le Guin goes further: 'There he is!' – there, if only for a moment. If I had to invent two entire worlds to get to him, two worlds and all their woes, it was worth it. If I could give the readers one glimpse of what I saw: Shevek, Mrs Brown, The Other, a soul, a human soul, "the spirit we live by . . ." '[18]

There is an odd contradiction here between the insistence on the need for solidity of characterisation (the 'ordinariness' of Mrs Brown) and the 'soul' or 'spirit' which the characters represent. But there are other problems raised by this subject-centred view of the novel.

Firstly, for a feminist reading, it raises the question of why Ursula Le Guin's 'people' are always men. She has explained this in terms of her own timidity and conventionality in her early work; but the same excuse cannot be given for her more ambitious later work. As we have seen, the very least that science fiction can offer a woman writer is a release from the constraints of the realist mode in which the subjecthood of men is paramount. I will leave aside the question of whether novels in general must be subject centred in order to achieve 'novelhood', saying only that it is not, as she ingenuously comments in the same essay, just a question of what is 'critically fashionable'.[19]

The second problem lies in her determination that the same criteria should apply to science fiction as to other forms of fiction. As Patrick Parrinder has put it in his response to Le Guin's essay, 'The Alien Encounter: Or, Ms Brown and Mrs Le Guin': 'In SF it is the new element, and not the need for subtle and rounded characterisation, which determines the basic rules of the genre.' He criticises both what Le Guin wants to characterise and how that characterisation should be achieved:

What is limiting about their [Woolf's and Le Guin's]

declarations of loyalty to Mrs Brown is not the stress on characterisation as such, but their belief that what is characterised most fully must always be the autonomous human beings of liberal individualism. Is it too much of a travesty of conventional fictional theory to say that the SF novelist must never desert Ms Brown, but that *his* [sic] Ms Brown is frequently an alien, quite possibly with six legs and certainly with a language of her own?[20]

It is perhaps a little strange that Parrinder should use feminist nomenclature for *his* alien (we may be trying to forge a language of our own but we don't have six legs), but it seems to me that he has pinpointed the central contradiction in Le Guin's later work. For despite her elaborate worlds, her millennia-spanning histories of Leagues and Ekumens, her ansible and her FTL ships, can her works really be called science fiction? Their doubtful identity perhaps explains their author's popularity outside the usual SF market: the science fiction is just so much background to a novel of individual psychology in the realist mode. With the backgrounding of the SF material, Le Guin turns her back on opportunities SF offers for political experimentation through form. These male heroes with their crises of identity, caught in the stranglehold of liberal individualism, act as a dead weight at the centre of the novels.

Genly Ai, the protagonist of *The Left Hand of Darkness*, is a representative from Earth to the planet Gethen, or Winter. He is, apparently, a trained anthropological observer, but his preconceptions of and prejudices towards women are positively prehistorical (in terms of the Hainish cycle twentieth-century earth qualifies as this). On Gethen there are meant to be no men: the human inhabitants are androgynes, with an oestrus cycle that brings them regularly into *kemmer*, when they can take on either female or male sexual characteristics. The novel is at least partly about the social and political consequences of this. But it is not the case that there are no men on Gethen; it is, rather, as Joanna Russ and others have pointed out, that there are no women. Even though the king is pregnant.

As is so often the case with Ursula Le Guin, she responds to criticism with self-criticism. In this instance, she regrets 'certain timidities or ineptnesses' in failing to follow up the psychic implications of Gethenian physiology. She wishes she had been familiar with the work of Jung, 'so that I could have decided whether a Gethenian had *no* animus or anima, or *both*, or an animum . . . But the central failure in this area comes up in the frequent criticism I receive, that the Gethenians seem like *men*, instead of menwomen.'[21]

The invisibility of women in the book is further compounded by showing the Gethenian protagonist, Estraven, in almost exclusively 'male' roles and, even more, by the use throughout of the generic 'he'. 'I utterly refuse to mangle English by inventing a pronoun for "he/she",' said Le Guin;[22] this comment conjures up, instantly and pervasively, the weight of male values in previous science fiction writing (let alone mainstream writing), where generic 'he' is not at odds with universes exclusively stocked with male characters. Writing only a few years later, Marge Piercy was able to create such a pronoun in *Woman on the Edge of Time* with remarkable effect and without injury to aesthetic considerations. Which is not to say that Ursula Le Guin *should* have, for it was perhaps those few years of explosive development in feminist consciousness that made it possible for Marge Piercy to conceive of such a linguistic revolution; however, the consequences, in terms of presenting a society of androgynes, are far-reaching. (Piercy's society is not androgynous: her use of 'person' and 'per' reflects and feeds into social and political rather than physiological change.)

The lack of women on Gethen can be seen as part of what Frederic Jameson calls most interestingly 'world-reduction'.[23] At first sight such a phrase is surprising, for Le Guin is generally considered to be one of the foremost practitioners of the 'world-building' school of science fiction writers; further, as Jameson points out, there is no lack of different kinds of narrative strands in *The Left Hand of Darkness*. Indeed he calls it a 'virtual anthology', including travel narrative, pastiche of myth, drama of court intrigue, straight SF, Orwellian dystopia, adventure story, multi-racial (though unisexual) love story. But where science fiction goes in for a systematic variation of the empirical and historical world around us through analogy and extrapolation, here there is 'ontological attenuation'. There is no history and no evolution: humans have surmounted historical determinism and are left alone to invent their own destinies. The mission of world-reduction, Jameson suggests, is the utopian exclusion of the fearful problematics of sex, 'an

intolerable, well-nigh gratuitous complication of existence' and
capitalism, seen as 'a disease of change and meaningless
evolutionary momentum.'

On Gethen there is no sexual difference: no sexual repression
and no sexual desire. There is no historical dialectic. Everything
is stripped down to the all-pervading cold and the individual
destiny of Genly Ai.

Rosemary Jackson offers a different perspective, but one that
stresses equally Le Guin's denial of conflict on both a personal
and a political level. She includes Le Guin in her analysis of
'romances of integration', suggesting that through Le Guin's
attempted syntheses of binary opposites (male/female, light/
darkness, life/death) she creates 'psychomyths', which offer 'a
promise of redemption on cosmic and personal levels'. She
continues: 'These miraculous unities are myths of psychic order
which help to contain critiques of disorder. Their utopianism
does not directly engage with divisions or contradictions of
subjects *inside* human culture; their harmony is established on a
mystical cosmic level.'[24]

While Rosemary Jackson does tend to lump together all
science fiction as being in Le Guin's style, allowing the SF genre
no radical history or potentiality, her analysis of the 'secondary
worlds' as 'compensatory' is pertinent to a reading of Ursula Le
Guin. These worlds, she argues, 'fill up a lack, making up for an
apprehension of actuality as disordered and insufficient. These
fantasies *transcend* that actuality . . . '[25] The texts she sees as
fulfilling this are those that move 'towards the realm of the
"marvellous" ' and which are, precisely, 'the ones which have
been tolerated and widely disseminated socially';[26] in distinction, that is, to fantastic texts that are subversive, that replace
presence by absence, that are interrogatory rather than compensatory, deconstructionist rather than transcendental.

While Le Guin insists in 'Is Gender Necessary?' that *The Left
Hand of Darkness* is 'a book about betrayal and fidelity', and
that the questions of sex and gender that it raises form only 'the
lesser half' of it I think that it is this lesser half that accounts for
the book's wide appeal. It contains such an amazingly interesting idea, a marvellous contribution to that tradition within
science fiction that has asked and continues to ask, 'what if
. . .?' The book is not, as readers innocent of science fiction
often think when they approach this kind of novel, in any sense

prescriptive. It is, as Le Guin herself stresses, 'a heuristic device, a thought-experiment'. Which is precisely what a great deal of science fiction is. Out of this 'rather neat idea' comes an experiment that is 'messy'. Le Guin picks out three of these 'dubious and uncertain results' as being of particular interest: the absence of war in 13,000 years of Gethenian history (although this is changing during the timespan of the novel); the absence of exploitation of the land; the absence of sexuality as a constant social factor (Gethenians are only sexual one fifth of the time).[27]

What is striking here is the 'negativity' of the results, the *absence* of all conflict. In its place is a search for balance (a balance that is being lost as one of the nations of Gethen develops into a nation-state) and integration. Ursula Le Guin states her philosophy quite clearly at the end of her comments on this 'lesser half':

> Our curse is alienation, the separation of yang from yin. Instead of a search for balance and integration, there is a struggle for dominance. Divisions are insisted upon, inter-dependence is denied. The dualism of value that destroys us, the dualism of superior/inferior, ruler/ruled, owner/owned, user/used, might give way [if men and women were genuinely equal in every way, 'socially ambisexual'] to what seems to me, from here, a much healthier, sounder, more promising modality of integration and integrity.[28]

Here, I think, lies the key to the popularity of *The Left Hand of Darkness* with women readers. The problematics of sexual desire are, quite simply, eliminated. The book offers a retreat from conflict, a retreat from the symbolic order and the construction of the subject within language, back to the pre-Oedipal imaginary order, or, as Frederic Jameson puts it, the ancient dream of freedom from sex.[29]

The Left Hand of Darkness can thus be seen as continuing a tradition found in 'hard' SF which holds a particular appeal to men: showing a world in which men can roam freely unconstrained by the difficulties that arise from sexual difference. But the appeal is shifted: it speaks to liberal rather than misogynistic male readers, to readers who feel at ease with the kind of feminism that seeks to remove conflict and difference.

Like *The Left Hand of Darkness*, *The Dispossessed* is

constructed around a set of binary opposites: scarcity/wealth, socialism/capitalism, individual/society. And like Gethen, the anarchic/socialist society of Anarres is set on a bare cold planet, stripped of environment and indeed of history; all we are told is that it was set up 600 years previously by the anarchist Odo. Since then apparently nothing has happened. At the centre of the novel is the physicist Shevek, who, like Genly Ai, is a stranger in a strange land, moving from his home world of Anarres to Urras with its capitalist bloc and its totalitarian bloc.

There is a lot of politics *talked* in this novel – more than in *The Left Hand of Darkness* (here at least the question of childcare is discussed) but very little is *shown*. It is as if the text is at odds with its purpose. In Samual Delany's terms, there is a gap between the foreground, that is, the incidents and events of the story, and the recit, or didacta, of the background, through which we are told (or lectured on) the social organisation and history of the worlds Le Guin is describing.[30] Or, as Tom Moylan puts it about Anarres: ' . . . while Le Guin's utopia expresses a libertarian and feminist value system, the gaps and contradictions in her text betray a privileging of male and heterosexual superiority and of the nuclear, monogamous family.'[31]

Poor old Takver, the token strong woman, keeps the home fires burning while Shevek is off changing the future of mankind; homosexuality is tolerated as adolescent experimentation but nothing more; Shevek's mother is horribly punished for being a career woman by being given a really unpleasant character. These could, of course, all be read as signs of the ambiguity of the utopia, for Anarres is an ambiguous utopia, as stated in the title. But it does not explain the secondary role assigned to any of the characters who might be said to be part of any political process, such as Takver herself, or Shevek's friend Bedap, or indeed the masses who rebel in Benbili and whose rebellion fizzles out leaving Shevek, as usual, and rather incredibly, centre stage. Moylan points out interestingly that Shevek's theoretical and political breakthroughs are always preceded by a sexual encounter, saying that Le Guin valorises the 'creative potency' of the male 'aided by lovers who are not equal co-workers and partners but rather stimuli for the solitary activity of the hero.' Shevek, he goes on, 'generates the entire action of the text.'[32]

Shevek's 'true voyage' of return brings him back to his ambiguous utopia with widened perceptions. Le Guin's vision eliminates all sense of interaction, of history or of change, indeed of human agency. Nadia Khouri compares this with the view of history presented by Marge Piercy in *Woman on the Edge of Time*: ' . . . the dominance of the past mode [in *The Dispossessed*] or of timelessness confirmed events in their irrevocable occurrence and characters in their essential unchangeability. In *Woman on the Edge of Time*, every past and present happening prepares the way for the modification of future events.'[33]

At the end of *The Dispossessed* differences are resolved without conflict or change. Utopia is seen as relative: the Hainish and the Terran envoys see it respectively in Anarres and Urras. Instead of a break from the closed structure of binary oppositions the reader is presented with, as Tom Moylan says, 'endlessly repeating options in the unified galactic cultural supermarket.'[34]

The Left Hand of Darkness and *The Dispossessed* raise a variety of questions about what a science fictional narrative can achieve, and how it is different from a mainstream narrative. This is because Ursula Le Guin attempts to deny that difference, and yet her heart lies with the former and not with the latter. The centrality of her protagonists, Genly Ai and Shevek, and the synthesis within them of the ideational oppositions of the narrative, push these works into the tradition of the bourgeois novel with its construction rather than deconstruction of the subject as hero. But the question must be asked: how successful are they? Le Guin believes that she has captured Mrs Brown, for as she says of *The Dispossessed*: 'The sound of axes being ground is occasionally audible. Yet I do believe that it is, basically, a novel, because at the heart of it you will not find an idea, or an inspirational message, or even a stone axe, but something much frailer and obscurer and more complex: a person.'[35] With such a definition she writes off a multitude of science fiction novels: *The Female Man*, *Walk to the End of the World*, *Up the Walls of the World*, *Les Guérillères*, *The Wanderground* (to choose examples only from novels already mentioned), countless works that do not have a 'person' at their heart.

But how 'realistic' *are* Genly Ai and Shevek? Who remembers what they look like? Or what they say? Or feel? Do they suffer, grieve, undergo any profound change? Yet I think nobody would deny that these two works *are* novels, and rich ones at that. And what makes them so is the wealth of ideas in them, however much Le Guin may turn her nose up at ideas as being unworthy to serve as the basis of a novel. Here are some marvellous science fictional ideas: a society free of sex roles, where the elimination of sexual aggression and repression simultaneously gets rid of all forms of institutional violence; a world that reflects east/west systems of state totalitarianism and rampant capitalism with, in the sky above it, on its own moon, a remarkable colony of anarchist/socialists that has existed for 600 years.

But rather than revelling in the open vistas of her outer space, or the curious contradictions of her inner lands, Ursula Le Guin chooses to ravel them all up in her dreary male heroes, the 'persons' she so anxiously seeks. She denies the freedom that science fiction offers for political exploration, not of the star wars kind, but of the kind that allows a writer to ask what it is that constructs a 'person'. She is nervous, it seems, of what she sees as her propagandising tendencies, insisting that 'my interest is aesthetic' while admitting ruefully that 'I am always grinding axes and making points.'[36] What is wrong with making points? And science fiction is full of axes being ground to tunes that are playful, inventive and challenging.

Her political disavowals, her attempts not to grind axes, seem to me to cause an aesthetic problem with both *The Left Hand of Darkness* and *The Dispossessed*, to provide the gaps and tensions in the texts pointed out by Delany, Khouri and Moylan. Her passion for synthesis at all costs leads to a surface calm that barely conceals the cracks beneath; in neither novel is the political potential lived in the language. In fact *The Dispossessed* does not offer complete closure, for Shevek's world-changing discovery – sequency and simultaneity within a unified field theory of time, which leads to the development of an instantaneous transmitter, the ansible – does not preclude later conflict. The harmony implied in the closing sequence of the novel is already shown to have broken down in Le Guin's earlier books, which are set later in the Hainish cycle.

It is perhaps this lack of a political problematic that allows Ursula Le Guin such ease and fluency with her 'left-handed'

Earthsea trilogy. In *The Encyclopedia of Science Fiction* Peter Nicholls makes high claims for it: 'Always gripping, often moving, and shot through with a complexly used but plain and almost puritanical imagery, it may be UKLG's most perfect work.'[37] It may seem odd to make such claims for a work that is ostensibly for children, but the trilogy is powerful and haunting in a way that neither *The Left Hand of Darkness* nor *The Dispossessed* quite achieve. Le Guin describes it very well herself, in her characteristically modest way, in terms of a lack of conflict between ideas and language: 'The ideas of the trilogy are more totally incarnated, less detachable from the sounds, rests and rhythms, less often stated as problems and more often expressed in terms of feeling, sensation and intuition. If you dissect the ideas out of those books you get things like Don't Meddle, Keep the Balance, Man is Mortal – Fortune-cookie ideas.'[38]

The three books of *Earthsea* are set in an ocean world with clusters of islands, where magic is one of the natural laws, and treat of the apprenticeship, maturity and death-quest of the magician Ged. Here Le Guin roams her inner lands without having to look over her shoulder at an array of social and political creations of her own that are forever coughing not so discreetly in the background, demanding their share of the action. In both *The Left Hand of Darkness* and *The Dispossessed* the ideas do remain ideas: in *Earthsea* they are integral to the language and so transcend the banality of their 'translation'.

But where there is an aesthetic problem with both *The Left Hand of Darkness* and *The Dispossessed*, there is not, interestingly, with the novella *The Word for World is Forest*, which to my mind is as fluid and integrated a piece of fiction as the *Earthsea* trilogy. It demonstrates that there *is* room in Le Guin's chosen territory of outer space and inner lands for the conjuncture of political and aesthetic concerns, although, with reference to this work, she has expressed uneasiness about such a possibility.

The Word for World is Forest was originally written in 1968 as *The Little Green Men*, when Ursula Le Guin was in England and so separated from the US peace movement, in which she had been an activist. It is set on the forested planet of Athshe. The Athsheans inhabit a world time and a dream time, and are being destroyed by a group of colonists and their leader, the evil

Captain Davidson, who are able to behave in this 'frontier' spirit because the lack of an ansible cuts them off from anyone they should be accountable to in the League of Worlds. Le Guin says of the late sixties: 'The victory of the ethic of exploitation, in all societies, seemed as inevitable as it was disastrous.' She had never written a story 'so easily, fluently, surely – and with less pleasure.' In her introduction she admits 'regret' for the 'moralising aspects' of the story which she believes are 'now plainly visible'.[39]

The story conjures up vivid images of the Vietnam war, of rape, murder, destruction. But while the characters are recognisably 'stock' – the bullying Davidson filled with fear and loathing of the 'creechies', and the liberal 'good guy' Lyubov – the central metaphor of the forest, which holds the unconscious of the Athsheans, rises above them. As in Vietnam, the oppressors see deforestation as the key to victory; the political points, far from detracting from its metaphoric power, increase it. This is a story about dreams and reality as well as about power and oppression. It is about corruption and change and the materiality of the unconscious. It is, significantly, more open-ended than much of Le Guin's later work. Possibly this is to do with her feelings of despair and isolation while she wrote. The Athsheans are rescued from total destruction at the hands of Davidson by the arrival of Le Guin's ubiquitous envoys from elsewhere, in this case Hainish and Cetian. But the knowledge of murder now exists in world time and cannot be driven back and contained in dream time. There is no integration or homecoming here.

Ursula Le Guin is a skilled writer of short stories, too. She can be comic and discursive, while the more obviously 'political' stories, such as 'The New Atlantis' or 'The Diary of the Rose' (both in *The Compass Rose*) show a concreteness of language that fuses the 'idea' with its fictional expression. The short story form perhaps offers a freedom from the search for the elusive 'person'.

In conclusion, then, I would say that of the writers looked at in the second half of this book, Ursula Le Guin is the least radical in her approach to sexual politics. Sexuality is, in her work, too integral a part of a philosophy of binary systems that leads, ineluctably, to stasis. This is related, I think, to her search for the whole person, for Mrs Brown, her idealistic hope that, there, symmetry or balance can be found. Her contribution to science fiction cannot be overestimated – she demands a seriousness from readers and from other writers that is enormously important – but her conception of her beloved outer space and her inner lands is too closely related to parameters set by mainstream narrative modes to explore to the full the explosive potential of science fiction. Le Guin speaks *with* the voice of authority – although it is a voice that is at once self-critical and encouraging to others – rather than against it. Where Tiptree, Charnas, Russ can perhaps be seen as stow-aways, taking over, redirecting the time-machine of the genre, seizing power in their own works to go this way and that, Le Guin is a traditional voyager. She invites the reader to accompany her as crew, not accomplice, and the reader is returned, dazzled perhaps, but unscathed.

13
The Absent Heroine: Suzy McKee Charnas

I

Feminists, when discussing the work of Suzy McKee Charnas, most often refer to her second novel, *Motherlines*. This is undoubtedly because, of her two science fiction novels, it is *Motherlines* that centralises women. There are, indeed, no men in it. Perhaps because of this separatist status it is often seen as a feminist utopia. In fact, neither of the two women-only societies portrayed in it is unmitigatedly utopian. Charnas herself has said of it, in an interview in *Algol, Motherlines* 'isn't a tract, a textbook, or a blueprint'. Another reason for the primacy given to *Motherlines* in feminist criticism is perhaps the novel's exploration of the contentious method of reproduction used by the Riding Women in their women-only society.

Walk to the End of the World, on the other hand, is often ignored, seen merely as providing a background to *Motherlines* and an origin for Alldera, the latter's 'heroine'. Alldera is a strange evasive figure, a kind of absent heroine, a blank on which are inscribed the myths, dreams and nightmares of the two books. The powerful yet shadowy role she plays in *Motherlines*, loses much of its impact, I feel, if *Motherlines* is read alone. The two books are best read together, although *Walk* does present certain problems to the reader. It depicts, as I will go on to describe, a patriarchal, militaristic culture in the process of disintegration; this is a *sine qua non* of the process of change sparked off by Alldera's escape into the Wild. It is, I think, a very feminist book, but its concentration on male characters and its depiction of a society in which women are slaves are, understandably, offputting to readers who are fed up to the teeth with women as slaves and want something ráther more inspiring.

Charnas describes in her essay 'A Woman Appeared' how *Walk* became imbued with her own developing feminist consciousness. At first the only female characters in the book were the work gangs of 'fems', 'debased and enslaved . . . the other face of the book's macho survival culture'. Then the three protagonists, all male, found themselves joined by another, a fem, who was 'filling the place taken in so many stories, SF and mainstream, by "the girl" – she who stands for (and invariably lies down for) that half of humanity that is otherwise absent from the foreground.' With no literary models for such a character (while there were plenty for the three men), Charnas approached her with unease and trepidation, to find that inventing her necessitated drawing on her own experience rather than other texts, and led to 'a series of revelations that gave the story a whole new balance of events, character and meaning.' What had started as a 'thin, familiar tale . . . about a young hero adventuring with two male companions in search of his father' turns out to be something very different.

I think it is worth quoting in full Charnas' comments on this sea-change, because they show so simply and so clearly how a political vision can become an integral part of the imagination; how important, in other words, politics is to art. They also show the energy of the ideas coming out of the women's liberation movement in the early 1970s, and how immediate was their influence on writing.

> Looking back, I now recognise the obvious. During that same winter of 1972–3 (while writing *Walk*), I was doing what so many other women were doing: reading books like Shulamith Firestone's *The Dialectic of Sex* (Bantam 1971) and *Sisterhood is Powerful* edited by Robin Morgan (Vintage 1970) and participating in consciousness-raising sessions with other women. As my awareness matured – and my anger at finding myself trapped in the powerless class of women – Alldera pushed her way more and more to the heart of the story I was writing, changing everything around her as my own perspective on her fictional world changed.[1]

In this chapter I shall look in some detail at both *Walk to the*

End of the World and *Motherlines*. Charnas originally intended them as the first two novels of a trilogy, but the third final novel has never appeared. Instead she has written two others, *The Vampire Tapestry* and *Dorothea Dreams*, as well as shorter pieces and work for children. The lack of a third book to complete the trilogy is, I think, inevitable; the lack encourages, as I will show, a different reading of these two.

The trilogy is a common structure in science fiction and fantasy partly, no doubt, because of market forces, but also because of its suitability as a narrative method for tales of romantic quest. (Many authors do not stop at the third book but carry on churning them out, like Stephen Donaldson with his immensely popular and lucrative *Illearth* books, creepy quasi-allegories in a sub-Tolkien style.) The romantic quest usually takes the form of an opening section introducing the hero/ine (childhood, or arrival on planet); a central section describing vicissitudes overcome; and a finale depicting the achievement of maturity, order, wisdom.

Science fiction, in its eclectic way, draws heavily on romance structures. I would suggest that these two books, *Walk* and *Motherlines*, set out along that road, but in fact turn out to be something quite different. Whatever Suzy McKee Charnas says about Alldera taking over the story ('Inevitably and almost effortlessly, the last pages of *Walk* grew to be Alldera's. At that point the story had become her story.'[2]), she is not a heroine in the romance tradition. Unlike the romance-based novels of Ursula Le Guin (who does not use the trilogy as a form, but uses a complex chronology to link her separate works) Charnas' fictions do not offer, in Rosemary Jackson's words, 'a promise of redemption on cosmic and personal levels'.[3] While Le Guin's protagonists become wiser if sadder men (and they are usually men), in a world to which some kind of order has been restored, Alldera, despite the 'chief lines' on her face at the end of *Motherlines*, is still a cipher.

Walk and *Motherlines* are essentially interrogative: of character, of order, of unity. They anatomise disintegration and decay (*Walk*) and process and change (*Motherlines*). The object of their interest is dissolution rather than resolution. And it is this, I think, that precludes a third book, a book that will 'round off' or 'complete' the trilogy, as in a traditional SF romance it would do. Interestingly, Charnas comments on heroic quests in the

Khatru symposium: 'The writer who makes use of the echoes of ancientry that this form automatically raises can't help raising those other sexist echoes as well.'[4] At that stage she thought there would be a third book; conscious on one level of the strictures of the form, it is as if she had not appreciated the tensions already in evidence between that form and what she had written.

The structure of the two books is similar: a shifting viewpoint moves the story from character to character and place to place. Both books have multiple protagonists. In *Motherlines* there are group protagonists; that is, besides the individual voices in the book, two groups of women, the Free Fems and the Riding Women, both tense with inner conflict, are major protagonists.

Charnas, describing the writing of the two books, says that while her method loosened up with *Walk*, the process became more flexible with *Motherlines*, when she asked for the participation of others. Again she points to the influence of the women's liberation movement: ' . . . it [*Motherlines*] demanded an approach that I think reflects some of the thinking about work and how to do it that has come out of the women's movement.'[5]

Walk to the End of the World has four protagonists, three men and one woman, through whose eyes, in turn, the story is told. It opens with a prologue, which briefly recapitulates the history of the Holdfast society, and ends, cataclysmically, with a section entitled 'Destination'.

The destruction of the old world has been caused not by nuclear holocaust, but by 'pollution, exhaustion and inevitable wars among swollen, impoverished populations'.[6] This Wasting, as it is called, has now played itself out, and the world is left to the wild weeds. The handful of officials that had access to shelters, the story goes, took some women with them for breeding purposes; denied them any role apart from that of reproduction; brutally accused them, when some of the women objected to being slaves, of having caused the Wasting. When the survivors emerge from the shelters they find virtually nothing: no fish, no animals, very little plant life. Continuing the 'heroic, pioneering tradition of their kind'[7] the men kill the few wretched mutants they find. So, finally, there is nobody left who is different from themselves; their world is made up of White able-bodied men and, of course, women. The men project the *description of walk*

blame for the Wasting on to everything outside themselves: non-White men, animals, youths who 'repudiated their fathers' ways' and above all the men's 'own cunning, greedy females'.[8] All these are called 'unmen'. 'Of all the unmen, only females and their young remain, still the enemies of men.'[9]

The Holdfast is a slave society. The women, or fems, do all the hard labour and are treated like pack animals. A few of them become 'pets', private slaves and sex objects, but it is a precarious existence because women's bodies are regarded as so foul and evil that only the most highly privileged of the 'Seniors' can afford to be seen to get enjoyment from them. The ethos is misogynist; everything male is clean, pure and honourable while everything female is foul, dirty, weak and dangerous. The men are caught in a fearful contradiction; they believe women to be the fount of all corruption and responsible for the Wasting but, on the other hand, know that without women there will be no more sons. Female children, once weaned, are dropped into the kitpits, there to fight for survival or to die; male children are brought up in a Boyhouse where they are inculcated with an intense repugnance for and loathing of everything female. Fathers and offspring do not know each other, so that the 'fated enmity of fathers and sons' can be avoided.[10] For it was the young men, too, corrupted by their mothers, who rose up against their fathers and so brought about the Wasting. Captain Kelmz muses on this when he first meets Eykar Bek, the only man in the Holdfast who knows who his father is. 'Old and young were natural enemies; everyone knew that. To know your father's identity would be to feel, however far off, the chill wind of death.'[11]

Elaborate rules, rituals and beliefs contain the men's fear of chaos and of the void, particularly as represented by women. Society is basically divided between men and unmen: men are further divided into Seniors and Juniors, those over and those under thirty. Social intercourse across the age divide is restricted, sexual intercourse taboo. The Juniors are organised militaristically, into work units, which move around from one job to another every five years. The Seniors indulge in political and social intrigue.

Alldera describes the Holdfast as a society in which 'a man's whim was law, and knowing this made men capricious'.[12] Nowhere are women referred to as women: they are always fems, and they are burnt, tortured, abused, hunted through the streets by packs of drug-crazed killers, mutilated and, finally, eaten.

Walk to the End of the World is extremely disquieting to read. All the references to fems, until we reach Alldera's section of the book, are insulting and abusive, as the three male protagonists share, to a greater or lesser extent, their peers' fear and loathing of women. 'Fem' is a swear-word in itself: 'Go eat femshit' and 'Go stick it up a fem' are typical abusive phrases. Like any slave race the fems are seen as fickle and devious; like any slave race they are the negative Other, forced to accept responsibility for all misfortunes and misdeeds, from the failure of a harvest to transgressions by a member of the ruling class. Alldera, for example, is blamed for the sexual assault made on her while she was 'unclean'. Similarly, Eykar Bek's mother has been burned 'on suspicion of having witched a man into breaking the Law of Generations . . .'[13]

Walk offers many details of the working of this grossly polarised society. Charnas portrays the strategies for survival amongst the fems; the oppressors' underestimation of the intelligence – and humanity – of those they oppress; the oppressors' need to control their own desires with ritual and taboo; the institutionalised release of energies that might otherwise grow dangerous. Suzy McKee Charnas is, I think, particularly skilled at fleshing out her vision with psychological detail. There is no idealisation of fems or their potential in _Walk_. Their lives are nasty, brutish and short; to ensure their lives _are_ that, at least, the older fems, the Matris, kill off any younger rebellious ones, any who might attract the avenging attention of men.

The older fems see the survival of humanity as paramount, as did their ancestors in the underground shelters who bowed their heads and agreed to bear children for men. Alldera has been chosen by the Matris, on account of her unusual skill in long-distance running, to escape into the Wilderness, whence she is to come back pretending she has met up with the mythical Free Fems and that these have pledged to come, when the time is ripe, to rescue the fems in the Holdfast. This is to immobilise young fems, to substitute dreams of the future for present action that may threaten the survival of all the fems. Alldera has no illusions about her fellow fems, nor about the possible response

of the Free Fems, if indeed such creatures exist. 'Fems knew if
anyone did that having been victimised was no guarantee of
courage, generosity, or virtue of any kind.'[14]

Our first close-up sight of the fems shows them labouring in a
laver-processing plant in Bayo. Servan d Layo, the protagonist
of this section of the book, is surprised when he enters the
work-room to hear them talking to each other, for 'the majority
of them were held to be incapable of any but the most limited
fem-to-master type of speech.'[15] When they realise that men
have entered the room, 'suddenly every fem in the place
acquired a slight stoop or cringe. The faces of the nearest ones
went slack and foolish before his eyes.'[16] It is details like these
that give credibility to this nightmare world. D Layo knows that
this transformation is not 'witchery', but a deliberate strategy on
the part of the fems; he is unusually perceptive for a Holdfast
man. To say that it is in the political interests of the fems to have
men underestimate their intelligence doesn't approach the
extremity of the women's oppression. As Charnas says, *Walk* is
about 'sexism carried to a logical extreme, and . . . the inherent
destructiveness of any society in which one portion of the
population enslaves and dehumanises another.'[17] In *Walk*
women are tolerated as a slave class; men are so mad that they
would kill all of them if they showed any signs of being anything
other than dumb beasts.

The insanity of this society springs from men's fear of death.
They have only themselves, their own 'manliness', to protect
them against everything other: fems, with their 'inner core of
animating darkness shaped from the void beyond the stars';[18]
the Wild outside the Holdfast which, on a windless day, is like
'the stillness of the void'.[19] When there is wind, the Wild is full
of 'the whispers of the ghosts of the vanished unmen'.[20] Such
fears are contained, as I said above, by ritual and taboo.
Aggression is safely channelled through spectator blood sports
with, of course, fems as the hunted (as I said earlier, this book
can be very disturbing); potentially anti-social desires are
expressed and defused through controlled drug-induced 'Dark-
Dreaming'.

But this is a society on the very verge of disintegration. When
this happens, the creation of *Motherlines* is possible. Within the
fictional timescale the societies depicted in the two books exist
simultaneously, but Alldera, the nominal heroine of the

duology, must be freed from the Holdfast before the dynamic possibilities of the Free Fems and the Riding Women are played out within her silent and shadowy psyche. Alldera the runner, with her deadpan face and her pretend stupidity, is the absent centre of *Walk to the End of the World*. She is the least memorable character in the book; perhaps she represents the void so feared by the men of the Holdfast, the 'emptiness' on which the patriarchy is constructed.

The three male protagonists, Captain Kelmz, Servan d Layo and Eykar Bek are travelling together towards a first, final and forbidden meeting with Raff Maggomas, the father of Eykar Bek. All three are outcasts in their various ways; all break taboos. All hold within them the seeds of the Holdfast's destruction.

Captain Kelmz is a man who has passed the age-divide but has refused a Senior's privileges so that he can carry on working with his beloved 'mad-eyed' Rovers, robot-like killers who are each locked into a solipsistic heroic vision and are kept under control with a drug, manna; they are liable, however, to outbreaks of uncontrollable behaviour, when they 'go rogue'. (Kelmz's Rovers are recognised by the fems as being 'clean' killers.) Kelmz is the most traditional and unquestioning of the three men; he is a rebel despite himself, accepting of the hierarchy but refusing to move up it. Indeed he recognises that the 'insidious lure' of DarkDreaming lies partly in the 'deliberate abolition of hierarchy'.[21] He expresses disgust at another man who dreams he is a fem, but he himself dreams he is a beast. There are no animals left in the Holdfast; but the beasts of the unconscious lie only a dream away. D Layo sneers at his upset: 'He should know as many men as I do who dream themselves a coat of fur or feathers when they get the chance!'[22]

Servan d Layo is more subtle than Kelmz. He recognises the importance of the dark recesses of the unconscious and does not underestimate the humanity of the fems. His cruelty is intelligent rather than conventional: Alldera understands how dangerous this is. D Layo is a practised DarkDreamer. He has lived outside the law since boyhood, when he was thrown out of the Boyhouse and left on the edge of the Holdfast to be picked up by Scrappers, who would castrate him and sell him to an old man as a bondboy. D Layo trusts no one except Bek, whom he loves. He knows that he is being used in a game of political intrigue and that when Maggomas is found his own life will be forfeit. But as he has escaped the castrators' knives so he hopes to escape further retribution. In the final scene of the book, with Kelmz long dead and Bek presumed dead, when the city of 'Troi has fallen heralding the collapse of the Holdfast, Alldera from her hiding place watches d Layo move like 'some hungry beast' or 'hunting predator'. She imagines him 'cutting down some less clever survivor and feeding on the flesh, rank or not . . . as innocently ruthless as any beast.'[23]

Eykar Bek, the only man who knows his father, symbolises the possibility of sons rising up, again, against their fathers, in a re-enactment of the Wasting. For this, he has been sent off to be Endtendant at Endpath, the place where men go to die. The Endtendant's duties are to mix and give the death-dealing poison, see to the disposal of the bodies, organise the inclusion of the dead one's name in ritual chants and, sooner or later, to mix a cup of poison for himself. To be Endtendant is a dubious honour. Usually Endtendants dispose of themselves quite quickly. Eykar Bek is the first ever to leave his post; worse, he has closed down Endpath.

Bek has seen through the myth of Endpath. He says to d Layo: 'Whatever they say about men choosing to come to Endpath, more are broken and desperate than are "ripe for release", whatever that may mean. Cancer drives them, madness drives them, passion drives them . . . '[24] He realises that he has been sent to Endpath to die but decides 'not to let himself be so easily discarded' and instead to take 'the shaping of his life into his own hands'.[25] Bek at first views fems with superstitious fear; but his contact with Alldera begins to change this.

As the economic base of Holdfast life crumbles – the laver harvest has failed over some years and the lammins (long kelps eaten by men only) are alarmingly scant – each taboo that is broken smashes holes in the superstructure. Bek has broken the father/son taboo and has returned to life from his place of death. Servan d Layo has outwitted death/castration, and remains apparently unpunished for his arcane knowledge of the chaos of the soul. The otherwise conservative Kelmz has rejected rank and status and gives his own life for the taboo Bek.

The final taboo is broken in the city of 'Troi, where the monstrous Maggomas has instituted cannibalism as a means of

better exploiting his resources before seizing power. This is at
once symptom and cause of the end of the Holdfast. Bek fulfils
the Oedipal myth, slays his father and brings destruction upon
the land.

What opposes these myths of disintegration? In contrast to
the scandal and intrigue amidst which sexual affairs are usually
conducted in the Holdfast, the relationship between Servan d
Layo and Eykar Bek shows at times a tentative tenderness that
is reminiscent of the famous love scene between Genly Ai and
Estraven in Ursula Le Guin's *The Left Hand of Darkness*. But it
is not a grand passion. D Layo is a survivor; the great gesture of
love is reserved for Kelmz, and it leads only to a messy death.

More important, perhaps, as a symbol of integration, is the
humanising power of language. Speech is a central metaphor in
Walk to the End of the World: it gives fems the only kind of
freedom that they know. They communicate with each other in
softspeech, which men cannot understand, and convey information up and down the land through news-songs. A secret
language is a common fantasy – and not always a fantasy –
amongst oppressed peoples. Children use elaborately made-up
languages to exclude adults. In science fiction Suzette Haden
Elgin has explored the idea of a secret language for women in
Native Tongue and its sequel *The Judas Rose*; there the women
develop one language that the men know about but do not
understand, so as to cover up their development of another,
much more complex, woman-centred language called Làadan.
The men of the Holdfast certainly recognise the empowering
nature of language: their response is to cut out tongues.

Speaking fems have a prime fantasy, of 'becoming the one
who, by sheer eloquence, drove through the barrier of men's
guilt and fear.'[26] Alldera approaches this: confined with Bek
when he is wounded in the fight that kills Kelmz, she begins to
speak to him with herself as subject. He is forced to recognise
her autonomy: refuses to rape her when, for a second time, the
opportunity arises (he has already raped her before) and, at the
end, connives at her escape. But the partial humanisation of one
individual has no power to change the whole social structure. It
is a mere drop of possibility that is swept away in the wave of
chaos that finally engulfs the Holdfast.

Walk to the End of the World is open-ended. The social order
collapses in murder, patricide, cannibalism and predation. Men

have become beasts, the very mythical monsters in the Wild they once feared. All their protective structures have collapsed to reveal darkness and death. *Walk* is a subversive fantasy that reveals the emptiness of the patriarchal order. Although it shares a setting with other feminist post-holocaust novels, such as Vonda McIntyre's *Dreamsnake* or Sally Miller Gearhart's *The Wanderground*, it shows none of their redemptive qualities. *Walk* is a novel of disintegration rather than renewal. It is only through the crumbling of the patriarchy that Alldera the runner is freed, and only against such scenes of destruction that the story of *Motherlines* can be told. ' "Unmen, the heroes are gone . . . " '[27] sings Alldera as she sets out on her long, hard run into the Wild. In the Holdfast there were only men and unmen and although Alldera, importantly I think, will retain that self-defined negativity, it is through her that we will, at last, see women.

There are no male characters in *Motherlines*. Charnas, describing her emergence, as a writer, from male conditioning, has said that at first she was 'scared' that she wouldn't be able to write a book about women only and that if she did it would be 'boring'.[28] *Motherlines* is far from boring. As Charnas says, she did write it, and 'without men there to hog all the interesting action and character development for themselves, the women blossomed out into whole and interesting people, or so I believe. The result is not . . . about the long-neglected female "half" of world experience but about a whole, complete and self-sufficient world of women.'[29] As Margaret Miller says in an essay on *Motherlines* and Charlotte Perkins Gilman's *Herland*, 'they both [Charnas and Gilman] assume that women are potentially omnicompetent, that there is no human task they could not perform were restraints on their activities removed. They also share the assumption that a society organised by women isolated from male pressures would be non-authoritarian and co-operative rather than competitive.'[30]

Motherlines shows us two societies of women: the Free Fems, victims of the culture of *Walk*, who 'try to heal themselves and succeed or do not succeed in a manless world' and, at the 'heart of the book', the Riding Women.[31] Between these two groups moves Alldera, who is not a heroine but who develops heroic qualities, accompanied, in the later stages of the book, by an *alter ego*, the hideously scarred ex-pet Daya, romancer and myth-maker.

In the symposium published in *Khatru 3 & 4* Suzy McKee Charnas praises SF's capacity for revealing 'the brilliance of the strange', and notes how 'everything becomes transmuted, fresh, newly-meaningful, full of writing-possibilities'. She goes on to say, 'Better yet, instead of having to twist "reality" in order to create "realistic" free female characters in today's unfree society, the SF writer can create the societies that would produce those characters, not as exceptions of limited meaning and impact, but as the healthy, solid norm . . . SF lets women write their dreams as well as their nightmares.'[32]

If the male-dominant slave society of the Holdfast is the nightmare, then the co-operative democratic society of the Riding Women is the dream. The Riding Women are descendants of a group who took control, during the Wasting, of a lab in which experiments in parthenogenesis were being conducted. Those women perfected the changes that had been made, so that each daughter would get a double set of traits from the mothers. They also continued breeding animals in the lab that would be able to live in the outside world after the Wasting: the sharu, small vicious creatures descended from rats; and the horses, bred for toughness and speed, which are now an integral part of the Riding Women's lives. The Riding Women live like tribal nomads, moving camp according to the season, living close to their horses and to the land. They depend on their horses not just for transport, but for meat and for the sperm that sets off the parthenogenetic process. Nenisi Conor, the strong Black woman who is one of Alldera's sharemothers, her friend and her lover, tries to explain what happens at a Gather, when the young women dance and mate with the horses, in terms of the Riding Women's way of life: 'The balance of all things includes us and acts on us, and animals – even the sharu in their way – are our links with that balance. We celebrate it every year at the Gather of all the camps, where young women mate. The Gather is part of our bond with each other too, you see. Every woman has trusted herself to a horse this way, or is blood kin to another woman who has.'[33] To Alldera, newly escaped from the Holdfast, whose only experience of sex is rape, and who has recently given birth to a 'cub' she didn't want, the image this conjures up is repugnant.

Charnas describes the Riding Women in loving detail, as if

she has made an anthropological study of her own invention and given them life through her imagination. As she describes it: 'My impulse was just to follow the Riding Women forever, recording what it was like travelling and camping with them, living their life – as if I were one of those nineteenth-century wanderers who vanished into the wild spaces of the world for years and came back to write books with titles like *My Life Among the Mongols* or *A Winter in Crow Camps*.'[34]

The Riding Women are non-possessive in both their sexual and their family relationships. Child-bearing and child-rearing feature prominently in *Motherlines*: indeed it is the women's biological experiences that give shape and rhythm to much of the celebration and ritual that is so much a part of their lives. This is in contrast to the attitudes towards women's bodies held by men and by fems in the Holdfast. And it is, too, a comment on women's experience of their own biology in the contemporary world. Nenisi, for example, when Alldera marvels at her own recovery from starvation, exhaustion and childbirth, replies, 'Everyone knows that any normal female is tougher and healthier in pregnancy than any other time in her life . . .'[35] Nenisi is rueful that she herself like the rest of her line is not a 'normal female'; she finds pregnancy very difficult.

When a child is born she is suckled by all the sharemothers: the women who will become her family, to whose tent she will belong, when, at puberty, she comes out of the childpack. The childpack roams around the edge of the camp; not all survive it. At menarche a girl is harried out of the pack and enters the adult world. Alldera reminds herself of the significance of the mother-and-child bond when she returns from the Free Fems to welcome her own child out of the childpack:

> The bloodmother looked at her child and saw her own image made young, her replacement in the world, Nenisi said. The child saw in her bloodmother the pattern for her own being. Women said it was best not to let this powerful connection unbalance all the other relationships that guided their two lives, and so it was appropriate that the bloodmother and child be separated for a time.[36]

This parallels the Holdfast men's attitude towards sons and fathers, but transforms it utterly. There, the father/son relationship is circumscribed with taboo to keep at bay the forces of death and destruction; here, the mother/daughter relationship is placed formally within a kinship system that incorporates the possibility of death and change within a view of life as process. Such an insight into the possibly harmful effects of too close or intense a relationship between biological parent and child is expressed, as noted before, in another feminist vision of the future, Marge Piercy's *Woman on the Edge of Time* where, again, a period of separation is enforced between a newly pubertal child and her parent.

The Riding Women are rough, tough, unsentimental. They are, as Margaret Miller puts it, 'grubby and smelly'.[37] They can be jealous, argumentative, aggressive. Sheel, another of Alldera's sharemothers, who formerly wanted to leave her to die in the wilderness, is all of those. Sheel recognises the threat posed by the Free Fems to the lives of the Riding Women; she knows that they bring unwelcome change, and she hates them for it. The different motherlines have their faults, passed on from mother to daughter; the bad teeth of the Conors, the quick tempers of the Fowersaths, the laziness of one line, the nosiness of another. But, to quote Miller again, the Riding Women are 'tough, proud, strong, joyous and loving, and they call no man – and no woman – master.'[38]

In contradiction to the Riding Women are the Free Fems, the band of ex-fems escaped over the years from the Holdfast. Their behaviour is dictated by their past lives, when they had to struggle for survival as individuals rather than as a group. The band is ruled by the massive and dumb Elnoa. Her dumbness is typically described in the casual way in which the cruelty of Holdfast life is referred to throughout *Motherlines*, as a background of horror to the present lives of the women.

> Decades ago when she had first bossed her master's femhold, one of the fems under her command had argued and denied a charge of theft instead of taking her punishment with her mouth shut. Following tradition, the master had ordered Elnoa's tongue removed to impress upon her that she was responsible for the silent submissiveness of those she bossed.[39]

Elnoa is all-powerful and, like any despot, has a band of courtiers in attendance who mediate for others and manipulate for themselves. The ethos of individualistic struggle for survival has survived beyond the Holdfast; each fem keeps a little cache of treasure in the hills, its whereabouts a jealously guarded secret; where the Riding Women have friendships, the Free Fems have alliances; where the Riding Women allow every woman her say in matters of dispute, for the Free Fems Elnoa's wish is law. The most important difference, perhaps, is that the Free Fems are a dwindling band and have only extinction to look forward to. Despite the use of herbal douches prepared by the solitary wise woman Fedeka, and despite prayers and invocations to Moonwoman, the Free Fems cannot reproduce. This is why Alldera's child takes on such a significance. The Riding Women are also dwindling, for there are no new lines to compensate for ones that die out; they hope that Alldera's child will start a new motherline.

There is no love lost between the Riding Women and the Free Fems. The former despise the latter for their Holdfastish ways, for their softness and slavishness and their inability to ride; the Free Fems suspect the Riding Women of foul unnatural practices with their horses and find them altogether monstrous. Now that the fems have stopped coming from the Holdfast, to be found by the patrolling Riding Women, as Alldera was, and passed on to the Free Fems, the only contact between the two groups comes via the Free Fems' trading wagons.

Alldera leaves the Riding Women. Their refusal to accept and validate her life as a fem makes her feel alien and outcast. The Riding Women do not accept difference; as Alldera now lives with them, then she must be one of them. They expect her to assimilate, but she knows she cannot. The difference comes home to Alldera when she tries out her 'self-song' on Nenisi. Each woman composes her own self-song: they typically include tales of horses raided from other camps, fights against the sharu, tales of passion and strength and laughter. Alldera sings:

> I don't look like anyone here,
> Where I come from there were many like me, sweating fear.
> That's left behind, but I lived it.
> Our heads were bent because we couldn't look our masters in the eyes.
> We just sidled by, nursing our lives along.
> That's left behind – [40]

Nenisi's response is: ' "No, that's not the idea at all. That song is all about fems, not about yourself." '41

That night Alldera tells Nenisi a story about Holdfast life, about how in the freezing winter two fems froze to death outside the hall where their masters slept. Nenisi replies: ' "Why didn't all you fems break into the hall and throw the men out to freeze?" '42 Nenisi is not being deliberately unsympathetic or obtuse. It is simply that the Riding Women cannot imagine even subservience, let alone slavery. The only men they have ever seen are those that stray out into the desert and these are only 'a quarry to hunt', 'wild-eyed and bestial' in their terror of approaching death.43 The Riding Women are mistresses of their world: the balance of their lives is achieved through co-existence rather than domination.

By denying the significance of Alldera's past the Riding Women deny she has anything to offer them in the present. They see her skills in running as weird, and are interested only in whether she can learn to ride, which indeed she does. Alldera's suggestions for strengthening the granaries to protect the grain from scavenging sharu are brushed aside: the Riding Women are opposed to change. It is only Sheel, Alldera's implacable foe in the camp, who realises that Alldera's arrival, in itself, signals change.

Alldera leaves her daughter in the childpack and goes to join the Free Fems, but they distrust her for the time she has spent with the Riding Women and suspect her of habouring contemptuous feelings towards the Free Fems. The Holdfast ethos is still strong, and Alldera gets caught up in a piece of intrigue hatched by Daya that almost breaks her. She is badly beaten up. Her body, streaked with blood and dirt, and her head hanging in 'that horrible, loose way',44 remind Daya of the runaway fems in the Holdfast that were captured and brought back to be hunted to death. For a while Alldera's spirit does seem broken, and she takes to alcohol. She becomes a focus for Daya, and the relationship that slowly ensues transforms both of them.

Daya the ex-pet is used to 'conversation, lively companions and the pleasing tension of intrigue'45 and uses all the skills acquired in the Holdfast to jockey for and maintain a position as Elnoa's favourite. She rarely smiles, for when she does, she feels 'the scars in her cheeks ruck up the skin into hideous lumps, making of her smiling face a fright mask'.46 Charnas' skill as a novelist is most apparent in her creation of characters like Daya:

characters who are not heroines, who lack virtue, grace and integrity, and yet who are revealed to be worthy of our interest. (I think it is remarkable that the three male protagonists of *Walk*, men so gross that they don't even recognise women as being of the same species, can be portrayed in such a way that not only interest but sympathy are aroused in the reader.) Poor Daya. When, as a result of some other intrigue, another woman mixes some awful burning poison into her douche – as they all, desperately, try to conceive – and she nearly dies, she thinks, deliriously, 'that she had offended them with her scarred smile, that they did not want to look at her. She promised not to smile again, ever.'[47]

Daya's real importance is as a myth-maker. She creates stories of the strong heroic Free Fems who will return to the Holdfast to rescue the fems still living there. Alldera rejects these as romances, just as she rejects Daya's version of the past, her stories of clever fems outwitting their masters. Alldera accuses Daya and the Free Fems of still being slaves, incapable of action, happy to 'sit around making excuses for their cowardice until they die!'.[48] But Alldera's vision is no more 'real' than Daya's, and in the end it will be Daya who wants to act on her dreams of return to the Holdfast.

Stories and dreams, Charnas suggests, are necessary. Who is to say that one thing is more real than another? Daya understands instinctively that the importance of belief does not have to be related to its truth. So, when Alldera points out the material basis for one of Fedeka's religious beliefs, Daya asks her not to reveal it to Fedeka. Alone with Alldera in Fedeka's camp, Daya slowly emerges from the restricting role of court favourite. Alldera steals some wild horses and breaks them in and Daya learns to ride. It gives her a new freedom and strength. She is released from a constant sexual tension that has made her unable to identify herself except through her sexual relationships. She and Alldera become lovers, then friends. She accompanies Alldera when she returns to Stone Dancing Camp to welcome her daughter out of the childpack at puberty and, having been introduced as kin, becomes kin.

Increasing numbers of fems 'defect' from Elnoa's camp. They create dissonance amongst the Riding Women with their secretive, gossipy, plotting ways, but they bring to Stone Dancing Camp qualities that the Riding Women lack: versatility, adaptability, perseverance and patience. They don't scorn hard, manual work. They dig foundations for the granaries so the sharu can't burrow in; they learn to ride; they demand that Alldera's child, Sorrel, be acknowledged as part fem as well as part Riding Woman.

Alldera doesn't want to jeopardise the Riding Women's lives by a return to the Holdfast, but she is not a prime mover of events. 'It seemed to her that the surface of the plain stirred slowly, purposefully, inexorably beneath her feet, carrying her and all of them east toward the mountains like waves to the rocks.'[49]

Daya has taken over Alldera's role as rescuer of the fems in the Holdfast. But Daya, despite the strengths she has revealed, is, like Alldera, a misfit, an outsider, heroic in her own way but not a heroine nor a leader of women. Daya is a storyteller, and it is her stories that have created the possibility of a return to the Holdfast. The stories that Alldera once rejected as romances may turn to tragedies. There is no way of telling whether the future will be a dream or a nightmare.

With great passion and with no sentimentality Charnas shows us a complex world of women who are strong, life-affirming and, importantly, believable. Although there are no male characters in *Motherlines*, Charnas' vision is not an essentialist one. Her Riding Women are strong because they live in freedom, co-operative because coercion has never been forced on them, life-affirming because they know that death is part of life. The question of what women and men are 'naturally' like does not arise; for once, in literature, women have been set free from societal constraints. It could, perhaps, only have happened in science fiction.

Behind *Motherlines* stands *Walk to the End of the World*: the dissolution of the nightmare of the latter gives Charnas the freedom to construct her dreams of the former. But *Motherlines*, too, is open-ended: the process of change that is heralded by Alldera's arrival amongst the Riding Women at the beginning has not reached a conclusion at the end. The Free Fems have served their purpose; their qualities of intelligence and endurance have been offered to the Riding Women, and now, with what they have gained from the Riding Women in terms of how it is possible to live free and proud, they will move on. The Riding Women have had their conservatism challenged. And they, too, may not survive unscathed the Free Fems' return to the Holdfast. If the Free Fems are smashed like waves on the rocks then the Riding Women too might be destroyed.

In *Walk* and in *Motherlines* the issues are not simply individual. For this is not just the story of how one woman moves from slavery to freedom. *Walk* is a depiction of that state of slavery, and its dissolution; *Motherlines* is a depiction of how it might be to live without men, not of how it would be. Both books are fired by a political vision coming from the heart of the women's liberation movement, one that is transformed by the power of Charnas' imagination into a rich and complex fiction. Most importantly, the vision is not presented to the reader to be passively consumed. The very negativity, or blankness, of the central figure, Alldera, disallows this. For *Walk* and *Motherlines*, finally, are not pedagogical fictions: they explore possibilities, but offer no solutions.

II

The Vampire Tapestry is not strictly science fiction, if anything ever can be called strictly science fiction. It is set in the contemporary world – America in the 1970s – described with Charnas' customary meticulous attention to realistic detail, and concerns one Dr Weyland, brilliant and respected professor of anthropology at Cayslin College, researcher into dreams, and vampire.

As in *Walk* and *Motherlines* there are multiple protagonists, each with a different relationship to the powerful, attractive and potentially deadly Dr Weyland. Weyland is reminiscent of Servan d Layo in *Walk*: both are predators; both have the physical grace of the large cats (Weyland is seen as lion and tiger as well as wolf) and the intellectual cunning needed for survival amongst humans.

The Vampire Tapestry offers no cosy coffins or echoing underground vaults into which the reader can push her discomfort along with the vampire. This is a world of rapes on college campuses, of murders in Central Park, of therapists who crack up. It is a modern world, and the vampire has modern guise; he comes though from the primeval past.

We are introduced to Weyland early on – after a brief glimpse of him emerging from his sleep lab and dabbing at his mouth with his handkerchief – as he gives his annual public address on 'The Demonology of Dreams'. He describes what a 'corporeal vampire' would be like, that is, one that was the product of 'forces of evolution'. He describes himself.

The vampire, 'if he existed', says Weyland, would have to be able to survive on a slim supply of blood so as not to draw too much attention to himself. If he were able to live off the blood of animals then he would do so, as humans are the most dangerous of animals; animal blood, it is safe to assume, would only tide a vampire over a lean patch. Periodically he would have to withdraw for his own safety and, by sleeping for several generations, would awake to an ignorant, and replenished, source of food. The vampire must be able to slow his metabolism. This, along with survival on scant rations, would help extend his life span. Long life would be preferable to reproduction; there would then be no rivals for the limited supply of blood. It can't be true, Weyland continues, that the vampire's bite turns the victim into a vampire – later, he snaps 'I am not a communicable disease' to his therapist Floria Landauer – nor that the vampire has fangs. He refers to the Polish version of the legend, in which the vampire has some kind of puncturing device, like a needle in the tongue, that secretes an anti-clotting agent. The wound thus made would be minimal, and the vampire could seal his lips around it so there would be no wasteful splashing of blood.

When one of the students in the audience asks if a vampire would sleep in a coffin, Weyland replies, 'Would you, given a choice?'[1] The vampire must have access to the world: coffins deny that. One of the most pressing problems for a modern vampire is to find a safe long-term sleeping place. Another is to keep up with the extraordinarily fast pace of change in the contemporary world. When one of the audience suggests that a centre of learning would be a suitable place for a modern vampire to settle in, Weyland agrees, and offers Cayslin College as an example. He denies any sexual element in the vampire's bloodsucking activities. In fact women are extremely attracted to him as Katje de Groot, the protagonist of this first section of the book, recognises. In the audience, she is the only one to recognise the games that Weyland is playing, and the 'Satanic pride' of his being, which he insistently denies.

Katje recognises the predator in Weyland and muses on the audience's reactions: 'For overcivilised people to experience the approach of such a predator as sexually attractive was not strange.'[2] Later, with Floria, when she pushes him on the subject of reproduction and he destroys the myth of communicable vampirism, she asks if he ever desires sexual intercourse and he replies, 'Would you mate with your livestock?'[3]

Katje recognises 'The Ancient Mind at Work', the title of this section, because she is herself a hunter. Weyland is attracted to her, seeing her as a prey worth pursuing, underestimating her own prowess at hunting. To defend herself she draws a gun, reminding herself that he is not a legendary immortal being, but 'just a wild beast, however smart and strong and hungry'.[4] She shoots him twice, in the chest and belly, sending him off in full flight.

Weyland ends up a prisoner in New York in an apartment belonging to the slightly crooked Roger, and there meets another hunter, Alan Reece. Reece is hungry for power, recognises Weyland as a real vampire and plans to make money and fame out of him. Weyland is released by Mark, Roger's fourteen-year-old nephew, who cannot bear to see the suffering that is inflicted on the vampire by Reece and, on Reece's orders, by Roger. Both Mark and Weyland are exiles from 'The Land of Lost Content', the title of this section. Mark offers himself to Weyland when he sees Weyland drinking his own blood in desperation, and Weyland sucks feverishly, almost draining the life from Mark (he has already over-sucked from, and killed, a young addict Roger found and brought in for him). At the last moment he flings Mark aside, unconscious, and, freed from his cell, takes Roger in his arms to drink his fill. He is about to kill Roger, but desists on Mark's pleading.

For Katje and Reece, the hunters, Weyland is the 'other', set up in opposition to themselves. He is the part of the self that they reject, that they must conquer. They are the descendants of the ancient vampire-hunters, in full cry with blazing torches held aloft, denying the vampire existence, stamping out the beast within.

For Mark and even more for Floria Landauer in the next section, 'Unicorn Tapestry', Weyland is the dark side of the self that they recognise, the 'other' that is also themselves. Mark is too young to offer his life freely, but Floria does so. She is a successful gestalt-based but eclectic therapist who feels she has lost control of her work; she has been paralysed by her mother's death and the significance that has for the 'inevitability of her own death'.[5] Her therapy is rooted in the here and now; it is light years away from the primitive structures of Weyland's mind. Weyland has been sent to Floria by the Dean of Cayslin College for treatment for his 'breakdown'. Floria is pulled further and further into the recesses of her own soul: she carries on as a professional, pretending that his vampirism is a fantasy, forcing him to 'speak for' the repressed parts of himself that she feels are disguised in his vampire fantasies, while at the same time believing him to be a vampire.

The complexity of their relationship is portrayed with remarkable skill through the notes Floria makes at the end of each session as well as through the main narrative. Eventually Floria forces Weyland to 'speak for' her – as therapist, as prey and as keeper – and describes this in her notes:

'W. whispered, "As to the unicorn, out of your own legends – 'Unicorn, come lay your head in my lap while the hunters close in. You are a wonder, and for love of wonder I will tame you. You are pursued, but forget your pursuers, rest under my hand till they come and destroy you.' " Looked at me like steel; "Do you see? The more you involve yourself in what I am, the more you become the peasant with the torch!" '[6]

But Floria means no treachery, and it is the unicorn who is the chaste one. When Weyland must move on, leaving nothing behind him that can point to his being a vampire, Floria 'rose to face the vampire'.[7] She yields control, accepting the possibility of her own death, saying to herself, 'What I feared I have pursued right here to this moment in this room.'[8] Weyland does not kill her. At her request, they make love, and he leaves her. She thinks of how they 'met hidden from the hunt, to celebrate a private mystery of our own . . . '[9]

Both Floria and Mark are saved by their 'love of wonder', by embracing the 'other' in themselves. Both are strengthened by their encounter with the dark force of death; both, one must imagine, are changed. Floria looks at her hands:

What I have in my hands is my own strength, because I had to reach deep to find the strength to match him . . . Time was beginning to wear them thin and bring up the fragile inner structure in clear relief. That was the meaning of the last parent's death, that the child's remaining time has a limit of its own.[10]

The Vampire Tapestry expresses an irreconcilable contradiction: the price you pay for survival is the knowledge of possible death. 'Unicorn Tapestry' forms the structural and gnostic centre of the book: the rational and the instinctive, the articulate and the dumb, the conscious and the unconscious, the modern and the primitive, meet and merge in a mystic embrace. The sexual union of Weyland and Floria Landauer is unrelated to procreation: they do not kiss, or hold each other; it is 'unlike closing with unlike'.[11] It is a union that does not defy death, but instead accepts it. Weyland is humanised by his encounters with Mark, and more particularly with Floria, and so made vulnerable. The rigid distinction between predator and prey, necessary for his own survival, is dissolving.

Weyland has begun to respond to art, too, first to the ballet and then to opera. He decides not to go back to Cayslin but takes a post instead at a college in New Mexico. Soon after his arrival he is taken to a performance of *Tosca* in an open-air opera house in the hills above Santa Fé. All the sexual passion that Weyland cannot feel, and in particular did not feel for Floria Landauer, is expressed by the villain Scarpia for Floria Tosca. This section 'A Musical Interlude' reads almost like comic relief after the emotional and intellectual rigours of 'Unicorn Tapestry'; the opera house becomes the setting for a comedy of manners with ambitions, disappointments and alliances lightly sketched in.

Weyland is aroused by Scarpia's 'fierce declaration of appetite'. He kills a man, a stranger, without need and without hunger, reverting to an 'ancient method'.[12] For the first time he has killed gratuitously, and for the first time the action is sexualised: 'But what elation in that instant of savage release! Thinking of it now he felt his muscles tingle, and his breath came in a sharp hiss of pleasure.'[13] Weyland feels that he is now open to the power of art, and he is fearful. Art's ability to speak to him of himself he sees as a 'perilous new pattern'.[14]

As he recognises himself in art, understanding how he is constructed as a vampire from the depths of the human unconscious, so, in the final section, 'The Last of Dr Weyland', he observes in human history the recurrent image of the beast. Until now, he has dismissed humankind as cattle, as prey for his superior predation, but on reading the oral history collected by his colleague Irv he again recognises himself, in an anecdote from a Spanish witch who transformed himself into a coyote to follow an enemy and 'trotted along a wagon track in the wild dark, ears pricked to the creak of wheels and slap of reins up ahead . . .'[15] He recognises the wolf in the cattle he so despises.

In this section he is recognised for what he is by a painter. Dorothea Winslow, who, like Floria, and like Mark with his dreams of a space colony, likes 'a world with wonders in it'.[16] She has spent twenty-two years in the desert and knows death. She reassures Weyland: ' "Just because you've noticed something doesn't mean it's yours to meddle with." '[17] Not so Reece, who has hunted Weyland down and now closes in for the kill. Weyland thinks back to Katje de Groot 'the huntress whom he had so disastrously hunted'.[18] Hating Reece with a passionate hatred, he uses all his skill and cunning to turn the tables on his enemy and wrest from him his advantage. Sucking him to death, he sates his 'hunger and hatred'.[19] Weyland's loathing for Reece is personal, the corollary of his involvement with other humans: Floria, Mark, Irv, Dorothea. He knows it is a weakness: by acknowledging the demands of the present he risks losing the strengths of the past. He must enter vampire sleep, must slough off human vulnerability and sink down to the primeval depths, to awake in years to come without the weakening entanglements of heart and memory. Dr Weyland must die for the vampire to survive.

Dorothea Dreams incorporates a range of Charnas' preoccupations and, although one of the central characters is dying slowly and painfully of cancer, is surprisingly upbeat. Dorothea Howard is a reclusive middle-aged artist who has finished but who cannot break herself away from a massive sculpture she has made and embedded in a New Mexican hillside. She has employed for her sculpture all the artefacts of modern life, the durables of plastic and glass others have thrown away as rubbish. Across the canyon, opposite her own sculpture, are ancient Indian rock carvings. Dorothea is troubled by dreams she can't understand, but she begins to interpret them with the help of her old friend Ricky who has come to her to die. Her dreams are of the French Revolution: as in *The Vampire Tapestry* Charnas depicts an individual pitting herself against the masses, perhaps a particularly American theme. In this case the individual is Dorothea's ghost, a judge, who urges on her the virtues of compromise and selfishness.

Another strand of the story tells of a young chicano brother and sister in nearby Albuquerque who get caught up in a confrontation with the police after the people of their street have tried to resist a property developer's scheme to buy them all out. Roberto is not obviously a political hero: he is macho, insecure, lacking in political vision. His sister is asthmatic. Both, quite simply, are oppressed by poverty and racism. The police provoke an incident and open fire. Roberto finds himself on the run, with a gun that he barely knows how to handle, and hijacks a van of students who are on their way to visit Dorothea.

The ensuing confrontation is finally resolved – though not without pain and suffering – as Dorothea rejects the advice of her ghost-adviser and risks her life for the safety of the others. Roberto finds her sculpture by moonlight and attempts to smash it. This frees Dorothea from its spell; she relinquishes it to the world by making it public and so frees herself for future work. The moral release afforded by her encounter with Roberto has led to an artistic release.

Dorothea seems to share more than a first name with the minor character Dorothea Winslow in *The Vampire Tapestry*. They are both artists, both recluses, both capable of visions: Dorothea Winslow recognises Dr Weyland for what he is; Dorothea Howard recognises and accepts the possibility of death. *Dorothea Dreams* is much less grim than *The Vampire Tapestry*. Although it deals centrally with death – and Dorothea's delicately developing relationship with dying Ricky is marvellously done – it is, finally, optimistic. The many conflicts with which it deals – of race, class, generation, between the living and the dying are finally reconciled.

There is a certain similarity between the relationship of *Walk* to *Motherlines*, and of *The Vampire Tapestry* to *Dorothea Dreams*. *The Vampire Tapestry* reworks many of the themes of *Walk*, within a setting of past and present rather than future.

Both deal with the dissolution of structures, with the centrality of death, with the amorphousness underlying intellectual and moral codes. At the end of *Walk* the Holdfast is destroyed so that, in fictional terms, Alldera may live. At the end of *The Vampire Tapestry* Weyland sleeps, so that Dorothea may dream. While I do not think that *Dorothea Dreams* has the same stature as *Motherlines* – it is, finally, not quite an adult book, perhaps because its optimism is too unrestrained – it is nonetheless a thoughtful and sensitive study of a woman who is an artist and, more unusually, who is in late middle age. She is strong, loving, creative, in short, a likely candidate for starting a motherline.

These two more recent books are not so obviously feminist as *Walk* and *Motherlines*; although the themes overlap I don't feel the push of sexual politics that speaks through the worlds of the Holdfast and the Wild. But science fiction is, I think, ideally suited to the fictionalisation of such political themes, and Charnas, in these two recent books, has chosen a different direction. It seems to me that her creation of the Riding Women, women that she feared she would not be able to portray for lack of ability to write about whole women, has freed her to create complex and interesting female characters such as Floria Landauer and Dorothea Howard. As she says, 'As a result of writing *Walk* and *Motherlines* I think I have changed my way of looking at real women in the real world.'[20] A further result has been the creation of fictional women in a fictional world that deals, in particular, with the meaning that death holds for us and how, as we struggle to invent it, it shapes our lives.

14
The Reader as Subject: Joanna Russ

Joanna Russ is the single most important woman writer of science fiction, although she is not necessarily the most widely read. Her science fictional output is not large: four full-length novels (*And Chaos Died*, *The Female Man*, *We Who Are About To . . .* and *The Two of Them*), of which one, *We Who Are About To . . .*, is noticeably shorter than conventional novel length; two collections of linked stories (*The Adventures of Alyx* and *Extra(Ordinary) People*), a novel for children (*Kittatinny*), and many short stories, some of which are collected in *The Zanzibar Cat*. Her novel *On Strike Against God* contains science fictional elements, but is usually classified amongst non-genre fiction. I make this claim about her importance because of the seriousness of her feminist and her aesthetic concerns: the two are married (and as in any marriage are at times in conflict) in her work in a way that is not achieved by – indeed is not the ambition of – any other contemporary writer of science fiction.

The importance of Joanna Russ's work as a critic has I hope been made apparent in the earlier part of this book. Here, I want to show how she is a modernist in her fiction writing, and how modernism – contrary to many people's view of it as abstract and isolated from wider social and cultural concerns – can act as the literary or aesthetic form of a revolutionary politics, or, in other words, the politics of feminism.

Like many other writers of science fiction, Joanna Russ makes use of the versatility of the short story (she is not quite so exclusively devoted to it as James Tiptree Jr) and, again like many others, lets her work move easily from short stories into longer forms. Science fiction enjoys a remarkable freedom from rigid rules about what constitutes a novel. All lengths of work are taken seriously by readers and critics, as can be seen from the multitude of prizes that are awarded annually: best short story, best novella, best novel (while the awards for illustration, fanzines, films, etc. reflect the cultural diversity of science fiction). Because of the magazine basis of science fiction publishing, novels often appear serially (as did *We Who Are About To* . . .). Or a short story or novella might later appear with a different formal status, such as *Picnic on Paradise*, published as a novella in 1968, and as part of *The Adventures of Alyx* in 1977.

This lack of rigid distinctions between categories seems to encourage, too, not just an insouciance towards the hierarchy of form, but an easy attitude towards the common stock of science fictional literature. That is, there is a lot of reference and self-reference, borrowing and modifying. A writer may take her own short story and rework it in another form; or she may take another writer's short story and rework that. Russ has dedicated her novel *The Two of Them* to her fellow writer Suzette Haden Elgin 'who has generously allowed me to use the characters and setting of her short story, "For the Sake of Grace", as a springboard to a very different story of my own.' This does not, perhaps surprisingly, create a body of work that seems inward-looking and exclusive; rather the opposite in fact. Russ's modification of sword-and-sorcery in the Alyx stories, for example, throws the genre wide open.

The response of readers to Joanna Russ is striking in two significant ways, both of which are useful for an interpretation of her fiction.

The first is the response of women readers. Most of the women who read Joanna Russ would probably define them-selves loosely as feminist – that is why they read her, and they are quite distinct – although of course overlap with – readers of, say, Ursula Le Guin or Anne McCaffrey. Russ is hailed as a feminist first and foremost for an aspect of her work that, in my view, is comparatively minor: her participation in the feminist utopian tradition with her creation of the planet Whileaway. This sub-genre of SF – as I have noted earlier – relies to a certain extent for its feminism on an essentialist, unitary view of women. The French feminist philosopher Julia Kristeva, in a categorisation that I think is very useful, describes this as a reflection of what she calls the 'second stage' of feminism: the rejection of the male symbolic order in the name of difference. This is a radical feminist position in which 'femininity is extolled'.[1] The biologism and essentialism that underpin notions of female superiority are often unconscious, but are nonetheless there. I have found that Russ's short story 'When It Changed' – in which the all-women world of Whileaway has its first encounter with men – seems to have a special resonance for women readers, and is regularly favoured over what Russ herself calls her 'feminist novel'[2] *The Female Man*, where Whileaway reappears, but in a quite different context from the unproblematic 'When It Changed': a context of multiple narratives and multiple narrators.

I would contend that Russ's feminism is to be found not so much in her utopian creations as in her deconstruction of gender identity, of masculine and feminine behaviour. For Kristeva, the third stage of feminism rejects the dichotomy between masculine and feminine as metaphysical. I am indebted here to Toril Moi's reading of Kristeva in which Moi insists on the importance of the second stage, that is the political necessity for feminists 'to defend women as women in order to counteract the patriarchal oppression that precisely despises women *as* women' *as well as* Kristeva's third stage which 'radically transforms our awareness of the nature' of the political struggle.[3]

I hope to show in this chapter not so much how Joanna Russ challenges woman-scorning patriarchal oppression by creating strong women characters who have an obvious appeal to feminists (those six SF readers in search of a woman character); but how the revolutionary nature of her writing is to be found, as Toril Moi says, in her deconstruction of 'the death-dealing binary oppositions of masculinity and femininity'.[4]

The second striking and significant response to Joanna Russ is that of male readers, who continue to be shocked and outraged by her. It is not the separatist utopian aspect of her work that elicits this response, precisely because the essentialist ideas that accompany this position allow the reader to 'take it or leave it'. In my experience male critics, students or readers are not fazed by Russ's invention of Whileaway. It is instead what I would call Russ's 'deconstructionist' works, and in particular the novel *The Two of Them* which analyses a heterosexual relationship, that call forth the cries of panic and alarm, the fear that here is a woman *who dares to hate men* – which, judging from her work, is most probably not the case. Or, when the critic is concerned to be sympathetic to feminism himself, the accusations of bitterness and hostility to men are transformed, at least, for example, in Samuel Delany's critique of *Picnic on Paradise*, into criticisms of coldness in the prose (and he is not, consciously, referring to the qualities of the planet Paradise, which is icebound).[5] This suggests that an attempt to deconstruct notions of masculine and feminine is more of a transgression against the male law than is a radical separatism.

Here, in a discussion of the 'relative gentleness' of feminist utopias, Joanna Russ gives an example of, and offers an explanation for, a man's reading of her novel *The Female Man*:

> However, it may well be that the feminist books [Russ is referring to their 'relative gentleness' which is perhaps 'surprising'], because their violence is often directed *by women against men* are perceived as very violent by some readers. For example, *The Female Man* contains only four violent incidents: a woman at a party practices judo on a man who is behaving violently toward her and (by accident) hurts him; a woman kills a man during a Cold War between the sexes after provocation, lasting (she says) twenty years; a woman shoots another woman as part of her duty as a police officer; a woman, in anger and terror, shuts a door on a man's thumb (this last incident is briefly mentioned and not shown). A male reviewer in *Mother Jones* quoted at length from the second and fourth incidents (the only quotations from the novel he used), entirely disregarding the other two. Ignoring the novel's utopian society, which is one of four, he called the book 'a scream of anger' and 'a bitter fantasy of reversed sexual oppression', although the only fantasy of reversed sexual oppression in the novel appears to be the reviewer's. There is one scene of reversed sex roles in the book and that involves not a woman and a man but a woman and a machine.[6]

I want now to look in some detail at *We Who Are About To . . .*, *The Female Man*, 'When It Changed', *The Two of Them* and 'Sword Blades and Poppy Seed'.

We Who Are About To . . . was written at about the same time as what Russ calls her 'feminist novel', *The Female Man*; it was published in part in *Galaxy* Magazine, in 1975 (the year *The Female Man* was published), 1976 and 1977. 1977 saw its publication as a novel. Not surprisingly, there are themes common to the two books, in particular political and aesthetic concerns.

Towards the end of *We Who Are About To . . .* the narrator, who is alone and dying in a cave on a planet untold thousands of light years from earth, remembers being woken with her lover one summer dawn by the banshee shriek of sparrow fledglings in a nest in the air-conditioner vent. Then she imagines the six people she has killed as screeching fledglings.

Feed me, feed me, feed me! (Am I one too?)
Read me, read me, read me![7]

The narrator is herself a greedy baby bird: she has got rid of the audience that won't listen to her, the six who imagine they can survive on an alien planet and so refuse to prepare themselves for death, and now demands another audience, us, her readers.

The narrator of *We Who Are About To . . .* is herself fragmented, like that of *The Female Man*, although the fragments, in both books, are underpinned by a woman's voice that is wry, resigned, intelligent, fierce and prickly. Russ is passionately concerned about her readers; in all her work they feature variously as voyeur, eavesdropper, willing or unwilling confidante. The reader is forced to take up a position, to engage with the text. This does, of course, mean that reading Russ is demanding, if not at times daunting: a reaction is forced from us, as the baby bird forces a reaction from its parent.

But Russ's readers are rewarded as well as being bullied and cajoled. In *The Adventures of Alyx* the reward is implied in the promise 'But that's another story' which appears at the end of each story until finally Alyx disappears and there are, at the end of 'The Second Inquisition', 'No more stories'. An ambiguous ending; meaning, perhaps, that the reader can no longer rely on the author but must stand on her own (an interesting reversal of the parent/child paradigm). 'Are you truly curious?' Russ asks the reader of 'Sword Blades and Poppy Seed', a short story narrated by George Sand about Amy Lowell and the sisterhood of writing women, 'Then read our books,' she commands.[8] The reward for the reader comes from the reading. Russ's position on authorship is radical in two ways. First, she insists that books have a political life and that her own work, and the work of other women, are effective texts. Second, she constitutes the reader as someone who can, and indeed must be affected; and, at the same time, she constitutes the reader as female.

At the end of *The Female Man* Russ apostrophises her book:

> Live merrily, little daughter-book, even if I can't and we can't; recite yourself to all who will listen; stay hopeful and wise. Wash your face and take your place without a fuss in the Library of Congress, for all books end up there eventually, both little and big! Do not complain when at last you become quaint and old-fashioned, when you grow as outworn as the crinolines of a generation ago and are classed with *Spicy Western Stories*, *Elsie Dinsmore*, and *The Son of the Sheik*; do not mutter angrily to yourself when young persons read you to hrooch and hrch and guffaw, wondering what the dickens you were all about. Do not get glum when you are no longer understood, little book. Do not curse your fate. Do not reach up from readers' laps and punch the readers' noses.
>
> Rejoice, little book!
>
> For on that day, we will be free.[9]

The reward Joanna Russ offers her readers is imaginative knowledge, understanding and independence. There is no sense in Russ's work (although she has been accused of it) of pedagogy, or of a privileged voice, for Russ puts herself and her narrators on a par with her readers. Her modesty about her 'little daughter-book' is not a false modesty: she believes passionately in the power of words skilfully used and the power of the reader to respond.

Russ uncovers the need of the author and her text for readers; beneath the shaking by the scruff of the neck, the uncomfortableness and the harshness meted out to the reader, the text is crying out, 'Read me!' Author, text and readers move around the paradigm of mother and child in a complex and at times contradictory way. The result is quite startling: the female reader addressed directly by the author becomes The Reader, as fragmented as the narrators on the page but no less intelligent and with no less an effective potential. The operation of the text itself, and the reading of it, become political acts. Such literary radicalism is remarkable in itself; within science fiction it is, I think, unique. Russ exploits the forms of science fiction with a seriousness that many of its practitioners would not dare to claim.

If Russ's readers are forced into a multiplicity of roles, then her narrators are let off no less lightly.

The narrator of *We Who Are About To* . . . is a musicologist by profession, by circumstance a dealer of death; although she denies being a secret agent – almost synonymous, in Russ's work, with being a dealer of death – she shares many attributes of Russ's other secret agents: Alyx, Irene, Jael and, in this novel, Nathalie. Early on in the narrative Nathalie strikes the narrator as being 'a death's head', but it is the narrator herself who both symbolises and is this. She sees herself in precisely those iconic roles: as court jester and as death-bringer, and as the latter she assumes the qualities of the six people she kills, including the one that she, or we, least want to die, Cassandra the prophet.

We Who Are About To . . . is ostensibly the story of what happens when eight humans from an advanced high-technology society crash on an uninhabited planet with a chance of rescue so small as to be negligible. Because of the manipulation of spacetime in space travel they do not even know where they are. As the narrator says, 'the light of our dying may not reach you for a thousand million years'.[10] It is the narrator who accepts, alone, and at once, the inevitability of death. The others, in various ways, set about reconstructing civilisation.

A major feature of this is, of course, the reproduction of the species. In these circumstances hierarchies dissolve and re-form with remarkable speed: fifty-year-old Valeria Graham, previously rich and powerful and as used to buying people as goods, suddenly loses value and becomes the cook. 'Good for nothing else, I suppose,' comments the narrator.[11] Her daughter, twelve-year-old Lori, becomes at once an object of enormous value. The narrator refuses to participate in the crazy scheme of mating; though what alienates her most from her companions is her insistence on questioning the desirability of a life without culture, history, tradition or future. She rejects their notion of civilisation. John Ude, who pretends to be a historian, tries to persuade her of the importance of her role as childbearer (as she is only too well aware, the chances for the older women, like herself, of surviving a first pregnancy and birth in such surroundings are not high).

'Civilisation must be preserved,' says he. 'Civilisation's doing fine,' I said. 'We just don't happen to be where it is.'[12]

Latrine digging, housebuilding and mating start in earnest, and the narrator, who is already scapegoat and sacrificial victim, makes her escape. The first killings are almost accidental: she bashes Alan, newly validated in his machismo, too hard on the head when he enters her cave to winkle her out; Ude and Nathalie are victims of their attempt to ambush her. Victor Graham, a participant in the first 'mating', has already died of a heart attack. The narrator seeks out and shoots Valeria and Lori, and finally despatches Cassie, too, to the world of ghosts. 'So I'm left talking to myself. Which is nothing and nobody.'[13]

Before the narrator's disintegration as narrator, she offers the reader, in her taped narrative of events, a satirical view of civilisation and the growth of patriarchy; she satirises, too, that old pioneering spirit beloved of many a science fiction writer, which insists on the colonisability of many a planet. She questions the idea that Marion Zimmer Bradley posits in *Darkover Landfall*, that women's first duty is to reproduce the species; and, further, that they would enjoy it. She rejects as illusory the comfort offered by myth (Adam and Eve and the virgin world) and by cliché. The cliché of kind old earth, for instance, which this unknown planet seems strangely to resemble.

Oh sure. Think of earth. Kind old home. Think of the Arctic. Of Labrador. Of Southern India in June. Think of smallpox and plague and earthquakes and ringworm and pit vipers. Think of a nice case of poison ivy all over, including your eyes. Status asthmaticus. Amoebic dysentery. The Minnesota pioneers who tied a rope from the house to the barn in winter because you could lose your way in a blizzard and die three feet from the house. Think (while you're at it) of tsunamis, liver fluke, the Asian brown bear. Kind old home. The sweetheart. The darling place.
Think of Death Valley . . . in August.[14]

We Who Are About To . . ., for all its brevity, can withstand a multiplicity of readings. If it is about how to die, then it is as much about how to live. It tells the story of a woman who more or less coldbloodedly kills her six companions in misfortune (including a twelve-year-old child), and it shows how notions of dignity, humanity and freedom are central to such circumstances. It depicts a woman trying to make sense of living and dying in the midst of the very process of fragmentation. In moments of extremity the surface gloss of social relations cracks; so too does the surface of the narrative.

The narrator herself 'loses track' in both space and time; she cannot recall nor recount the exact sequence of events. Similarly, her narrative is full of breaks and stops. In the passage from voice to tape to typed script the conventional nature of the written word is revealed. The narrator has once been a political activist, but ran away from the responsibility it entailed. As she recalls the past, the distinction between memory and hallucination grows dim; facing death she makes a bid for immortality via the vocoder, turning all experience, including herself, into narrative.

> Everything's being sublimed into voice, sacrificed for voice; my voice will live on years and years after I die, thus proving that the rest of me was faintly comic at best, perhaps impossible, just an organic backup for conversation. Marvelous, marvelous conversation! The end of life.[15]

Towards the end of the book the narrator is visited in her cave by the ghost or hallucination of a five-year-old girl, Kennedy ('the only child I ever knew who was named after an airport'[16]) who had been killed in a car crash. These young girls recur in Russ's tales, often bearing indecipherable messages, speaking to the narrator across the chasm of years, already expressing need but not yet confined by it.

The ghosts that wander in and out of the rooms of the narrator's mind have no other habitation. The planet on which the story has apparently unfolded comes to look increasingly like a construct, the stage setting for a drama of life and death. The supporting roles are played by ghosts; the central character has wiped herself out of the script. There is little comfort for the reader, who must make what she may of it. But then that perhaps is Russ's aim: to refuse to take on the voice of authority, and so to challenge the relationship between author, reader and text.

Male science fiction critics often express disgruntlement with Joanna Russ's high-minded (in their view) ways with (their) science fiction. In the British Science Fiction Association magazine *Vector* (Dec 86/Jan 87) L.J. Hurst reviews *The Two of Them* and moans: 'Why Joanna Russ had to set it off planet and far away when everything she attacks is clearly here on earth and close at hand remains a mystery.' What is here on earth and close at hand is, of course, men: Joanna Russ is attacking systems of male dominance. This, I think, accounts for the reviewer's tone of annoyance. But Russ is quite clear about what SF offers to her as a writer. In the *Khatru* symposium she says:

> One of the best things (for me) about science fiction is that –
> at least theoretically – it is a place where the ancient dualities
> disappear. Day and night, up and down, 'masculine' and
> 'feminine' are purely specific, limited phenomena which have
> been mythologised by people. They are man-made (not
> woman-made). Excepting up and down, night and day
> (maybe). Out in space there is no up or down, no day or
> night, and in the point of view space can give us, I think there
> is no 'opposite' sex – what a word! Opposite what? The
> Eternal Feminine and the Eternal Masculine become the
> poetic fancies of a weakly dimorphic species trying to imitate
> every other species in a vain search for what is 'natural'.[17]

Throughout her work Russ is both constructing a space for women and at the same time deconstructing the 'death-dealing binary oppositions' of masculine and feminine. There is not necessarily a contradiction here: it is only when those 'ancient dualities' have been interrogated and revealed as 'specific, limited phenomena' that women can take responsibility as subjects, and as readers.

In the 1960s Russ wrote a series of stories that were later published as *The Adventures of Alyx*. For the first time a space is cleared in what Samuel Delany calls the 'over-masculinised society' of sword-and-sorcery for a woman who is not just a female sword-and-sorcery hero, like C.L. Moore's Jirel, but who, in Delany's words again, represents a 'proto-feminist consciousness'. In his perceptive if idiosyncratic essay on Alyx in *The Jewel-Hinged Jaw* (when he complains about the coldness of Russ's prose) Delany points to the centrality of relationships between women in the stories: 'Bluestocking', 'Picnic on Paradise' and 'The Second Inquisition' are variations on a theme, that of a worldly woman overseeing the maturation of one who is not so worldly (Alyx and Edarra, Alyx and Iris, and the 'visitor' and the narrator respectively). The Alyx stories are wonderful: vigorous, playful and joyfully at ease with the richness of the sword-and-sorcery tradition with its expression of conflict between cultures and histories, between magic and rationalism. Tanith Lee is the only other woman writer I know to grasp the subversive potentialities of sword-and-sorcery while retaining its popular framework. As Delany says, the Alyx stories are set in an overdetermined universe, which is what one learns living on the margins. 'The Second Inquisition' signals, according to Delany, the end of 'early Russ'.[18] Certainly it seems as if a proto-feminist consciousness has become a feminist one.

'When It Changed' shows a separatist utopia, in existence for thirty generations, about to be changed for ever by the reappearance of men. In a short introduction to its reprinting in *The Zanzibar Cat* Russ gives it a political history: 'This story won the Nebula Award, given by the Science Fiction Writers of America, for 1972. Three years before, feminism had hit the university at which I was then teaching and in the crash of failing marriages and the sturm-und-drang of fights at parties, this story wrote itself. (My feminist novel, *The Female Man*, was a later and very different project.)'[19]

Although I think *The Female Man* is a very different project (whether in the same way as Russ suggests is another question —you certainly have to be on your toes with her elliptical asides) it is a little disingenuous to suggest that 'When It Changed' wrote itself: it is very much more carefully crafted than Joanna Russ would like us to believe. It is a simple story that is full of surprises and challenges, that immediately demands of the reader a political involvement. It is worth quoting in full the opening paragraph to show the consummate cunning with which Joanna Russ challenges notions of the normal.

Katy drives like a maniac; we must have been doing over 120 km/hr on those turns. She's good, though, extremely good, and I've seen her take the whole car apart and put it together again in a day. My birthplace on Whileaway was largely given to farm machinery and I refuse to wrestle with a five-gear shift at unholy speeds, not having been brought up to it, but even

> on those turns in the middle of the night, on a country road as bad as only our district can make them, Katy's driving didn't scare me. The funny thing about my wife, though: she will not handle guns. She has even gone hiking in the forests above the 48th parallel without firearms, for days at a time. And that *does* scare me.[20]

There is nothing particularly odd about what we learn in the first three sentences, except that Katy is really remarkably good with cars, which is perhaps a little bit unusual in twentieth-century terms although not in science fiction. It is in the fourth sentence that the strangeness sets in: what is so funny about a wife not handling guns? Although she is obviously an unusual one, surely many wives don't handle guns? But that 'will not' is odd: it somehow throws a question mark over the word – usually unproblematic – 'wife'. What kind of a world is this, where it seems a 'wife' is expected to handle a gun as part of the normal course of things?

What is called into question here is the relationship between the narrator and Katy. Who is the narrator? If Katy is a wife then we are prompted by a learned devotion to dualism to supply the narrator with the label 'husband'. But what husband ever spoke in quite such egalitarian terms? It is only later that we discover that the narrator, too, is a wife: that on Whileaway women who are committed to each other, who are raising daughters, are all 'wives'. A 'wife' is no longer one half of a binary 'whole': thus the absence of a hierarchical tone in the opening paragraph. The reader has been forced to reflect on what she brings to the text, what expectations are brought to the description of any relationship between two people in a patriarchal world.

The men that come to Whileaway are trapped by notions of oppositional sexual dualism that blind them to the fact that an all-female society has not simply existed for six centuries but has actually developed. Whileawayans have reached the point where an industrial revolution is a real possibility: they are approaching it with intelligence and caution. What the men completely fail to see are the glories of Whileaway – everything, in fact, that makes it a utopia. Janet, the narrator, has fought three duels, borne two children, and is the chief of police. The economy is based on agriculture; but physical labour underwrites physical freedom.

What is invigorating about the inhabitants of Whileaway is their boldness. Janet foresees the inevitability of change, and asks her daughter, sadly and curiously, to imagine the future.

> 'Yuki,' I said, 'do you think you could fall in love with a man?' and she whooped derisively.
> 'With a ten-foot toad!' said my tactful child.[21]

The men are 'heavy as draft horses' and speak in 'blurred, deep voices'. Their assumption of their own necessity, and, further, their superiority, is portrayed with economy and wit. But the story rests on a basis of essentialism: the women are great because they are women, the men oppressive and horrible because they are men.

I think much of the appeal to feminists of 'When It Changed' is to do with when it was written. Even if it didn't 'write itself', it seems all of a piece with the early days of sixties and seventies feminist consciousness: the bold simplicity of the parameters; what seemed like the sudden glaring obviousness of male oppression; the ease with which men can be mocked and the danger of doing so (Russ has been and continues to be vilified; it must get very wearing); the centrality of lesbian relationships. Although the importance of this latter remains throughout Russ's work, many of her stories of the eighties explore sexuality more through a questioning of gender identity, as in the linked stories of *Extra(Ordinary) People*.

The Female Man is a more complex undertaking. Its changing styles and changing voices make it quite difficult to read. It is both a novel and a polemic. It is inventive, wild, funny and, as Marilyn Hacker has said, it 'invents itself as it goes along'.[22]

I will begin with a quote about life on Whileaway, which makes up the whole of section XVLLI or Part Four of *The Female Man*:

> There's no being out too late in Whileaway, or up too early, or in the wrong part of town, or unescorted. You cannot fall out of the kinship web and become sexual prey for strangers, for there is no prey and there are no strangers – the web is worldwide. In all of Whileaway there is no one who can keep you from going where you please (though you may risk your life, if that sort of thing appeals to you), no one who will

follow you and try to embarrass you by whispering obscenities in your ear, no one who will attempt to rape you, no one who will warn you of the dangers of the street, no one who will stand on street corners, hot-eyed and vicious, jingling loose change in his pants pocket, bitterly bitterly sure that you're a cheap floozy, hot and wild, who likes it, who can't say no, who's making a mint off it, who inspires him with nothing but disgust, and who wants to drive him crazy.

On Whileaway eleven-year-old children strip and live naked in the wilderness above the forty-seventh parallel, where they meditate, stark naked or covered with leaves, sans pubic hair, subsisting on the roots and berries so kindly planted by their elders. You can walk around the Whileawayan equator twenty times (if the feat takes your fancy and you live that long) with one hand on your sex and in the other an emerald the size of a grapefruit. All you'll get is a tired wrist.

While here, where *we* live — !23

On Whileaway women enjoy the physical and spiritual freedom that allows them not to be women, but to be human. For on Whileaway there are no men to define women, and to constrain them in that definition. The impossibility of being a woman and human is the central paradox around which *The Female Man* is constructed. This paradox remains unsolved: though Russ reveals it to us, unpicks its various strands. Her method is exemplified by the above quotation. The vision of Whileawayan freedom is tempered, and modified, by the comment at the end. Where is 'here' and who is 'we'? When Joanna Russ chooses to play the omniscient author she refuses to put on the mantle of its corollary, the absent author. Russ as author is present throughout *The Female Man* in a variety of guises. The reader may choose to think that 'we' refers to herself and Joanna Russ the author, and indeed that 'here' refers to the contemporary Western capitalist world: in this case the reader may be correct, but her assumption rests on shifting sands.

The Female Man breaks all formal rules of narrative fiction. It has no beginning-middle-end, no clear relationship between author and characters and, indeed, no clear relationship between text and meaning. While flagrantly flouting what can be seen as patriarchal conventions (for a fascinating discussion of the 'metaphor of paternity', with its conflation of fatherhood, mastership and ownership into the very word 'author', see the opening pages of Sandra Gilbert's and Susan Gubar's *The Madwoman in the Attic: The Woman Writer and the Nineteenth-Century Literary Imagination* – the notions they discuss are not confined to the nineteenth century), it resists, too, any attempt to substitute a feminine convention for a masculine one.

Here the female man is describing how she first had to turn into a woman before she could turn into a man (Part Seven, section 1):

> You will notice that even my diction is becoming feminine, thus revealing my true nature; I am not saying 'Damn' any more, or 'Blast'; I am putting in lots of qualifiers like 'rather', I am writing in these breathless little feminine tags, she threw herself down on the bed, I have no structure (she thought), my thoughts seep out shapelessly like menstrual fluid, it is all very female and deep and full of essences, it is very primitive and full of 'ands', it is called 'run-on sentences'.[24]

Russ's refusal of conventional narrative techniques is mocked as 'the tired tricks of anti-novelists' in a section (Part Seven, section III) of previews of the book, which starts, 'We would gladly have listened to her (they said) *if only she had spoken like a lady*. But they are liars and the truth is not in them.'[25] Russ consistently refuses to speak as a lady, just as she refuses to speak as a woman. *The Female Man* challenges the simple notion of an author speaking and her readers hearing. (Poul Anderson's 'Reply to a Lady', mentioned earlier, includes a marvellously disingenuous sentence – 'I think she simply let her fervor in a cause run away with her' – which is surely echoed in such phrases here as '. . . really important issues are neglected while . . . another shrill polemic which the . . .' Here, of course, I am suggesting that there is an easily decodable relationship between the text and real world but it is one I cannot resist.)

Defining her own book, and then mocking that definition, undermines the authority of the author as much as the authority of the critic. Russ speaks always from the margins, from the area that Mary Ellmann describes in *Thinking About Women*, and from where she too speaks (and *The Female Man* wittily fictionalises many of Ellmann's 'sexual analogies'), the area of ironic anti-authoritarianism. Or, in Kristeva's terms, she exploits the subversive potentiality of the margins.

The book is divided into nine parts, each subdivided 'into sections of varying length, some consisting of a few words or lines, others of several pages. Some sections have titles ('How Whileawayans Celebrate' or 'The Great Happiness Contest (this happens a lot)') but most don't. None of the Parts are titled, although section I of Part Nine consists of the sentence 'This is the book of Joanna.'[26] The sections are made up of a narrative of events around the various Js – Janet, Jeannine, Joanna, Jael – who in some sense are the 'characters' of the book, and also include dialogue, meditation, polemic, satire and factual accounts from any of the histories that are recounted.

The speaking 'I' constantly changes: sometimes it represents Janet Evason, sometimes Joanna, sometimes (though less often) Jeannine Dadier (who exists in a slightly different late 1960s from the one we are familiar with) and sometimes, and powerfully, Jael, otherwise known as Alice-Jael Reasoner, assassin, who appears briefly at the beginning of Part Two to warn of, or threaten, her later reappearance. Russ also offers both the 'us' of readers and author, and the 'us' of author and Janet. The 'I' of Jael sometimes takes over from the authorial 'I': both are intrusive, bullying, anguished and disagreeable.

For example, when Jeannine imagines she has fallen in love with an actor, this Jael/'I' first sneers, then 'shouted at her and beat her on the back and on the head; oh I was an enraged and evil spirit there in the theatre lobby, but she continued holding poor X by the hands – little did he know what hopes hung on him as she continued (I say) to hold on to his hands and look into his flattered eyes.'[27] The next day Jeannine decides, finally, that she will marry her old love Cal (even though he's so rude to her cat), and the 'I' stands 'like Atropos in the corner, with my arm around the shadow of her dead self . . .'[28]

We have seen the narrator as death before; we also have the author as voyeur, insinuating (or intruding) between reader and text to reveal the reader's own complicity. For example, Janet Evason finds herself an all-American family to stay with in Anytown, USA and, despite the Whileawayan taboos against cross-age sex, falls passionately, and mutually in love with the teenage daughter of the house, Laura Rose Wilding. (It is perhaps in Laura, and not in any of the Js, that the most realistic picture is given of the conflicts forced by a patriarchal culture on an ambitious, intelligent young woman; it is Laura who recognises the dead hand of self-denial that her culture is forcing on her simply because she is female.) The omniscient, organising 'I' of Jael, who has been hanging by a claw from the window curtain while the preliminary declarations of love and lust are being made, follows Janet and Laura upstairs making sententious comments the while ('God will punish, I said'), but there's no way she's going to sacrifice her authorial prerogative of being there. 'They'll be doing it with the dog next', she says (and you can imagine her rolling up her ghostly eyeballs), as they passionately, tenderly and clumsily make love.[29]

In the final part of the book, Part Nine, the scene is re-enacted. This is the 'book of Joanna' and the ghostly authorial, voyeuristic 'I' has been banished: the author is now a character in her own fiction as well as narrator. The reader is now voyeur and is forced to look at the political meaning of a woman making love to a woman.

> Now they'll tell me it's because I'm a Lesbian, I mean that's why I'm dissatisfied with things. That's not true. It's not because I'm a Lesbian. It's because I'm a *tall, blonde, blue-eyed Lesbian*.
>
> Does it count if it's your best friend? Does it count if it's her mind you love through her body? Does it count if you love men's bodies but hate men's minds? Does it count if you still love yourself?[30]

Here, it seems to me, by parodying normative adolescent heterosexual anxieties through placing them within a marginal sexual position, Joanna Russ is ironically and gracefully opening up the subversive possibilities of the representation of lesbianism. She transforms the idea of a girl's rite of passage by refusing its previous meaning of entrance into the 'death-dealing binary' of woman and man.

The plot of *The Female Man* could cause quite a headache if mulled over too long. It is based on the science fictional premise of parallel probable worlds, but is subversive of the classic SF paradox of time travel in which the present is changed by travel into the past, resulting in a mirror-like multiplication of selves as in Heinlein's 'By His Bootstraps' and 'All You Zombies', or a view of history as upside down causality as in Garry Kilworth's 'Let's Go to Golgotha'.

As is explained in Part One, section VI:

> . . . the paradox of time travel ceases to exist, for the Past one visits is never one's own Past but always somebody else's; or rather, one's visit to the Past instantly creates another Present (one in which the visit has already happened) and what you visit is the Past belonging to that Present – an entirely different matter from your own Past. And with each decision you make (back there in the Past) that new probable universe itself branches, creating simultaneously a new Past and a new Present, or to put it plainly, a new universe . . .[31]

And so the relationship between our here and now and Whileaway is explained:

> Thus it is probable that Whileaway – a name for the Earth ten centuries from now, but not our Earth, if you follow me – will find itself not at all affected by this sortie into somebody else's past. And vice versa, of course. The two might as well be independent worlds.
> Whileaway, you may gather, is in the future.
> But not *our* future.[32]

Whileaway is thus placed in a relativistic position to our own world just as strong, handsome, woman-loving, duelling Janet is placed in a relativistic position to the other Js. Nothing so simple as role models is offered here. Whileaway is more complex than it appeared in 'When It Changed', and more complex than the positivistic universe in Marge Piercy's *Woman on the Edge of Time*, where the existence of Mattapoisett depends upon a conscious choice made by people in the present. This latter reflects a kind of revolutionary idealism and faith in the efficacy of agency, or indeed of cause and effect. Joanna Russ is much less certain.

The plot of *The Female Man* culminates in a choice offered by Jael to her 'otherselves', whom she has gathered together in the hope that they might put their universe at the service of the war being waged by her people, the Womanlanders, against the Manlanders. The soppy, dreamy Jeannine rather takes to Jael; more, anyway, than fastidious Joanna does, or indeed Janet 'whom we don't believe in and whom we deride but who is in secret our savior from utter despair, who appears Heaven-high in our dreams with a mountain under each arm and the ocean in her pocket'.[33] But this is not a choice that exists outside of the text. Indeed, all the different 'I's are waved goodbye to at the end: Janet, Joanna, Jeannine, Jael, Joanna Russ. Jael, the 'specialist in disguises' will reappear in *Extra (Ordinary) People*, where her visit as a Faery Prince to a feudal kingdom which she describes briefly here ('I lived in a dank stone castle with ghastly sanitary arrangements and worse beds for a year and a half'[34]) is the subject of the hilarious 'What Did You Do During the Revolution, Grandma?' Joanna Russ, as we know, reappears.

Although the Js, it transpires, are all variations on the same genotype (Jeannine, Joanna and Janet being, in Jael's view, the Young, the Weak and the Strong) they do not form the different parts of one whole. For Joanna Russ's view is not a holistic one; her concern is not to construct a 'whole' or consistent self, but instead to deconstruct, to pick apart, to open up. There is no 'real' J which the others express parts of, just as there is no 'real' world which others parody or satirise. The desire the reader may have for Joanna's world to be ours (it is contemporary and she does share a name with the author) is disallowed by the author who recreates herself as a prickly fictional character. Indeed it is hard to imagine a more discontented grumbling fractious crowd of Js than jostle through these pages.

The final section of Part Seven, section V, begins: 'Jeannine, Janet, Joanna. Something's going to happen.'[35] Each of these three speaks at some length, and uninterrupted, before, in Part Eight, they are 'collected' by Jael. Joanna, who is not necessarily the authorial 'I' but who sometimes seems very close to her, attempts to describe the construction of herself as a woman.

> There is the vanity training, the obedience training, the self-effacement training, the deference training, the dependency training, the stupidity training, the placation training. How am I to put this together with my human life, my intellectual life, my solitude, my transcendence, my brains and my fearful, fearful ambition? I failed miserably and thought it was my own fault. You can't unite woman and human any more than you can unite matter and anti-matter; they are designed not to be stable together and they make just as big an explosion inside the head of the unfortunate girl who believes in both.[36]

The Female Man describes this explosion and Joanna Russ watches it. We are not (really) allowed to choose any of the women in the book as role models (although the author is not so cruel as to disallow all feelings of affection between reader and character) because of the position from which the book is written, a position in which 'there is no "opposite" sex'. From there we can see what it is that makes up 'woman': nothing can be taken for granted.

In the same way, the choice that Jael offers is not a real one. The reader is not allowed to make a political choice vicariously, for there is no coherent 'I' with whom she can identify. Russ disclaims the conventional authorial role of seeming to offer a resolution. Instead, as shown earlier, she apostrophises the book itself, claiming for it political effectiveness and demanding responsibility from her readers.

I think Marilyn Hacker describes the book well when she says 'Its events reverberate in the reader's mind, setting off possibilities, just as the four protagonists reverberate in each other's.' This is one of the reasons she gives for why she wants to read it again and again.[37]

Before we leave *The Female Man* I would like to offer one last extract from this eminently quotable book for no other reason than it makes me laugh out loud every time I read it:

> I know that somewhere, just to give me the lie, lives a beautiful (got to be beautiful), intellectual, gracious, cultivated, charming woman who has eight children, bakes her own bread, cakes and pies, takes care of her own house, does her own cooking, brings up her own children, holds down a demanding nine-to-five job at the top decision-making level in a man's field, and is adored by her equally successful husband because although a hard-driving, aggressive business executive with eye of eagle, heart of lion, tongue of adder, muscles of gorilla (she looks just like Kirk Douglas), she comes home at night, slips into a filmy negligée and a wig, and turns instanter into a Playboy dimwit, thus laughingly dispelling the canard that you cannot be eight people simultaneously with two different sets of values. *She has not lost her femininity*.
> And I'm Marie of Rumania.[38]

The Two of Them (1979) turns out to be a more pessimistic novel than *The Female Man*. It tells the story of how two espionage agents, colleagues and lovers from parallel universes, visit a quasi-Islamic, newly formed, grossly misogynistic society called Ka'abah, and kidnap, or liberate, a twelve-year-old girl, Zubeydeh, who passionately wants to become a poet but whose likely fate is to turn into a medicated mother-of-sons like her own mother, or to be locked up in an excrement-smeared cell like her mad Aunt Dunya, who also wanted to be a poet. As Zubeydeh says later, as a kind of refrain, 'the gentlemen always think the ladies have gone mad'.[39]

The abduction becomes a watershed in the relationship between the two TransTemp agents, Irene Waskiewicz and Ernst Neumann, partly, although certainly not entirely, because their forced hasty departure means they have to leave Zubeydeh's mother behind – not that she wants to come, but this is something Irene does not or will not recognise. The novel is partly (and I would stress partly) about Irene and Ernst; she with a passionate active sexuality and a fine tough intelligence, he so handsome with 'the beaked nose, high cheek-bones, and deep-set dark eyes of a desert prophet'[40] and a sexuality that responds to Irene, that does not trammel or constrain. But alas, this is not a comedy, 'where Ernst would marry Irene in the end.'[41]

The journey back from Ka'abah to Centre becomes a rite of passage both for Irene and for Zubeydeh. Irene as secret agent, wife-stealer (a fearful monster from a Ka'abahan play-cycle), lover, as female man, comes to recognise that it is not just on Ka'abah that conditions are different for women and for men; indeed that it is different conditions – social, economic, political – that inform the differences that make up sexual, racial and class oppressions everywhere.

Irene, existing as a female man under the Law of the Father, fails to recognise the variety and the contradictions of desire. Her analysis allows only for internalised oppression; it is Ernst's vision that is broad enough to allow for conflict, but that is because he sees, and speaks, from a privileged position. Irene learns from the girl-child Zubeydeh of the needs and wants that she, grown up, has repressed in herself. The figure of the girl-child is exremely important in Russ's work, and it is linked here with a mother-figure – Irene's 1950s mother Rose, the original 'friend' of Ernst – who also must be faced up to and come to terms with. The theme is powerfully reworked in a 1982 story 'The Little Dirty Girl', in which Russ appears as Russ and is pushed into a reconciliation with her former five-year-old self and with her own mother.

Ernst Neumann represents the Law of the Father, under which women are either silenced or speak, like Scheherazade, only as a strategy for survival. Irene, with infinite regret, recognises that she is 'too old for a Daddy'.[42] Once she questions her own position as female man, then Ernst, who had 'judged her worthy . . . now [he] judges her mad'.[43] He instructs the ship's computer to reject her in all her various identities, but she re-enters herself as Irenee (the name that Ernst had earlier given her). Then she shoots him.

Here Russ is deliberately testing her readers' responses. She insists on her role as author.

> It occurs to me that she only stunned him, that soon he'll get up, facing nothing worse than a temporary embarrassment (because they can't find him in the computer), that he'll come looking for her, penitent, contrite, having learned his lesson.
> Well, no, not really.[44]

What is the lesson? It is something to do with the traditional romance or comic forms that make up science fiction. John Clute describes the lesson of both *The Female Man* and *The Two of Them* as 'you think I'm telling you X; well I wouldn't tell you X if my life depended on it. In fact my life depends on my not allowing you to get away with hearing X from my lips. Your willingness to suspend disbelief so as to luxuriate in the telling of X is tantamount to complicity with the invidious systemic violation of women in this world, whose roots are homologous with the engendering impulses behind traditional genre fiction, or X, baby.'[45]

For John Clute *The Two of Them* fails because 'Irene is too much for it' and '. . . reality has intruded'. But it is the shooting of Ernst that seems to stick, for in his criticism of the formal failings of the story the subjective note nonetheless intrudes, as in the final clause of this sentence: 'Irene finds she cannot any longer live with Ernst, despite his humanity and his lack of any avowedly sexist tendencies, though Irene does seem entirely capable of shaping his responses into a sexist mould.'[46] Well, she does criticise him for saying 'people' when he means 'men'. But for me it is not just his 'humanity' that makes the shooting of Ernst distressing; it is also his sexiness (and you don't find much of that in science fiction).

But the book does not end with the shooting of Ernst. Who indeed are 'The Two of Them'? This title can describe Irene and Zubeydeh as well as Irene and Ernst. Irene has killed the Father, but her journey into adulthood is predicated also upon the acceptance of her girl-child self, and of her mother back in the world very like our own. This is where the book ends: Irene has become a thirty-year-old divorcee in a hotel room in Albuquerque, with a child to support. And she dreams, of a valley of bones, dead, dry, sterile, over which a faint wind blows, whispering, *'Shall these bones live?'* and again, louder, *'Shall these bones live!'* For Irene, 'It is nothing living but only the memory of another voice, the voice of Dunyazad, Shahrazad's sister, that mad, dead, haunted woman who could not tell stories, who could not save herself.'[47]

This is what John Clute describes as 'a splitting grey morning headache in Albuquerque', the end of a lesson that is the result of Irene's inability to 'ultimately inhabit genre'. [48] Whereas for some readers *The Two of Them* seems to fail as a story, for me it works because it throws open the traditional genre narrative. Underlying any formal criticism is the position of the reader as a gendered subject. Any reading is subjective, and it is an awareness of that subjectivity that Joanna Russ insists upon in her readers.

In the 'author's comments on the story' (so dear to the hearts of editors of science fiction anthologies) preceding 'Sword Blades and Poppy Seed' in Jessica Amanda Salmonson's *Heroic Visions*, Joanna Russ writes: 'Samuel Delany once said that the question, "Where do you authors get your crazy ideas?" couldn't be answered because the question itself was a mistaken one. Obviously, he was mistaken.'[49] Joanna Russ then quotes as an epigraph from Ellen Moers' *Literary Women*: 'For this was something new, something distinctive of modernity itself, that the written word in its most memorable form . . . became increasingly and steadily the work of women.'[50]

'Sword Blades and Poppy Seed' is narrated by the ghost of George Sand, describing the very moment of her metamorphosis from the twenty-seven-year-old Aurore Dudevant. It affords a gently ironic commentary on the poem of the same title by Amy Lowell (to be written ninety years later) and on Amy Lowell herself, the 'sister of the President of Harvard'. This short short story offers more than one answer to Delany's question, it seems to me. First, it places the genesis of ideas within a tradition, or a community, of women writers; such a simple acknowledgment does much to undermine the bourgeois notion of the solitary (male) genius. Further, through the figure of the narrator/protagonist Aurore Dudevant, it conjures up, without having to describe, the physical, material and social obstacles that women must overcome in order to write. The epigraph refers us at once to Ellen Moers' inspiring work, where she quotes from George Sand's *Histoire de ma Vie* (which runs to twenty volumes). Sand describes how in Paris, on the advice of her mother (who had done the same thing herself but for solely economic reasons – no money for dresses), she dressed as a man.

> So I had made for myself a *redingote-guérite* [the long, shapeless man's outer coat of the 1830s – Moers] in heavy gray cloth, pants and vest to match. With a gray hat and a large woolen cravat, I was a perfect first-year student. I can't express the pleasure my boots gave me: I would gladly have slept with them, as my brother did in his young age, when he got his first pair . . . No one knew me, no one looked at me, no one found fault with me; I was an atom lost in that immense crowd . . . I could make up a whole novel as I walked from one side of town to another without running into someone who would say: 'What the devil are you thinking about?'[51] [This is a shorter version of the extract quoted by Ellen Moers.]

Again, as in Tiptree's work, the need to be invisible as a woman before living as a human. Sand here is taking on the protective coloration of those around her, that (other) half of the human race for whom the streets of the city are wide open; but, as Ellen Moers describes, this is only one aspect; for Sand, by dint of extraordinary hard work and versatility, did not have to become a Female Man in order to succeed. Instead, she begins, declares Moers, 'a literary lifestyle distinctly modern in its middle-class informality, and child-centred domesticity, and dominating presence: the efficient, versatile, overworked, modern mother.'[52]

All this, the cost, the difficulty, the determination, is implied by Joanna Russ. The actual story shows us Aurore Dudevant, with her first novel *Indiana* as yet unfinished, emerging from the theatre one night in her man's guise and going to the shop of an old man, or possibly an old woman, who is a *Marchand des Mots*, where she finds, and claims as hers, the sword blades and poppy seed, the 'dreams and visions', and the 'hard edged weapons' with which to transform them into words. It is the shopkeeper, the magician, who gives Aurore her name, her own name as a writer: George Sand. There she learns of the other women who have been there before her, Jane Austen, Harriet Beecher Stowe, Mary Shelley and many many others, who have each found, and claimed, something different.

The story is also about the danger of this undertaking and the price that is exacted for it. Aurore looks around the shop, and describes her feelings:

> Did my head go round? Did I weep? Well, it may be that I wept a little, thinking of my ambition, my unhappy marriage, *Indiana*, my poverty. It was unthinkable then for a woman to write . . . but whatever I intended, I heard these words come out, 'Which of these is for me?' But the French is stronger; it says *à moi*, which means Mine.[53]

Joanna Russ shows us the responsibility that writers have towards their ideas, towards their art; and at the same time she forces a reciprocal responsibility upon readers. The ghost narrator ends by saying: 'I have told you (with some help from Madame Lowell) where we got the tools of our trade, but do you now want to find out what those tools really were? Are you truly curious? *Then read our books.*'[54] Again, it seems to me, Joanna Russ has constituted the reader not only as subject but as female subject.

Ideas do not come from an indescribable realm to which only 'the artist' has privileged access. Writing has a material base, and the claims made by an artist on her art must be paid for. Aurore Dudevant must pay to become George Sand.

> Unlike the sister of the President of Harvard, who affects to be revolted at this point (but don't believe it; it's all the exigencies of the metre), I am of good bourgeois stock, at least on one side, and know that what one gets one must pay for. But how? In what currency? And that was exactly the question I asked. 'With time,' said the old man. 'And work.

The work of a lifetime, Madame.' And then he called me by a name that was not my own . . .[55]

Joanna Russ transforms Amy Lowell's poem into a story of sword-and-sorcery, no less. In it we hear the clash of magic and rationalism, of the dialectical relationship between the imagination and its material base. Joanna Russ situates herself within a tradition of women writing and struggling to write, or living and struggling to live. And she, like Ursula Le Guin and Alice Sheldon and many other women, has found that science fiction offers room for that struggle.

Notes

Introduction

1 Brian Aldiss, with David Wingrove, *Trillion Year Spree: The History of Science Fiction*, p 25.
2 Kingsley Amis, *New Maps of Hell*, p 99.
3 ibid, p 54.
4 Jeanne Gomoll, 'An Open Letter to Joanna Russ'.
5 ibid.

1 Representation and the Natural Woman

1 Joanna Russ, 'The Image of Women in Science Fiction'.
2 ibid.
3 ibid.
4 ibid.
5 ibid.
6 ibid.
7 Joanna Russ, unpublished letter, August 1987.
8 Poul Anderson, 'Reply to a Lady'.
9 Philip K. Dick, 'An Open Letter from Philip K. Dick'.
10 Mary Ellmann, *Thinking About Women*, pp 148–150.
11 Joanna Russ, *The Female Man*, pp 140–41.
12 Susan Wood, 'Women and Science Fiction'.

2 Science Fiction Narratives

1 Peter Nicholls and John Clute, *The Encylopedia of Science Fiction*, p 159.

2 Rosemary Jackson, *Fantasy: The Literature of Subversion*, p 63.
3 ibid, p 99.
4 Brian Aldiss, with David Wingrove, *Trillion Year Spree*, p 52.

3 Travelling Heroinism

1 It is odd, and presumably coincidental, that the name of Le Guin's enigmatic founder of the colony Anarres is the same as that by which the Piedmontese Jews refer to Christ, a term described by Primo Levi as 'completely cryptic and indecipherable' in his fascinating account of the secret jargon of his people in *The Periodic Table* – a book which must surely rank as the most marvellous fusion of science and literature (New York: Schocken, 1984; London: Michael Joseph, 1985, trans. Raymond Rosenthal). The passage referred to is on p 10, Abacus edition, 1986.
2 Ellen Moers, *Literary Women*, p 126.
3 ibid, p 91.
4 ibid, p 91.
5 ibid, p 93.
6 Rosemary Jackson, 'Frankenstein: A Myth for Women'.
7 Josephine Saxton, *The Travails of Jane Saint and Other Stories*, p 40.
8 ibid, pp 18–19.
9 ibid, p 89.
10 ibid, p 45.
11 Josephine Saxton, introductory note to *The Travails of Jane Saint and Other Stories*, 'A Plea to my Readers'.

4 Amazons: Feminist Heroines or Men in Disguise?

1 Joanna Russ, '*Amor Vincit Fœminam*'.
2 Joanna Russ, 'The Clichés from Outer Space'.
3 Susan Wood, 'Women and Science Fiction'.
4 Jessica Amanda Salmonson, *Amazons!*, p 14.

5 When Women Write of Women's Rule

1 Marion Zimmer Bradley, *The Ruins of Isis*, p 43.
2 ibid, p 45.
3 ibid, p 64.
4 ibid, p 230.
5 ibid, p 250.
6 ibid, p 233–4.
7 ibid, p 285.
8 ibid, p 284.
9 Another favourite is the way that women without men seem to organise their societies as if they were ants or bees, so desperate are they for the order of hierarchies. See, for example, John Wyndham's novella, *Consider Her Ways* (collected in *Consider Her Ways and Others*, London: Michael Joseph, 1961). So horrified is the heroine by the future all-female society whose citizens are rigidly defined by function – mothers, servitors, workers – that when she gets back to the present day she is determined to destroy the possibility of its coming into existence by killing the scientist who is responsible for the virus that wipes all men from the face of the earth. Alas, her research is not sufficiently rigorous, and she murders the wrong man.
10 Marion Zimmer Bradley, *The Ruins of Isis*, p 258
11 Jayge Carr, *Leviathan's Deep*, p 105.
12 Peter Nicholls, *The Encyclopedia of Science Fiction*, p 666. It is, however, described as ingenious.
13 Esmé Dodderidge, *The New Gulliver*.

6 The Dream of Elsewhere: Feminist Utopias

1 Russ's article is a consideration of eleven books and stories: Monique Wittig's *Les Guérillères*, Ursula Le Guin's *The Dispossessed*, Joanna Russ's *The Female Man*, Samuel Delany's *Triton*, Marion Zimmer Bradley's *The Shattered Chain*, Marge Piercy's *Woman on the Edge of Time*, Sally Miller Gearhart's *The Wanderground*, Catherine Madsen's 'Commodore Bork and the Compost', two stories by Alice Sheldon, 'Your Faces, O My Sisters! Your Faces Filled of Light!' (as Raccoona Sheldon) and 'Houston, Houston, Do You Read?' (as James Tiptree Jr) and Suzy McKee

Charnas' *Motherlines*.
2 Carol Pearson, 'Coming Home: Four Feminist Utopias and Patriarchal Experience'. *Future Females*, ed Marleen S. Barr, p 63.
3 ibid, p 68.
4 ibid, p 67.
Jóanna Russ, 'Recent Feminist Utopias'. *Future Females*, p 73.
6 ibid, p 76.
7 ibid, p 77.
8 ibid, p 79.
9 ibid, p 80.
10 ibid, p 71.
11 ibid, p 83.
12 Ann J. Lane, introduction to *Herland*, p xix.
13 ibid, p xx.
14 For a fascinating account of feminist involvement in the socialist utopian movements see Barbara Taylor's *Eve and the New Jerusalem*, London: Virago, 1983.
15 Ann J. Lane, introduction to *Herland*, p xi.
16 Shulamith Firestone, *The Dialectic of Sex: The Case for Feminist Revolution*, p 211.
17 ibid, p 135.
18 ibid, p 169.
19 Dale Spender, *For the Record*, p 89.
20 Shulamith Firestone, *The Dialectic of Sex*, pp 169–71.
21 ibid, p 192.
22 Joanna Russ, 'Recent Feminist Utopias', p 83.
23 Marge Piercy, *Woman on the Edge of Time*, p 31.
24 ibid, p 106.
25 ibid, p 134.
26 Joanna Russ, 'Recent Feminist Utopias', p 84.
27 Marge Piercy, *Woman on the Edge of Time*, p 141.
28 Sally Miller Gearhart, *The Wanderground*, p 2.
29 ibid, pp 2–3.
30 ibid, p 4.
31 ibid, p 125.
32 ibid, p 106.
33 ibid, p 110.
34 ibid, p 198.
35 ibid, p 201.

36 ibid, p 64.
37 ibid, p 81.
38 ibid, p 157.
39 ibid, p 208–209.
40 Joanna Russ, 'Recent Feminist Utopias', p 81.

7 The Reduction of Women: Dystopias

1 Daphne Patai, Introduction to *Swastika Night* (1985), p xi.
2 For a detailed analysis of *Swastika Night* and *Nineteen Eighty Four*, see Daphne Patai's 'Orwell's Despair, Burdekin's Hope: Gender and Power in Dystopia', *Women's Studies International Forum*, Vol 7, No 2, pp 85–95.
3 Zoë Fairbairns, 'On Writing *Benefits*', *No Turning Back*, p 255.

8 The Vicissitudes of Love

1 Shulamith Firestone, *The Dialectic of Sex*, p 121.
2 Joanna Russ, *The Female Man*, p 199.
3 Angela Carter, *Heroes and Villains*, p 83.
4 ibid, p 89.
5 ibid, p 89.
6 ibid, p 72.
7 ibid, p 68.
8 ibid, p 72.
9 ibid, p 86.
10 ibid, p 107.
11 ibid, p 107.
12 ibid, p 9.
13 ibid, p 41.
14 ibid, p 26.
15 ibid, p 72.

9 Authority and Sentiment: Is There a Women's Science Fiction?

1 Virginia Woolf *Contemporary Writers*, p 124.
2 Mary Ellmann, *Thinking About Women*, p 172.

3 ibid, p 163.
4 ibid, p 166.
5 Jenny Wolmark, 'Science Fiction and Feminism'. *Foundation*, No 37, p 50.
6 ibid, pp 50–51.

10 Feminism and Science Fiction

1 Susan Wood, 'Women and Science Fiction'.
2 Rhoda Lerman, epigraph to *The Book of the Night*.
3 Pamela Zoline, 'The Heat Death of the Universe'.
4 ibid.
5 ibid.
6 ibid.
7 ibid.
8 See Colin Greenland's, *The Entropy Exhibition* (London: Routledge, Kegan, Paul, 1983) for a detailed analysis of the major, male, 'new wave' writers.
9 James Tiptree Jr, 'The Women Men Don't See'.

11 Who is Tiptree, What is She?: James Tiptree Jr

1 James Tiptree Jr, in Charles Platt's, 'Profile: James Tiptree Jr'. *Isaac Asimov's Science Fiction Magazine*, April 1983, p 42.
2 ibid, p 42.
3 James Tiptree Jr, in *Khatru 3 & 4*, p 104.
4 Ursula K. Le Guin, introduction to *Star Songs of an Old Primate*, p ix.
5 ibid, pp x–xi. And Le Guin goes on to explore the broader ramifications of the success of Tiptree's disguise: '. . . it makes a point which no amount of argument could have made. Not only does it imperil all theories concerning the woman writer and the writer as woman, but it might make us question some of our assumptions concerning the existence of the writer *per se*.'
6 Tiptree, 'I'm too big but I love to play'.
7 Tiptree, 'And I awoke and found me here on the cold hill's side'.

8 Tiptree, 'Houston, Houston, Do You Read?'
9 ibid.
10 Tiptree, introduction to 'Your Haploid Heart' in *Star Songs*.
11 Tiptree, 'A Momentary Taste of Being'.
12 Lillian Heldreth, 'Love is the Plan, the Plan is Death: The Feminism and Fatalism of James Tiptree Jr'. *Extrapolation*, Vol. 23, p 23.
13 Tiptree (as Raccoona Sheldon), 'The Screwfly Solution'.
14 ibid.
15 ibid.
16 ibid.
17 Tiptree in *Khatru*, p 18.
18 ibid, p 17.
19 ibid, p 17.
20 ibid, p 18.
21 ibid, p 60.
22 Tiptree, 'Mama Come Home'.
23 Platt, 'Profile: James Tiptree Jr.', p 43.
24 Tiptree, 'All the Kinds of Yes'.
25 Tiptree, 'Angel Fix'.
26 Tiptree, 'Time-Sharing Angel'.
27 ibid.
28 ibid.
29 Platt, op cit, p 33.
30 ibid, p 33.
31 ibid, p 34.
32 ibid, pp 34–5.
33 ibid, p 35.
34 ibid, p 38.
35 ibid, p 38.
36 ibid, p 38.
37 Tiptree, 'On the Last Afternoon'.
38 ibid.
39 Tiptree, 'Slow Music'.
40 ibid.
41 Tiptree, 'Out of the Everywhere'.
42 *The Starry Rift* is made up of three linked tales, which form a history lesson for two young *Comenor* of the future, chosen for them by the chief assistant librarian in the Great Central Library of Deneb University. The structure recalls

Joanna Russ's *Extra(Ordinary) People*; but where her teacher/mentor is a computer, Tiptree's is a somewhat anthropomorphised snuffly amphibian. It has been pointed out that the first tale, 'The Only Neat Thing To Do', which tells of suicide with honour, strangely foretells Tiptree's own death. Tiptree's sentimental streak is perhaps over-much to the fore in this and in her previous novel, *Brightness Falls from the Air*. Interestingly, her post-humously published story, 'Yanqui Doodle' (*IASFM*, July 1987), shows a return to the passionate ferocity of some of her earlier work. And, to make another connection with her own life, it can be seen to refer back to her own earlier rejection of US military involvement in other countries.

43 Tiptree, in *Khatru*, p 60.
44 Platt, op cit p 41.
45 ibid, p 42.
46 ibid, p 42.
47 Judith Hanna, 'The Greenskins are Here: Women, Men and Aliens'. *Contrary Modes*, p 126.
48 Robert Silverberg, introduction to *Warm Worlds and Otherwise*, p xii.
49 ibid, p xv.
50 Tiptree, 'The Women Men Don't See'.
51 Silverberg, op cit, p xviii.
52 ibid, p xvi.
53 Tiptree, 'The Women Men Don't See'.
54 ibid.
55 ibid.
56 ibid.
57 ibid.
58 ibid.
59 ibid.
60 ibid.
61 ibid.
62 ibid.
63 Hanna, op cit, p 126.
64 Tiptree, 'With Delicate Mad Hands'.
65 ibid.
66 ibid.
67 Heldreth, op cit, p 23.

12 Inner Space and the Outer Lands: Ursula K. Le Guin

1 Ursula Le Guin, 'A Citizen of Mondath'. *Foundation*, No 4, July 1973, p 20.
2 ibid, p 24.
3 ibid, p 23.
4 See Joanna Russ, 'The Image of Women in Science Fiction'.
5 Ian Watson, 'Le Guin's *The Lathe of Heaven* and the Role of Dick: The False Reality as Mediator'. In the notes to this article Ian Watson provides a useful chronological chart for Le Guin's Hainish works, which were not written in chronological sequence.
6 These introductions are collected in *The Language of the Night*, ed Susan Wood. (Page references given are to *The Language of the Night*.)
7 Le Guin, introduction *Rocannon's World*, pp 133–4.
8 Le Guin, *Rocannon's World*.
9 Le Guin, introduction *Planet of Exile*, p 140.
10 ibid, pp 140–1.
11 ibid, p 143.
12 Le Guin, introduction *City of Illusions*, p 147.
13 ibid, p 147.
14 Le Guin, 'A Citizen of Mondath', p 23.
15 Le Guin, introduction *City of Illusions*, p 146.
16 Le Guin, 'Science Fiction and Mrs Brown', pp 24–5.
17 ibid, p 16.
18 ibid, pp 26–7.
19 ibid, p 16.
20 Patrick Parrinder, 'The Alien Encounter: Or, Ms Brown and Mrs Le Guin'.
21 Le Guin, 'Is Gender Necessary?', (page references are to *The Language of the Night*, pp 161–9.) pp 167–8.
22 ibid, p 168.
23 Frederic Jameson, 'World-Reduction in Le Guin: The Emergence of "Utopian Narrative"'.
24 Rosemary Jackson, *Fantasy: The Literature of Subversion*, p 154.
25 ibid, p 173.
26 ibid, p 173.

208

27 Le Guin, 'Is Gender Necessary?', pp 162–4.
28 ibid, p 169.
29 Frederic Jameson, op cit.
30 See Samuel Delany's essay 'To Read *The Dispossessed*', pp 218–283, in *The Jewel-Hinged Jaw*.
31 Tom Moylan, *Demand the Impossible*, p 102.
32 ibid, p 110.
33 Nadia Khouri, 'The Dialectics of Power: Utopia in The Science Fiction of Le Guin, Jeury, Piercy'.
34 Moylan, op cit, p 119.
35 Le Guin, 'Science Fiction and Mrs Brown', p 26.
36 Le Guin, interviewed by Win McCormack and Ann Mendel, 'Creating Realistic Utopias: the obvious trouble with anarchism is neighbours', *Seven Days*, 11 April 1977, quoted in *The Language of the Night*, p 128.
37 Peter Nicholls, *The Encyclopedia of Science Fiction*, p 347.
38 Le Guin, reponse to the UKLG issue of *Science Fiction Studies*.
39 Le Guin, introduction *The Word for World is Forest*, pp 151–2.

13   The Absent Heroine: Suzy McKee Charnas

I

1 Charnas, Suzy McKee, 'A Woman Appeared'. *Future Females*, ed. Marleen S. Barr, p 104.
2 ibid, p 104.
3 Rosemary Jackson, *Fantasy: The Literature of Subversion*, p 154.
4 Charnas, in *Khatru 3 & 4*, p 65.
5 Charnas, 'A Woman Appeared', p 107.
6 Charnas, *Walk to the End of the World*, p 3.
7 ibid, p 4.
8 ibid, p 4.
9 ibid, p 4.
10 ibid, p 22.
11 ibid, p 22.
12 ibid, p 150.
13 ibid, p 41.
14 ibid, p 148.

15   ibid, p 53.
16   ibid, p 53.
17   Charnas, 'A Woman Appeared', p 104.
18   Charnas, *Walk*, p 55.
19   ibid, p 140.
20   ibid, p 140.
21   ibid, p 45.
22   ibid, p 46.
23   ibid, p 213.
24   ibid, p 79.
25   ibid, pp 115–6.
26   ibid, p 149.
27   ibid, p 214.
28   Charnas in *Algol*, p 22.
29   ibid, p 22.
30   Margaret Miller, 'The Ideal Woman in Two Feminist Science Fiction Utopias', p 196.
31   Charnas, 'A Woman Appeared', p 106.
32   Charnas, in *Khatru*, p 9.
33   Charnas, *Motherlines*, p 102.
34   Charnas, 'A Woman Appeared', p 106.
35   Charnas, *Motherlines*, p 37.
36   ibid, pp 227–8.
37   Miller, op cit. p 196.
38   ibid.
39   Charnas, *Motherlines*, p 112.
40   ibid, p 85.
41   ibid, p 85.
42   ibid, p 87.
43   ibid, p 18.
44   ibid, p 135.
45   ibid, p 107.
46   ibid, p 136.
47   ibid, p 146.
48   ibid, p 159.
49   ibid, p 239.

II
1   Charnas, *The Vampire Tapestry*, p 37.
2   ibid, p 41.
3   ibid, p 142.

4 ibid, p 48.
5 ibid, p 121.
6 ibid, p 162.
7 ibid, p 171.
8 ibid, p 171.
9 ibid, p 177.
10 ibid, p 178.
11 ibid, p 177.
12 ibid, p 213.
13 ibid, p 213.
14 ibid, p 223.
15 ibid, p 239.
16 ibid, p 256.
17 ibid, pp 256–7.
18 ibid, p 269.
19 ibid, p 280.
20 Charnas, 'A Woman Appeared', p 107.

14 The Reader as Subject: Joanna Russ

1 See Toril Moi, *Sexual/Textual Politics*, p 12.
2 Joanna Russ, preface to 'When It Changed', *The Zanzibar Cat*, Baen edition, p 9.
3 Toril Moi, op cit, p 13.
4 ibid, p 13.
5 Samuel Delany, 'Alyx', *The Jewel-Hinged Jaw*, pp 191–209.
6 Russ, 'Recent Feminist Utopias', p 81.
7 Russ, *We Who Are About To . . .*, p 160.
8 Russ, 'Sword Blades and Poppy Seed'.
9 Russ, *The Female Man*, pp 213–4.
10 Russ, *We Who Are About To . . .*, p 8.
11 ibid, p 61.
12 ibid, p 31.
13 ibid, p 115.
14 ibid, p 20.
15 ibid, p 128.
16 ibid, p 166.
17 Russ, in *Khatru 3 & 4*, p 47.
18 Samuel Delany, 'Alyx', p 191.
19 Russ, *The Zanzibar Cat* (Baen edition), p 9.

20 Russ, 'When It Changed', p 10.
21 ibid, p 20.
22 Marilyn Hacker, 'Science Fiction and Feminism: The Work of Joanna Russ', p 74.
23 Russ, *The Female Man*, p 82.
24 ibid, p 137.
25 ibid, p 140.
26 ibid, p 201.
27 ibid, p 125.
28 ibid, p 131.
29 ibid, p 74.
30 ibid, p 209.
31 ibid, p 7.
32 ibid, p 7.
33 ibid, pp 212–3.
34 ibid, p 188.
35 ibid, p 149.
36 ibid, p 151.
37 Marilyn Hacker, op cit, p 76.
38 Russ, *The Female Man*, pp 118–9.
39 Russ, *The Two of Them*, p 147.
40 ibid, p 1.
41 ibid, p 164.
42 ibid, pp 129 and 139.
43 ibid, p 147.
44 ibid, pp 163–4.
45 John Clute, review in *Foundation*, No 15, Jan 1979, pp 103–5.
46 ibid, p 105.
47 Russ, *The Two of Them*, p 181.
48 Clute, op cit, p 105.
49 Russ, introduction to 'Sword Blades and Poppy Seed' in *Heroic Visions* ed Jessica Amanda Salmonson, p 157.
50 Ellen Moers, *Literary Women*, preface, p ix.
51 ibid, p 9.
52 ibid, p 11.
53 Joanna Russ, 'Sword Blades and Poppy Seed'.
54 ibid.
55 ibid.

Bibliography

UK and US first editions are given wherever possible. Editions that appear in parentheses are those used for page references in the text.

Aldiss, Brian, with Wingrove, David, *Trillion Year Spree: The History of Science Fiction*. London: Gollancz, 1986.

Amis, Kingsley, *New Maps of Hell; A Survey of Science Fiction*. New York: Harcourt Brace, 1960; London: Gollancz, 1961; (London: NEL, 1969).

Anderson, Poul, 'Reply to a Lady'. *Vertex*, Vol 2, No 2, June 1974, pp 8 and 99.

Atwood, Margaret, *Survival: A Thematic Guide to Canadian Literature*. Toronto: Anansi, 1972.

The Handmaid's Tale. London: Cape, 1986.

de Beauvoir, Simone, *The Second Sex*, trans. H.M. Parshley. London: Cape, 1953; Penguin, 1972.

Bellamy, Edward, *Looking Backward: AD 2000–1887*. Boston: Tickner, 1888.

Brackett, Leigh, 'The Lake of the Gone Forever'. *Thrilling Wonder Stories*, 1949; reprinted *More Women of Wonder*, ed. Pamela Sargent.

Bradley, Marion Zimmer, *The Shattered Chain*. New York: DAW, 1976; London: Arrow, 1978.

The Ruins of Isis. Norfolk, VA: Donning/Starblaze, 1978; London: Arrow, 1980.

'The Wind People'. *If*, February 1959; reprinted in *Women of Wonder*, ed Pamela Sargent.

Brantenberg, Gerd, *The Daughters of Egalia*, trans. Louis

MacKay. London: Journeyman, 1985.

✓ Burdekin, Katharine, *Swastika Night*. London: Gollancz, 1937 (under the name Murray Constantine); London: Lawrence & Wishart, 1985. 1984 *before Orwell*

Butler, Octavia E.,
Patternmaster. New York: Doubleday, 1976.
Mind of my Mind. New York: Doubleday, 1977; London: Sidgwick & Jackson, 1978.
Survivor.New York: Doubleday, 1978; London: Sidgwick & Jackson, 1978.
Wild Seed. New York: Doubleday, 1980.
Clay's Ark. New York: St Martin's, 1984.
Dawn. New York: Warner, 1987.

Butler, Samuel, *Erewhon* and *Erewhon Revisited*. Trubner & Co, 1872, revised 1901; Grant Richards, 1901.

Carr, Jayge, *Leviathan's Deep*. New York: Doubleday, 1979; London: Sidgwick & Jackson, 1980 (London: Futura, 1980).

Carter, Angela, *The Passion of New Eve*. London: Gollancz, 1977.
Heroes and Villains. London: Heinemann, 1969 (London: Penguin, 1981).

Charnas, Suzy McKee, *Walk to the End of the World*. New York: Ballantine, 1974; London: Gollancz, 1979.
Motherlines. New York: Berkley, 1978; London: Gollancz, 1980.
The Vampire Tapestry. New York: Simon & Schuster, 1980.
Dorothea Dreams. New York: Arbor House, 1986.
Interview in *Algol*, conducted by Neal Wilgus, Winter 78/79, pp 21–5.
'A Woman Appeared'. *Future Females: A Critical Anthology*, ed. Marleen Barr. Bowling Green State University Press, 1981, pp 103–8.

Clute, John, review of *The Two of Them* in *Foundation*, No 15, Jan 1979, pp 103–5.

Delany, Samuel, *Babel–17*. New York: Ace 1966; London: Gollancz, 1967.
'To Read *The Dispossessed*'. *The Jewel-Hinged Jaw: Notes of the Language of Science Fiction*. New York: Berkley, 1977, pp 218–83.
'Alyx'. Introduction to *Alyx* by Joanna Russ, Gregg Press,

1976; *The Jewel-Hinged Jaw*, pp 191–209.

Dick, Philip K., 'An Open Letter from Philip K. Dick'. *Vertex*, Vol 2, No 4, October 1974, p 99.

Dodderidge, Esmé, *The New Gulliver, or The Adventures of Lemuel Gulliver Jr in Capovolta*. New York: Taplinger, 1979; London: Dent, 1980; The Women's Press, 1988.

Elgin, Suzette Haden, *Native Tongue*. New York: DAW, 1984; London: The Women's Press, 1985.

The Judas Rose. New York: DAW, 1986; London: The Women's Press, 1988.

Ellmann, Mary, *Thinking About Women*. New York: Harcourt Brace/Harvest, 1968; London: Virago, 1979.

Fairbairns, Zoë, *Benefits*. London: Virago, 1979.

Stand We At Last. London: Virago, 1983.

Here Today. London: Methuen, 1984.

'Relics'. *Despatches from the Frontiers of the Female Mind*, ed. Green and Lefanu. London: The Women's Press, 1985.

'On Writing *Benefits*'. *Women and Writing Newsletter*, 1980. Reprinted in *No Turning Back*. London: The Women's Press, 1981, pp 255–8.

Firestone, Shulamith, *The Dialectic of Sex: The Case for Feminist Revolution*. New York: Morrow, 1970; London: Cape, 1971 (London: The Women's Press, 1979).

Forbes, Caroline, *The Needle on Full*. London: Onlywomen Press, 1985.

Gearhart, Sally Miller, *The Wanderground: Stories of the Hill Women*. Watertown, Mass: Persephone Press, 1979; London: The Women's Press, 1985.

Gentle, Mary, *Golden Witchbreed*. London: Gollancz, 1983.

Gilbert, Sandra M. and Gubar, Susan, *The Madwoman in the Attic: The Woman Writer and the Nineteenth-Century Literary Imagination*. Yale University Press, 1979.

Gilman, Charlotte Perkins, *Herland*. Serialised in the *Forerunner*, 1915; New York: Pantheon, 1979; London: The Women's Press, 1979 and 1986.

The Yellow Wallpaper. First published 1892. Collected in *The Charlotte Perkins Gilman Reader*, ed Ann J. Lane. New York: Pantheon, 1980; London: The Women's Press, 1981.

Gomoll, Jeanne, 'An Open Letter to Joanna Russ' in *Aurora*, Vol 10, No 1, Winter 1986–7, pp 7–10.

215

Hacker, Marilyn, 'Science Fiction and Feminism: The Work of
Joanna Russ'. *Chrysalis*, No 4, 1977, pp 67–79.
Hall, Sandi, *The Godmothers*. London: The Women's Press,
1982.
Hanna, Judith, 'The Greenskins are Here: Women, Men and
Aliens'. *Contrary Modes: Proceedings of the World Science
Fiction Conference, Melbourne, Australia, 1985*, ed. Jenny
Blackford et al, Ebony Books,. 1985, pp 122–32. (A brief
summary of the ideas developed in this article appears in
Judith Hanna's editorial column in *Interzone*, No 15, Spring
1986.)
Heinlein, Robert, 'By His Bootstraps'. *Astounding Science
Fiction*, Oct 1941 (as Anson MacDonald).
'All You Zombies'. *The Magazine of Fantasy and Science
Fiction*, March 1959.
Heldreth, Lillian M., 'Love is the Plan, the Plan is Death: The
Feminism and Fatalism of James Tiptree Jr'. *Extrapolation*,
Vol 23, No 1, Spring 1982, pp 22–30.
Hurst, L.J., review *The Two of Them* in *Vector*, Dec 86/Jan 87.
Jackson, Rosemary, *Fantasy: The Literature of Subversion*.
London: Methuen, 1981.
'Frankenstein: A Myth for Women'. *Women's Review*, No
12, Oct 1986, pp 16–17.
Jameson, Frederic, 'World-Reduction in Le Guin: The Emerg-
ence of "Utopian Narrative"'. *Science Fiction Studies*, No 7,
Nov 1975, pp 221–31.
Jones, Gwyneth, *Divine Endurance*. London: George Allen &
Unwin, 1984.
Escape Plans. London: Unwin, 1986.
Khouri, Nadia, 'The Dialectics of Power: Utopia in the Science
Fiction of Le Guin, Jeury, Piercy'. *Science Fiction Studies*,
Vol 7, 1980.
Kilworth, Garry, 'Let's Go to Golgotha', *Gollancz/Sunday
Times Best SF Stories*. London: Gollancz, 1975.
Lane, Ann J., Introduction to *Herland* by Charlotte Perkins
Gilman. (Pantheon and The Women's Press.)
Lane, Mary Bradley, *Mizora: A Prophesy*. Serialised in the
Cincinnati *Commercial* in four instalments, 1880–81; G.W.
Dillingham, 1890; Boston: Gregg Press, 1975.
Lee, Tanith, *Death's Master*. New York: DAW, 1979; London:
Hamlyn, 1982.

Sabella, or The Blood Stone. New York: DAW 1980.
'Sirriamnis'. *Unsilent Night*. The NESFA Press 1981.
Collected in *Dreams of Dark and Light: The Great Short
Fiction of Tanith Lee*. Sauk City, WI: Arkham House, 1986.
The Silver Metal Lover. New York: DAW, 1982; London:
Unicorn, 1986.
'Northern Chess'. *Amazons!*, ed. Jessica Amanda Salmon-
son. DAW, 1979.
Le Guin, Ursula K., *Rocannon's World*. New York: Ace, 1966;
UK: Tandem, 1972; Gollancz, 1975.
Planet of Exile. New York: Ace, 1966; UK: Tandem, 1972;
Gollancz, 1979.
City of Illusions. New York: Ace, 1967; London: Gollancz,
1971.
A Wizard of Earthsea. New York: Parnassus, 1968;
London: Gollancz, 1971.
The Tombs of Atuan. New York: Atheneum, 1971;
London: Gollancz, 1972.
The Farthest Shore. New York: Atheneum, 1972; London:
Gollancz, 1973 (revised). (These three volumes form the
Earthsea trilogy.)
The Left Hand of Darkness. New York: Ace, 1969;
London: MacDonald, 1969.
The Lathe of Heaven. New York: Avon, 1971; London:
Gollancz, 1972.
The Dispossessed. New York: Harper & Row, 1974.
London: Gollancz, 1974.
The Word for World is Forest (revised from novella). New
York: Berkley, 1976; London: Gollancz 1977.
Short fiction:
'The New Atlantis'. *The New Atlantis*, ed. Robert Silver-
berg, Hawthorn Books, 1975.
'The Diary of the Rose'. *Future Power*, ed. Gardner Dozois
and Jack Dann, Random House, 1976. Both stories are
collected in *The Compass Rose*. New York: Harper & Row,
1982; London: Gollancz, 1983.
Critical work:
'A Citizen of Mondath'. *Foundation*, No 4, July 1973, pp
20–24.
'Science Fiction and Mrs Brown'. *Science Fiction at Large*,
ed. Peter Nicholls, Gollancz, 1976; reprinted as *Explora-*

tions of the Marvellous, Fontana, 1978, pp 15–33. (Page references are to *Explorations of the Marvellous*.)
Introduction to *Star Songs of an Old Primate* (see James Tiptree, Jr). Reprinted in *The Language of the Night*, ed. Susan Wood, pp 179–184.
'Is Gender Necessary?'. *Aurora: Beyond Equality*, ed. Vonda N. McIntyre and Susan Janice Anderson; reprinted in *The Language of the Night*, ed. Susan Wood, pp 161–9. (Page references are to *The Language of the Night*.)
A response to the Ursula K. Le Guin issue of *Science Fiction Studies*. *Science Fiction Studies*, No 8, Vol 3, March 1976, pp 43–6.
Introductions to: *Rocannon's World* (Harper & Row edition, 1977); *Planet of Exile* (Harper & Row edition, 1978); *City of Illusions* (Harper & Row edition, 1978); *The Word for World is Forest* (Gollancz edition, 1977); *The Left Hand of Darkness* (Ace edition, 1976). All these introductions are reprinted in *The Language of the Night*, pp 133–59.
Lerman, Rhoda, *The Book of the Night*. New York: Holt, Rinehart & Winston, 1984; London: The Women's Press, 1986.
Call Me Ishtar. New York: Doubleday, 1973.
Lessing, Doris, *Canopus in Argos: Archives*. London: Jonathan Cape.
(*Shikasta*. 1979.
The Marriages Between Zones Three, Four, and Five. 1980.
The Sirian Experiments. 1981.
The Making of the Representative for Planet 8. 1982.
The Sentimental Agents in the Volyen Empire. 1983.)
MacLean, Katherine, 'Contagion'. *Galaxy Science Fiction*, October 1950; reprinted in *Women of Wonder*, ed. Pamela Sargent.
McCaffrey, Anne, 'The Ship Who Sang'. *Magazine of Fantasy and SF*, April 1961; reprinted in *Women of Wonder*, ed. Pamela Sargent; and as part of *The Ship Who Sang*, London: Walker & Co, 1969.
McIntyre, Vonda N., *The Exile Waiting*. Greenwich, CT: Fawcett, 1977; London: Gollancz, 1976.
Dreamsnake. New York: Houghton Mifflin, 1978; London: Gollancz, 1978 (London: Pan, 1979).
'Of Mist, and Grass, and Sand'. *Analog* October 1973;

reprinted in *Women of Wonder*, ed. Pamela Sargent; and as part of *Dreamsnake*.

Aurora: Beyond Equality, Amazing Tales of the Ultimate Sexual Revolution, ed. with Susan Janice Anderson. Greenwich, CT: Fawcett, 1976.

Merril, Judith, 'That Only a Mother'. *Astounding Science Fiction*, June 1948; reprinted in *Women of Wonder*, ed. Pamela Sargent.

Miller, Margaret, 'The Ideal Woman in Two Feminist Science Fiction Utopias'. *Science Fiction Studies*, Vol 10, 1983, pp 191–7.

Mitchison, Naomi, *Memoirs of a Spacewoman*. London: Gollancz, 1962; The Women's Press, 1985.

Moers, Ellen, *Literary Women*. London: The Women's Press, 1978.

Moi, Toril, *Sexual/Textual Politics*. London: Methuen, 1985.

Moore, C.L., 'Shambleau'. *Weird Tales*, Nov 1933. Collected in *The Best of C.L. Moore*, ed. Lester Del Rey, Ballantine, 1975.

'Jirel Meets Magic'. 1935; reprinted *More Women of Wonder*, ed. Pamela Sargent.

'No Woman Born'. *Astounding Science Fiction*, Dec 1944. Collected in *The Best of C.L. Moore*.

Morris, William, *News from Nowhere*. Serialised in *The Commonweal*, Jan–Oct 1890; Reeves and Turner, 1891.

Morton, A.L., *The English Utopia*. London: Lawrence & Wishart, 1952 & 1978.

Moskowitz, Sam, ed., *When Women Rule*. New York: Walker, 1972.

Moylan, Tom, *Demand the Impossible: Science Fiction and the Utopian Imagination*. New York and London: Methuen, 1986.

Nicholls, Peter, and Clute, John, eds, *The Encyclopedia of Science Fiction*. London: Granada, 1979.

Palmer, Jane, *The Planet Dweller*. London: The Women's Press, 1985.

Parrinder, Patrick, 'The Alien Encounter: Or, Ms Brown and Mrs Le Guin'. *Science Fiction Studies*, Vol 3, Part 1,March 1976; reprinted in *SF: A Critical Guide*. London: Longman, 1979.

Patai, Daphne, Introduction to Katharine Burdekin's *Swastika*

219

Night (1985).
Pearson, Carol, 'Coming Home: Four Feminist Utopias and Patriarchal Experience'. *Future Females*, ed. Marleen S. Barr, Ohio: Bowling Green University Popular Press, 1981, pp 63–70. This is a revised version of 'Women's Fantasies and Feminist Utopias' in *Frontiers: A Journal of Women's Studies*, Fall 1977, pp 50–61.
Piercy, Marge, *Woman on the Edge of Time*. New York: Knopf, 1976; London: The Women's Press, 1979; reissued 1987.
Piserchia, Doris, *Star Rider*. New York: Bantam, 1974; London: The Women's Press, 1987.
Mr Justice. New York: Ace 1973; London: Dobson, 1977.
Platt, Charles, 'Profile: James Tiptree Jr'. *Isaac Asimov's Science Fiction Magazine*, April 1983, pp 27–49. (The interview from which this profile was derived was conducted with Shawna McCarthy, then editor of *IASFM*.) Reprinted in Charles Platt's *Dream Makers II*, New York: Berkley, 1983, pp 257–72. (Page references are from *IASFM*.)
Radcliffe, Ann, *The Mysteries of Udolpho*. London: G.G. and J. Robinson, 1794; Oxford University Press, 1966.
Reed, Kit, 'Songs of War'. *Nova* 4, 1974; reprinted in *The New Women of Wonder*, ed. Pamela Sargent.
Rice, Anne, *Interview with the Vampire*. New York: Knopf 1976; London: MacDonald, 1976.
The Vampire Lestat. Knopf, 1985.
Roberts, Michèle, *The Book of Mrs Noah*. London: Methuen, 1987.
Russ, Joanna, *Picnic on Paradise*. New York: Ace, 1968; London: MacDonald, 1969; included in *Alyx*, Boston: Gregg Press, 1976; and *The Adventures of Alyx*, New York: Pocket Books, 1983; London: The Women's Press, 1985.
And Chaos Died. New York, Ace, 1970.
The Female Man. New York: Bantam, 1975; London: Star, 1977; (The Women's Press, 1985).
We Who Are About To . . . . New York: Dell, 1975; London: Methuen, 1978. (The Women's Press, 1987.)
The Two of Them. New York: Berkley, 1978; London: The Women's Press, 1986.
The Adventures of Alyx. New York: Simon & Schuster, 1983; London: The Women's Press, 1985.

220

Extra(Ordinary) People. New York: St Martin's, 1984; London: The Women's Press, 1985.
Kittatinny. US: Daughters, 1978.
The Zanzibar Cat. Sauk City, WI: Arkham House, 1983.
The Zanzibar Cat (a slightly different collection). New York: Baen, 1984.
On Strike Against God. Out & Out Books, 1980; The Women's Press, 1987.
Short fiction:
'When It Changed'. *Again, Dangerous Visions*, ed. Harlan Ellison. New York: Doubleday, 1972. Collected in *The Zanzibar Cat*; also reprinted in *The New Women of Wonder*, ed. Pamela Sargent.
'The Little Dirty Girl'. *Elsewhere*, Vol II, ed. Terri Windling and Mark Alan Arnold. New York: Ace, 1982.
'Sword Blades and Poppy Seed'. *Heroic Visions*, ed. Jessica Amanda Salmonson, pp 157–162.
'The Clichés from Outer Space', *Women's Studies International Forum*, Vol 7, No 2, 1984; reprinted in *Despatches from the Frontiers of the Female Mind*, ed. Green and Lefanu.
Critical work:
How To Suppress Women's Writing. Austin: The University of Texas Press, 1983; London: The Women's Press, 1984.
'The Image of Women in Science Fiction'. *Red Clay Reader*, 1971; reprinted in *Images of Women in Fiction: Feminist Perspectives*, ed. S.K. Cornillon, Ohio: Bowling Green University Popular Press, 1972, pp 79-94; reprinted in *Vertex*, Vol 1, No 6, Feb 74, pp 53–7.
'Speculations: The Subjunctivity of Science Fiction'. *Extrapolation*, Vol 15, No 1, Dec 1973, pp 51–9.
'*Amor Vincit Fœminam*: The Battle of the Sexes in Science Fiction'. *Science Fiction Studies*, Vol 7, 1980, pp 2–15.
'Recent Feminist Utopias'. *Future Females: A Critical Anthology*, ed. Marleen S. Barr. Ohio: Bowling Green University Popular Press, 1981, pp 71-85.
Salmonson, Jessica Amanda, ed., *Amazons!*. New York: DAW, 1979.
ed., *Amazons II*. New York: DAW, 1982.
ed., *Heroic Visions*, New York: Ace, 1983.
Sargent, Pamela, ed., *Women of Wonder: Science Fiction Stories*

by Women about Women. New York: Vintage, 1974; Harmondsworth: Penguin, 1978.

ed., *More Women of Wonder: Science Fiction Novelettes by Women about Women*. New York: Vintage, 1976; Harmondsworth: Penguin, 1979.

ed.,*The New Women of Wonder: Recent Science Fiction Stories by Women about Women*. New York: Vintage, 1978.

Saxton, Josephine, *The Hieros Gamos of Sam and An Smith*. New York: Doubleday, 1969.

The Travails of Jane Saint. London: Virgin, 1980.

The Travails of Jane Saint and Other Stories. London: The Women's Press, 1986.

Queen of the States. London: The Women's Press, 1986.

'The Triumphant Head'. *Alchemy & Academe*, 1970; reprinted in *The New Women of Wonder*, ed. Pamela Sargent.

Scott, Jody, *Passing for Human*. New York: DAW, 1977; London: The Women's Press, 1986.

I, Vampire. New York: Ace, 1984; London: The Women's Press, 1986.

Shelley, Mary, *Frankenstein, or the Modern Prometheus*. London: 1818. Harmondsworth: Penguin, 1987.

Silverberg, Robert, 'Who is Tiptree, What is He?'. Introduction to *Warm Worlds and Otherwise*. New York: Ballantine, 1975.

Slonczewski, Joan, *A Door Into Ocean*. New York: Arbor House, 1986; London: The Women's Press, 1987.

Smith, Jeffrey D., ed., *Khatru 3 & 4*, November 1975. Baltimore: Phantasmicon Press.

Spender, Dale, *For the Record*. London: The Women's Press, 1985.

Swift, Jonathan, *Gulliver's Travels*. London: 1726, revised 1735. Harmondsworth: Penguin, 1987.

Tiptree Jr, James (also Alice Sheldon and Raccoona Sheldon), *Up the Walls of the World*. New York: Putnam's, 1978; London: Gollancz, 1978.

Brightness Falls from the Air. New York: TOR, 1985.

The Starry Rift. New York: TOR, 1986.

Short fiction:

'Birth of a Salesman'. *Analog*, March 1968. Collected in *10,000 Light Years from Home*, New York: Ace, 1973;

London: Eyre Methuen, 1975.
'Fault'. *Fantastic*, August 1968. Collected in *Warm Worlds and Otherwise*, New York: Ballantine, 1975.
'Mama Come Home'. *If*, 1968 (as 'The Mother Ship'). Collected in *10, 000 Light Years from Home*.
'Faithful to thee, terra, in our fashion'. *Galaxy*, 1968 (as 'Parimutuel Planet'). Collected in *10, 000 Light Years from Home*.
'The Last Flight of Dr Ain'. *Galaxy*, 1969 (later revised, for Harry Harrison's *Author's Choice*, No 4, 1974). Collected in *Warm Worlds*.
'Your Haploid Heart'. *Analog Science Fiction/Science Fact*, September 1969. Collected in *Star Songs of an Old Primate*, New York: Ballantine, 1978.
'I'm too big but I love to play'. *Amazing*, 1970. Collected in *10, 000 Light Years from Home*.
'Painwise'. *Fantasy & Science Fiction*, Feb 1971. Collected in *10, 000 Light Years from Home*.
'And I awoke and found me here on the cold hill's side'. *Fantasy & Science Fiction*, March 1971. Collected in *10, 000 Light Years from Home*.
'All the Kinds of Yes'. *New Dimensions II*, ed. Robert Silverberg, 1972. Collected in *Warm Worlds*.
'On the Last Afternoon'. *Amazing Stories*, 1972. Collected in *Warm Worlds*.
'The Man Who Walked Home'. *Amazing*, May, 1972. Collected in *10, 000 Light Years from Home*, and in *Byte Beautiful*, New York: Doubleday, 1985.
'The Women Men Don't See'. *The Magazine of Fantasy and Science Fiction*, December 1973; collected in *Warm Worlds*; reprinted in *The New Women of Wonder*, ed. Pamela Sargent.
'Love is the Plan, the Plan is Death'. *The Alien Condition*, ed. Stephen Goldin, 1973. Collected in *Warm Worlds*, and *Byte Beautiful*.
'The Girl Who Was Plugged In'. *New Dimensions III*, ed. Robert Silverberg, 1973. Collected in *Warm Worlds*.
'Angel Fix' (as Raccoona Sheldon). *Worlds of If*, July/Aug 1974. Collected in *Out of the Everywhere*, New York: Ballantine, 1981.
'A Momentary Taste of Being'. *The New Atlantis*, ed.

Robert Silverberg, 1975. Collected in *Star Songs of an Old Primate*.
'Houston, Houston, Do You Read?' *Aurora: Beyond Equality*, ed. Vonda N. McIntyre and Susan Janice Anderson. Fawcett, 1976. Collected in *Star Songs of an Old Primate*.
'Beaver Tears' (as Raccoona Sheldon). *Galaxy*, May 1976. Collected in *Out of the Everywhere*.
'Your Faces, O My Sisters! Your Faces Filled of Light!' (as Raccoona Sheldon). *Aurora: Beyond Equality*. Collected in *Out of the Everywhere*.
'The Screwfly Solution' (as Raccoona Sheldon). *Analog Science Fiction/Science Fact*, June 1977 (special women's issue). Collected in *Out of the Everywhere*.
'Time-Sharing Angel'. *The Magazine of Fantasy and Science Fiction*, Oct 1977. Collected in *Out of the Everywhere*.
'We Who Stole *The Dream*'. *Stellar*, No 4, ed. Judy-Lynn Del Rey, 1978. Collected in *Out of the Everywhere*.
'Slow Music'. *Interfaces*, ed. Ursula Le Guin and Virginia Kidd. Ace, 1980. Collected in *Out of the Everywhere*.
'Out of the Everywhere'. *Out of the Everywhere*, 1981.
'With Delicate Mad Hands'. *Out of the Everywhere*, 1981 (and in *Byte Beautiful*.)
'Morality Meat' (as Raccoona Sheldon). *Despatches from the Frontiers of the Female Mind'*, ed. Jen Green and Sarah Lefanu, 1985.
Tuttle, Lisa, 'A Spaceship Built of Stone'. *Isaac Asimov's Science Fiction Magazine*, September 1980. Collected in *A Spaceship Built of Stone and Other Stories*. London: The Women's Press, 1987.
'Mrs T'. *Amazing Science Fiction*, September 1976. Collected in *A Spaceship Built of Stone*.
'The Wound'. *Other Edens*, ed. Christopher Evans and Robert Holdstock. London: Unwin, 1987.
Vinge, Joan, 'Tin Soldier'. *Orbit* 14, 1974. Reprinted in *More Women of Wonder*, ed. Pamela Sargent.
Watson, Ian, *The Book of the River, The Book of the Stars. The Book of Being*. London: Gollancz, 1984, 1984, 1985.
'Le Guin's *The Lathe of Heaven* and the Role of Dick: The False Reality as Mediator'. *Science Fiction Studies*, Vol 2, Part 1, 1975.

224

Wilhelm, Kate, *Margaret and I*. Little, Brown, 1971.
Wittig, Monique, *Les Guérillères*. Trans. David Le Vay, London: Peter Owen, 1971; London: The Women's Press, 1979.
    Across the Acheron. Trans. David Le Vay, London: Peter Owen, 1971; London: The Women's Press, 1988.
Wolf, Christa, 'Self-Experiment: Appendix to a Report', trans. Jeanette Clausen. *The New German Critique*, No 13, Winter 1978 (Milwaukee). I am indebted to Kate Fulbrook of Bristol Polytechnic for drawing this story to my attention.
Wolmark, Jenny, 'Science Fiction and Feminism'. *Foundation*, No 37, Autumn 1986, pp 48–51.
Wood, Susan, 'Women and Science Fiction'. *Algol/Starship*, Vol 16, No 1, Winter 78/79, pp 9–18.
    ed., *The Language of the Night*. New York: Putnam, 1979.
Woolf, Virginia, 'Mr Bennett and Mrs Brown'. *The Captain's Death Bed and Other Essays*, London: Hogarth, 1924.
    Contemporary Writers, London: Hogarth, 1965.
Wylie, Philip, *The Disappearance*. Rinehart & Co, 1951; London: Gollancz, 1951.
Yarbro, Chelsea Quinn, *Hotel Transylvania: A Novel of Forbidden Love*. New York; St. Martin's, 1978.
    A Flame in Byzantium. New York; TOR, 1987.
Zoline, Pamela, 'The Heat Death of the Universe'. *New Worlds*, July 1967. Reprinted in *The New Women of Wonder*. Collected in *Busy About the Tree of Life and Other Stories*. London: The Women's Press, 1988.
    'Instructions for Exiting this Building in Case of Fire'. *Despatches from the Frontiers of the Female Mind*, ed. Green and Lefanu, 1985. Collected in *Busy About the Tree of Life*.

Index

228

230

Sarah Lefanu's publications include *Sweeping Statements: Writings from the Women's Liberation Movement 1981–1983* (co-editor) (The Women's Press, 1983) and the original science fiction anthology *Despatches from the Frontiers of the Female Mind* (co-editor) (The Women's Press, 1985). Her articles and reviews have appeared in a variety of publications, including *Foundation* and *Marxism Today*. She works as an editor for The Women's Press, and lives in Bristol with her family.